T0349978

KATHERINE PANGONIS is a historian specialising in the medieval world of the Mediterranean and Middle East. She holds MA degrees in literature and history from Oxford University and University College London. She has a particular interest in rewriting the voices of women into the historical narrative, re-examining understudied areas of history and bringing her findings into the public eye. Travel is central to her research process, and that is how she spends most of her time.

Also by Katherine Pangonis

Queens of Jerusalem

TWILIGHT CITIES

Lost Capitals of the Mediterranean

KATHERINE PANGONIS

WEIDENFELD & NICOLSON

First published in Great Britain in 2023 by Weidenfeld & Nicolson,
This paperback edition first published in 2024 by
Weidenfeld & Nicolson,
an imprint of The Orion Publishing Group Ltd
Carmelite House, 50 Victoria Embankment
London EC4Y 0DZ

An Hachette UK Company

3 5 7 9 10 8 6 4 2

ISBN (Mass Market Paperback) 978 1 4746 1413 9
ISBN (eBook) 978 1 4746 1414 6
ISBN (Audio) 978 1 3996 0644 8

Typeset at The Spartan Press Ltd,
Lymington, Hants

Printed and bound in Great Britain by Clays Ltd,
Elcograf S.p.A.

MIX
Paper | Supporting
responsible forestry
FSC
www.fsc.org   FSC® C104740

www.weidenfeldandnicolson.co.uk
www.orionbooks.co.uk

I dedicate this book to the people of the Mediterranean, who have been so generous with me, even when they had little to share.

In particular, I dedicate it to those who lost their lives, or their homes and livelihoods in the 2023 earthquakes.

CONTENTS

AUTHOR'S NOTE

This book has been a journey. It started on a sailboat in stormy seas, limping into the harbour of Syracuse. I was twenty-one years old and it was my first time in Sicily – immediately the history of the island and the warmth of its people inspired me. That visit prompted me to study for a Master's degree in Mediterranean history, and after many twists and turns led me to writing this book. I will always remember the awe and curiosity I felt as I caught my first glimpse of Syracuse over the waves, the skyline glowing gold in the sunset. I remember walking into the Piazza Duomo, soaked through with sea water, and seeing the baroque facade of the duomo, and beneath it the bones of a Greek temple, which had once been topped with a golden sculpture of Athena's shield – a beacon at the heart of the Mediterranean Sea.

My research took me around the Mediterranean basin, to Tyre, Carthage, back to Syracuse, and on to Ravenna and Antioch, with many other places in between. I arrived in each city with one idea of its history and identity, and left with a new understanding. I swiftly learned that the histories and identities of these cities are being kept alive by their living residents, as much as by history books.

In writing this book I have included the stories of many different people, as a way of illustrating the living spirit of each place. In some cases, I have taken small steps and some artistic license to conceal identities. Covid disrupted my research and so, in some instances, my visits to cities were made over multiple trips instead of just one, but for simplicity I have condensed them.

The most difficult part of writing and researching this book has been witnessing the devastation and destruction in Antakya following the February 2023 earthquakes, and I encourage readers to donate to aid organisations working in the disaster area of southern Turkey and northern Syria.

INTRODUCTION

THE MEDITERRANEAN: *MARE MAGNUM NOSTRUM*

The Mediterranean Sea is bordered by three continents and lined with sandy coves and unforgiving cliffs. The surface is scattered with islands. For a thousand years this body of water was the conduit of global trade, and the stage of warfare that dictated the fate of empires.

It is a mythic region, steeped in history that has blurred with legend. This coastline has witnessed the life cycle of some of the world's greatest civilisations from conception to devastation. The beaches now populated by serried banks of sun loungers were once battlefields; just metres below the white sand lies the dust of generations of unnamed soldiers who fought and died for control of the Mediterranean Sea. The churning surface conceals tragedies in its depths: the remnants of lost civilisations, treasure ships, and the bones of long-drowned sailors and modern refugees. This almost tideless body of water, now a magnet drawing tourists from around the world, was once the key to global power.

Carved around the ancient coastline are cities among the oldest in the world. Tyre, Carthage, Syracuse, Ravenna and Antioch are some of the most culturally rich of these, but today their grandeur is all eroded. The gap between greatness and obscurity is surprisingly narrow. These cities are palimpsests, with layer upon layer of history, culture and identity drawn over one another, each obscuring the last, but with glimpses stealing through. In the architecture and spirit of these cities, their antique and medieval pasts collide and coalesce with their twenty-first-century realities.

In November 2021, a conceptual artist named Gea Casolaro unveiled an exhibition in the National Museum of Ravenna on Italy's Adriatic coast, entitled *Mare Magnum Nostrum*. Our Great Sea.

In 2013, a ship was wrecked near the Italian island of Lampedusa between Malta and Tunisia: 350 migrants crossing from Libya to Italy lost their lives. In response, the Italian government launched a new humanitarian initiative to prevent these disasters, called *Mare Nostrum*, reflecting the ancient Roman name for the sea. Inspired, Casolaro designed her project.

A museum usually dedicated to Ravenna's ancient past, and filled with objects thousands of years old, the National Museum of Ravenna was perhaps a strange choice for this interactive art installation. Casolaro wished to put the present in dialogue with the past. Her concept was one of conversation and connection – with the Mediterranean Sea at its centre. To this end, she created a white cube, large enough for visitors to step into. The floor and parts of the walls were painted deep blue, and on the walls the Mediterranean coastline was drawn, a continuous block of white above the water. There were no frontiers marked, only land and sea. Viewers stepping into the artwork found themselves standing in the heart of the sea, taking in the unmarked continents surrounding them. Over the coastline, photographs submitted by the public in every Mediterranean country were fixed. The photos from Lebanon were surprisingly similar to those from southern Spain, despite the nearly 4,000 miles of sea water separating them.

People were invited to consider the Mediterranean Sea from a new angle and through a new lens. Standing in the middle of the sea, they looked out at those surrounding them: one people, the product of centuries of shared cultural history and collision. The point was to stop them looking out from their own countries, or from their 'side' of the sea, to make viewers stand, immersed, at its centre and take in a view of the region starting from the sea itself.

It is sometimes tempting to view the Mediterranean as a dividing force, something separating the people of Africa from those of Europe and the Levant. In reality, the sea connects. Cultures around the Mediterranean basin have sprung up dependent on the sea and the opportunities it offers, to swim, to sail, to trade and to conquer. Since the dawn of history this sea has formed the shared horizon of innumerable native cultures. It was the crossing place and the meeting place: the centre of the world. Maritime routes criss-crossed its vast surface, ships transported pottery, food, crafts and men from one side to another. These travellers took with them languages, cultures, ideas. Sometimes they took weapons too.

Tyre, Carthage, Syracuse, Antioch and Ravenna represent five of the most intriguing cities of the Mediterranean. All of them are beautifully situated, and for layers of history and cultural riches they are rivalled only by their sister cities of Rome, Istanbul and Jerusalem. Their fates have been remarkably different from those of their more famous counterparts. Visitors flock in their millions each year to Rome, Istanbul and Jerusalem; tourists and pilgrims alike travel thousands of miles to stand awash in the august history and culture of these fabled cities whose names are known around the world. No such numbers converge on the ruins of Antioch, on Syracuse or on Ravenna. Carthage is a suburb of Tunis; Tyre is a forgotten city dangerously near to the closed Israeli–Lebanese border. Few pilgrims make the journey to the obscure city of Antakya in southern Turkey, close to the border with Syria, where 'Antioch the Golden' once stood, despite it perhaps being home to the earliest site of Christian worship: a cave church purportedly founded by St Peter himself. Syracuse and Ravenna do attract visitors but on nowhere near the scale of Rome. Most who do reach these places are drawn to these small cities by the promise of leisurely Italian lunches, convenient beaches and the occasional pretty church, rather than the millennia of varied history or to see the sites of devastating sea battles and ancient subterfuge. The names of these cities do not conjure the recognition that their glorious pasts deserve. The voices of those who long ago made these cities great are heard only as whispers, if they are heard at all.

This book is an attempt to bring to light the hidden pasts of these cities, to understand them, and to see what is left of the great but vanished empires and civilisations of the Mediterranean.

TYRE

Nobilissima et pulcherrima
– Jerome, fifth century AD

Tyre and the isthmus, 1848

Each day before dawn, darkly tanned feet churn the sand in the coves around the city of Tyre. The fishermen take to the boats laden with nets, as they have done for generations. As the first half-light of the sun permeates the sky around the horizon, the rosy-pink stain spilling over the crest of the sea, they launch their craft, striking out into the waters of the Mediterranean Sea. They are hunting for fish to bring back and sell to harbour restaurants, and pack in ice, perhaps to send up the coast to Beirut. When they have finished, many will swim. If they're lucky, they might skewer an octopus or two.

The rays of the Tyrian sun have beaten down on the faces of fisher-men on this coastline for thousands of years. The city was founded by an

enigmatic race of Semitic seafarers who in ancient times flitted across
the Mediterranean, trading glass, purple dye, sturdy cedarwood and
sometimes people. History has remembered them as the Phoenicians.
Ever since the day of foundation, men have put to sea from the natural
harbour that became the port of Tyre.

The port that the little boats chug out from today looks to the north,
towards Beirut and Saida, and was known in ancient times as the
Sidonian harbour. Another looked south, towards Egypt: the Egyptian
harbour. An island city with two ports, it is small wonder that the
Tyrians would establish themselves as the first rulers of the waves.

Tyre lies at the easternmost reaches of the Mediterranean. The oldest
part of the city juts out from the coast of south Lebanon on a tiny
peninsula, connected to the mainland by an uneven isthmus. The sea
around it glitters. When the Phoenicians first constructed their city,
the land they built on was an island, not connected to the mainland at
all and lying roughly a kilometre from the coast. It was chosen for its
natural harbours and easy defensibility. There was an older settlement
on the coast which acted as a supply centre for the island. The Anastasi
Papyrus, discovered in ancient Egypt and dating to 1200 BC, described
Tyre as 'a city in the sea'.

Three thousand years ago this island capital, cradled by waves, was
the glory of the Mediterranean: rich beyond measure as the mother city
of Carthage, Cadiz and the trade networks that crossed the middle sea.
The vanity and wealth of the Tyrians would grow, to such an extent that
the Old Testament prophet Ezekiel cursed Tyre, likening it to a treasure
ship careening towards wreckage. He wrote that the Lord said to him:

> O Tyre! I will bring up many nations against you, as the sea brings
> up its waves. They will destroy the walls of Tyre and break down her
> towers. I will scrape her soil from her and make her a bare rock. She
> will be a place where fishing nets are spread, surrounded by the sea.

Ezekiel's prophecy came true. Not only would Nebuchadnezzar besiege
the city for thirteen years, but it would fall victim to siege after siege.
For centuries following the Mamluk sack of the city in the thirteenth
century, Tyre was reduced to ruins, scarcely inhabited, populated only
by the dwellings of abiding fishermen, who spread their nets over the
docks. As their descendants paddle out through the city's shallows,
walking out at low tide to rocky islets from which they can raise a catch
with rods, their feet pass over the ruins of the empires that came before.
Jutting out of the waves that surround the city are granite and marble

columns; half buried in the sand are the handles of amphorae, rusted coins and crosses. The sea rushes out and in to the port of Tyre, just as fate has variously abandoned the city, and raised it up again with immeasurable riches.

The sea remains the source of much of Tyre's wealth, certainly in the old city. Fishermen depend on the catch, and the azure-blue waters bring hordes of tourists in the summer months. Somewhere off the Tyrian coast, reserves of natural gas have the potential to help lift Lebanon out of poverty.

Tyre has been reborn in the last century, but the great monuments of its past have been worn away by the churning sea, devastating earthquakes, multiple sackings and the slow turn of centuries. The towers cursed by Ezekiel have today given way to modest homes and high-rises. Occasionally, the balconies fall off: cheap concrete is not as strong as cedar. Steadily businesses have sprung up along the coastal strip and the urban sprawl has spread inland. Locals are eager to show photos of the city fifty or a hundred years ago: 'It was only sand,' they explain.

Today, modern Tyre is known primarily as the nerve centre of Hezbollah, the stomping ground of UNIFIL, and for a vast strip of pristine beach on which turtles hatch their young. There is some irony that members of the Lebanese militia group with their reputation for kidnap and extortion buy their phone credit and cigarettes from the same shops as UN personnel posted in Lebanon to monitor the Israeli border. In the summer, they bask side by side on the white sands. The United Nations Interim Force in Lebanon is as much a part of the fabric of modern Tyre as Hezbollah. They host an army of 10,000 soldiers and 800 civilian peacekeepers, and have been there since 1978. The force was established by the UN Security Council in the wake of the Israeli invasion of south Lebanon, which in itself was a response to Palestinian militants launching deadly attacks from Lebanese soil. The peacekeepers spend their evenings idling in bars in the small Christian quarter, watching sunsets, adopting dogs and propping up local businesses with their appetite for local beer and imported whiskey.

The road to Tyre is lined with scars of war, and green and yellow Hezbollah flags pulled ragged in the wind. Pictures of radical leader Nasrallah, martyrs and the assassinated Iranian general Soleimani cluster the highway, alongside adverts for Botox. The first apartment I stayed in in Tyre had a holographic image of Nasrallah on the fridge, held in place by *Simpsons* fridge magnets. Lebanese military checkpoints bisect the roads. Sometimes protestors block the way with burning tyres, but usually they are courteous enough to extinguish the fires and allow

women travelling alone to pass through. The highway follows the coast
and a railway line that for a century linked Beirut to Palestinian Haifa.
Now Haifa is an Israeli city, and no trains have crossed that border since
1948. The train tracks can still be glimpsed – rusted and overgrown with
ivy and glowing marigolds. In fact, the border is not a border at all. The
area separating Lebanon from Israel – two countries still technically at
war – is known as the Blue Line. It is the UN-monitored boundary over
which nothing – not even animals – is allowed to cross. Birds can get
away with it – at a pinch. In practice, though, this is difficult to enforce.
In 2021, seven cows crossed provoking an international dispute. The
Lebanese claimed the cows were stolen. UNFIL employees recorded
that only six out of the seven were returned, and speculated with some
amusement about what happened to the seventh.

Like all the cities in this book, Tyre has experienced successive
conquests, experiencing Greek, Roman, Byzantine and Ottoman rule
– eventually passing into French mandate, and finally an independent
Lebanon. Where Tyre proves exceptional among the other cities however
is that its history goes further back. Before the Greeks spread Hellenic
culture, before Alexander marched to India. Its history is one of continuous inhabitation as far back as the third millennium BC, placing it
as a rival to Jericho as the longest inhabited city of mankind. What also
marks it out is the still current collective memory of violence. For many
Mediterranean cities, invasion, conquest and occupation are a distant
memory, something for the history books alone – or an upbeat anecdote
to tell tourists as they lean over the railings of archaeological sites. In
Tyre, the memories are recent. Not quite in Israel's occupied security
zone, the city was still occupied by Israel for nearly three years from
1982 to 1985. In 1995 gunboats blockaded the harbour and stopped
fishermen sailing out for their catch. It was the first time in living
memory that boats did not launch from the harbour at dawn. At the
time of writing, the thunder of Israeli rockets could be heard in the city
of Tyre, a retaliation to those fired from Lebanon days before.

The Phoenicians who began the tradition of sailing out from Tyre
were a mysterious people: clever traders who built ships from the
cedars of Mount Lebanon and traded their wares far and wide. They
were merchants and explorers rather than conquerors, and the word
Phoenician meant nothing to them. They identified themselves by their
city of origin, rather than as a unified people or race. Tyre was not the
only city the Phoenicians built: Sidon, Beirut, Byblos and Arwad all also
had Phoenician founders. The word Phoenician derives from the Greek
word phoenix, referring to the reddish-purple colour of the famous dye

the Tyrians extracted by the tonne from the plentiful murex sea snails that crawled in their shallows, and became their signature product. It became the term the ancient Greek writers applied to these tribes of Levantine sailors who built the best ships of antiquity, perfected the art of navigation, purportedly invented the alphabet, and whose skin was stained dark from the dye trade.

Whatever they called themselves, the founders of Tyre were industrious and curious. Their skills and determination would eventually take them to every corner of the Mediterranean, and indeed beyond it, into the Atlantic Ocean. Hemmed in on their east by high mountains, hostile civilisations and the dense cedar forests which they used to build their ships and temples, the Phoenicians always looked west. The sea beckoned to them, as it beckons today to modern Tyrians. Talking to my friend Bachir in a seaside café, he laughs and pushes dark curls out of his eyes. 'It's not that the sea calls me, it's simpler than that: I am the sea, the sea is me. It's my livelihood, it was my parents' livelihood. It's everything for us. We are Phoenicians, it's in our blood, in our DNA.'

In the Middle Ages, the term Phoenician fell out of use. But the residents of the Lebanese coast never gave up their passion for international trade and exploration. Many Frankish sources refer to 'Syrian merchants' across Europe, and while we cannot be sure where exactly they hailed from, it is safe to assume that a good number came from Tyre and the surrounding region. The talent for exploration is reflected in the mentality of the modern Lebanese. Driven from home by economic crises, war and general instability, the Lebanese diaspora has fanned out across the globe. Strong Lebanese diaspora communities exist in all five continents. Today, in the wake of the many crises racking Lebanon, more and more Lebanese are seeking to move abroad. In 2023, there were more Lebanese living abroad than in Lebanon. Soon, even Bachir will leave his beloved city to travel to Switzerland. He believes the landlocked country holds more opportunities for him than Tyre, but you can read the pain he feels at leaving. He hopes he will at least be able to dive in the lakes.

Tyre and its Phoenician founders conjure certain connotations in the minds of visitors. Guidebooks will enthusiastically assert that the Phoenicians invented the alphabet, but what does that really mean? They will say that Europa – the demigod who gave her name to Europe – was kidnapped from Tyre, and her brothers Cadmus and Phoenix searched for her. They will say Dido set sail from here when she went to found Carthage. The Phoenicians were famous for their worship of Baal, Astarte, Melqart, Eshmun. Myths and facts have blended inextricably,

and it is all so ancient that it has become easier to parrot the myths as
fact, than to try and tease out the reality.

Keen to see for myself what these elusive seafarers left behind, I
make a date to go swimming with Bachir. He tells me that in the sea
around Tyre, I can get a greater sense of the Phoenicians and what they
did than in any of the museums on land.

We meet on a small beach, with the sun high overhead, in the sliver
of shade cast by a crusader watchtower that glows gold and guards the
tiny cove. I point to the sun and am thinking of my pale skin, wondering
if now is a wise time to go. Bachir laughs – swim enough, and you will
look like me, he smiles, gesturing to his deep tan. I am sceptical. I can
already feel the sunburn creeping up on me, but now is the right time,
he assures me: the water is very clear.

I spread my yolk-coloured fouta on the sand to claim my space,
quickly fold my clothes and follow Bachir out to the sea. After lunch,
fishermen come to the beach to relax, with speakers and hookah pipes,
their day's work complete, and this little beach can become crowded.
In the morning it is always empty. Picking my way carefully through
the rocks, crabs and shards of broken tile that cluster at the shoreline,
my eyes scan hopefully for murex, the sea snails whose shells yielded
the purple dye that made Tyre famous. Reaching a natural ledge, I dive
into the water. It is choppy, with the sort of waves that slap you in the
face when you surface to take a breath. My eyes sting, and beneath the
surface I hear the crackle of the live coral: it sounds like the muttering
of ghosts. When archaeologists come here they dive with full scuba kit.
It is necessary as they are, after all, digging – but for people like me who
just want to see, goggles and decent lung capacity will suffice.

Bachir swims every day without fail, even in winter, and has brought
fins with him. I have to work hard to match his pace as we swim out
towards the modern fishing harbour and the sea wall, the crusader
tower retreating behind us. Fifty metres out, I turn onto my back and
look back at the city. Ottoman house fronts stand over the water, some
dilapidated, some restored, painted in yellow, ochre and white. The tip
of the Virgin Mary's crown is just visible over the sea wall. She stands
in the middle of the fishing harbour, her palms upturned, welcoming
visitors to the town. She cuts a strangely incongruous figure in the Shīa-
dominated capital of South Lebanon. I can only pause for a moment;
Bachir has gone beneath the surface and is beckoning me to follow.

Breaking the surface, I enter another world, swimming over submerged columns. Ancient monoliths of granite from Roman times lie
end to end along the bottom of the sea, barely six metres down. The

water is clear, obscuring nothing, and my eyes dart around, taking in every detail. It is dreamlike, gliding over the remains of this ancient city, as if I've stumbled on the suburbs of Atlantis. I've read about these ruins: for centuries, travellers have written home about the remains of ancient Tyre, half submerged in the glittering waters. Now I am among them.

Diving deeper, I touch the stones – lichens, weeds and moss-like sea plants cover them. I run my hands over them, trying to make out the colour underneath, hoping there might be marble as well as granite. Something catches my eye, moving on the seabed. Distracted, I swim closer, and see rippling legs: an octopus. He eyes me warily, with blinking, milky eyes, and wafts himself under a rock. Bachir pulls me away. When we resurface he tells me, 'Normally I would play with them, but he's hurt, someone tried to catch him. He's afraid.' I don't blame him: Bachir has already invited me to eat octopus that evening. Octopus hunting is a cruel and unsophisticated business. The creatures are skewered through their heads with a metal spike, and hoiked from the water.

We swim on past the columns. Bachir dives again, summoning me and pointing to the seabed. Here, I can see blocks, and different levels. These limestone blocks, likewise covered in browny-green marine plants, are the remains of the ancient Phoenician harbour of Tyre. We resurface briefly. 'Bronze Age,' Bachir tells me. We dive again, and I look at the ancient blocks that once made up the jetty from which those famous ships were launched. The Phoenicians had a profound impact on the cultural development of civilisations around the Mediterranean basin: it all started from here. I think about the ancient ships that sailed here, and the ancient sailors who drowned here. Looking at photographs from ongoing excavations later, I see that some of the blocks are inscribed with runes, but their meaning has yet to be deciphered and I cannot hold my breath long enough to find them.

Bachir points to something below us, gesturing me to swim deeper. I see movement – a blotched brown shell propelled by mottled fins. One of Lebanon's sea turtles has decided to join us. Lazily she glides along the seabed, and a ghostly plastic bag wafts between us.

The sea off this part of the Lebanese coastline, far to the south and near the Blue Line, is filled with ancient stones, and occasionally treasure. If I had sharper eyes, and a good deal more time, I might find gold. One fisherman recounted to me in a café how he once found a solidus, a solid-gold Byzantine coin, in the sand while he was hunting octopus. He sold it for US$1,500. His eyes grew misty at the memory: times had been hard, but the ghosts had looked after him.

Political tension and august history are always close at hand in the modern city. Two archaeological sites dominate the landscape, and new discoveries are made all the time. The summer in which I was writing, I volunteered with an archaeological excavation that uncovered the remains of a Roman temple beside the Shīa cemetery and the ruins of the crusader cathedral. There is much more to be discovered, submerged in the waters off the coast. Marine archaeology was pioneered in Tyre by a British archaeologist, Honor Frost. Born in the ancient Mediterranean capital of Nicosia in Cyprus, she swam daily in her childhood, and – despite being orphaned and moving to London – the affinity with the sea remained strong. She would write, 'Time out of the water is time wasted.' She came to Tyre having glimpsed the aerial photographs taken by spy-cum-archaeologist Antoine Poidebard in the early twentieth century. His aerial images of Tyre provoked interest in unearthing the remains of the Phoenician harbours that once sent out the ships that would dominate Mediterranean trade.

Situated on the edge of the fertile crescent, Tyre is one of the early centres of civilisation.

THE PURPLE PEOPLE

Two and a half millennia ago, a traveller from Halicarnassus paid a visit to Tyre, specifically to see a temple of wondrous beauty that he had heard about at home. It was richly furnished and adorned, with uncommon extravagance. The traveller spoke to the priests, who told him that by that point, the city and the temple had already stood for 2,300 years. That traveller's name was Herodotus, and he had travelled to Tyre to visit the legendary temple of Heracles-Melqart – the city's patron divinity. In *The Histories* he wrote:

> I made a voyage to Tyre in Phoenicia, because I had heard there was a temple there, of great sanctity, dedicated to Heracles. I visited the temple, and found that the offerings which adorned it were numerous and valuable, not the least remarkable being two pillars, one of pure gold, the other of emerald which gleamed in the dark with a strange radiance. In the course of conversation with the priests I asked how long ago the temple had been built ... they said that the temple was as ancient as Tyre itself, and that Tyre had already stood for two thousand three hundred years.

Yet the god venerated in this temple is not the Heracles or 'Hercules' that Western readers will imagine. Equally strong, but eminently more divine, a bearded figure more often clad in a loin cloth than lion pelt, the god of this temple was the Lord of Tyre, the Phoenician god Melqart, who counted Hannibal of Carthage among his loyal devotees, and to whom temples sprang up across the Mediterranean in the wake of Phoenician settlement. In the Greek imagination, Heracles and Melqart became conflated and interchangeable.

For all this, their myths and identities were quite different. Heracles is a demigod, famous for his labours. Melqart is one of the most important gods of the Phoenician pantheon – a son of Baal the creator, patron deity of Tyre, lord of sailors and exploration. He died each year at the end of winter, was entombed, and three days later was resurrected, in a cycle known as the *egersis* or 'awakening' of Melqart.

The Phoenician temple of Melqart has been long since lost. No trace of it has been found in the various archaeological sites of Tyre. However, in 2018, a team of archaeologists from the universities of Barcelona and Warsaw chanced on something. Digging in the overgrown field adjacent to the ruins of the crusader cathedral, known as 'the jungle' by the men working on the site, they began to uncover a processional road of white stone that led to the remnants of a building built on monumental, monolithic foundations. They soon realised they had found a temple, but they didn't have the necessary proofs to announce it to the public until 2021. When they did, it made international headlines.

As they excavated it the archaeologists began to notice strange elements in the architecture. This was not a typical Roman temple – certainly it was Roman, from the age and the type of stone used, but it was not designed like any other Roman temple they had seen in Lebanon. It had a completely different structure: a narrow entryway, two massive columns and a strange subterranean chamber, almost like a tomb, but quite empty. It was built in the style of a Canaanite temple, and its entrance once stood fifteen metres high.

As they excavated, the archaeologists waited impatiently for the summer solstice on 22 June. If on that day the sun went down behind the monumental altar, then that – they felt – might be enough to tell them that this was not just any temple, but the Roman temple of Melqart – the Phoenician deity still worshipped by the people of Tyre well into the Roman period – an interloper in the Roman pantheon. Melqart's resurrection was linked with the summer solstice – Melqart was, after all, a sun god – so this seemed to be a clear indication that the temple was associated with him. Beyond this, why else would a Roman temple be built in the Phoenician/Canaanite style? And why else would there be an empty subterranean tomb, if not for the ritual of the god's death and rebirth – the *egersis* of Melqart? Without a clear inscription and dedication, they do not have enough evidence to announce to the world that this is Melqart's temple, they cannot definitively prove it, but most of them are convinced. When I saw the red disc of the sun slip down in the centre of the altar, I felt convinced too.

It is ironic of course that a people so often credited with the creation of the alphabet left next to no literature of their own. The Phoenicians have slipped between the lines of written history. Most of what they wrote themselves was on flimsy papyrus that has not survived, and subsequent civilisations did not preserve their works the way they did those of the Greeks, Romans and Israelites. Inscriptions do emerge, carved in stone and clay, but these are few and far between, and never take the form of true narrative history. Tantalising references to Tyre and her people are found across cultures, in the writings of the Egyptians, Assyrians, Babylonians, Persians, Hebrews, Greeks, Romans and more. Praise for their skill in sailing and handicrafts crops up everywhere from the *Iliad* to the Bible. For Homer, they were exemplars of master craftsmen and traders. He gives us our first written mention of Phoenicians, albeit Sidonians not Tyrians – though in many cases the word Sidonian seems to have stood for Tyrian or Phoenician in general, rather than specifically a citizen of Sidon. Homer mentions the quality of the goods they traded, offering their cunningly worked silver bowls as prizes in the funeral games of Patroclus. Hecuba similarly offers a robe embroidered by Phoenician women as a gift to Athena when her son Hector goes to fight.

The name Phoenicians is familiar to many, but few details are known about who they were and how they saw themselves, or even where they came from. Nevertheless, records attest that it was the Phoenicians who built the city, who made Tyre great and who forged its reputation as a shining jewel of the Mediterranean. The city was established on an island 600 metres from the coast. The island city had impregnable walls that rose out of the sea, and sophisticated, multistorey houses. As an island it was easily defensible, but in peacetime maintained strong links with communities on the mainland and regularly exchanged supplies brought over from settlements on the mainland and the fertile hinterland surrounding the coast. Of paramount importance were the two natural harbours of the city. Today, the Egyptian harbour is silted up, but the (now much diminished) Sidonian harbour is where the fisherman moor their boats, presided over by the Virgin Mary.

Melqart's priests told Herodotus that the city was founded in 2750 BC. The archaeological record backs this up, showing it was inhabited from early in the third millennium BC. As Tyre is among the oldest cities in the world, its early history is hard to piece together. Like so many ancient cities, Tyre's origins are unclear. Some sources say it was founded by Sidonians, while the cuneiform tablets found at Ugarit in Syria record that the city was founded by one 'Uzus'. Others say Melqart himself founded it, and named it in honour of his beloved mistress Tyrus. It was this same Tyrus whose disobedient dog bit into a murex shell while running along the Tyrian coast, staining his fangs a rich purple colour that Tyrus had never seen before. Once her initial panic at the dark liquid flowing from her pet's mouth abated, she marvelled at the colour and demanded from her lover a dress in the same shade. Melqart obliged, collecting all the murex snails he could lay his hands on and boiling them to extract the rich dye. The purple of Tyre would tint the robes of emperors for centuries. The Byzantine emperor and empress Justinian and Theodora stand resplendent in Tyrian purple in the Basilica of St Vitale in Ravenna.

While the foundation myth of Melqart and Tyrus is seductive, it is likely to be an invention of later centuries. The early name for the city came from the ancient Canaanite word for rock, ṣūr, and the modern Arabic name of the city itself, Sour, derives from this, but where the name Tyre came from, is unclear. The Phoenicians and Canaanites are often deemed interchangeable by historians. The people who came to be known by the Greeks as Phoenicians arrived in Tyre in the fourteenth century BC, and founded the city under the name by which it is now known, either due to Melqart, or some other unknown reason. They resulted from the mingling of the native Canaanites and the newly arriving, and somewhat disruptive, 'Sea Peoples'. These Sea Peoples are still largely unidentified in modern scholarship, with their title serving the purpose of a question mark over this obscure group who began to attack Egypt just before and during the Bronze Age collapse.

The citizens of early Tyre were first and foremost traders and craftsmen. They were the masons who built the temple of Solomon, the shipbuilders who gave the pharaohs of Egypt their navies, the weavers and dyers who made the purple mantles of emperors. They were talented glassblowers and metal workers whose handiworks were given to Trojan heroes, and navigators who crossed the Mediterranean and sailed out into the Atlantic. They are a people who – while they have not left written records of their own history – have left their footprints across the Mediterranean basin, culturally and archaeologically – most interestingly of all – genetically.

*

Nostalgia for the Phoenicians remains strong in Tyre, among the Christian community at any rate as I learn from my conversation with Bachir. On Saturday nights the wealthier Christian Tyrians and weekenders from Beirut flock to a rooftop hotel named El for a Phoenician deity, and quaff expensive cocktails named 'Astarte' and 'Tyrian Purple'. Nevertheless, a friend from a Shīa background tells me bluntly that Tyrians today are Arabs, and that the Phoenicians are ancient history – just a myth: 'You won't find any Phoenicians in Tyre,' he tells me. He laughs at my naivety, explaining that the only Lebanese who consider themselves Phoenicians live in the north, in Christian parts of the country. Tyre is a Shīa town.

Broadly, this is true. There are fewer than 3,000 Christians in Tyre, a city of 200,000 people. If I spoke to the vast majority of the citizens, they would echo what my friend said. This is part of a broader political and religious trend of those of Christian backgrounds identifying with the Phoenicians as their ancient ancestors, and those of Islamic backgrounds identifying with the Arabs. 'Phoenicianism', as it has become known, was championed by various political parties following the creation of modern Lebanon, most notably those with Christian and Druze leaders. This took on a darker side during the devastating civil war from 1975 to 1989, when 'New Phoenicianism' was picked up by far-right Christian militias and used as a way of differentiating the Christians from the Muslims, taking on a distinctly racist current. It's no wonder the Shīa communities of Tyre aren't convinced by the suggestion of common Phoenician ancestors. In some contexts, Phoenicianism, and the revival of interest in Lebanon's Phoenician past, is little more than a racist reaction to Pan-Arabism.

After our swim, over a beer served in a frosted, salt-rimmed glass and mixed with lemon juice, I ask Bachir about this. Ambivalent to the political baggage, he shrugs and simply asserts that he knows he is Phoenician. He says it isn't to do with politics, and mentions DNA again. When I press him, I realise the allusion to DNA is not exaggeration: 'They did a test. They proved that Tyrians have Phoenician genes.' I ask who proved this. The answer is *National Geographic*. Bachir directs me to a café in the harbour to find out more. Apparently, the owner was on the cover of the magazine, billed as 'the Last Phoenician'.

As promised, I find that the owner of the café – Charbel – a man tanned even more deeply than Bachir, and sporting a white goatee and gold earring – produces a copy of the magazine. Rifling through the pages, he opens it to a double-page spread, with a full-page portrait of himself – shirtless – and superimposed over an image of the Byblos figurines, the votive statuettes of Phoenician men. There is an uncanny resemblance between his long facial features and those of the figurines. The caption does indeed hail him as the Last Phoenician.

This article confirms to a degree what Bachir told me: that a team of geneticists led by a Lebanese professor named Pierre Zalloua and funded by *National Geographic* did indeed carry out genetic tests on volunteers across Lebanon, and particularly in Tyre. Charbel was one of the volunteers for their research project, and gave a swab of his cheek cells and a vial of his blood for the scientists to test for the 'Phoenician genetic trace'. His participation in this project and uncannily 'Phoenician features' earned him the full-page portrait – shirtless and steely eyed, posing as the last of a noble race of mariners.

The 'genetic trace' that Pierre Zalloua was searching for in Charbel's DNA is a certain Y chromosomal gene present in male DNA, passed down the generations from Phoenician ancestors. The Y chromosome usually does not merge DNA with other chromosomes between generations, which can render it a historic tag, allowing the movement of historic populations to be mapped. His results showed that this genetic tag, while only found in 6 per cent of men across the entire Mediterranean basin, was found in 30 per cent of Tyrians. So Bachir is sort of right: at least 30 per cent of the Tyrians are indeed descendants of the Phoenicians.

For the Lebanese however, Phoenicianism must be dismantled and rebuilt. This important part of Lebanese history must not be used for division. The Lebanese, 30 per cent of them at least, *are* the descendants of those famous purple traders. But it is not just the Christians. These Y chromosomes are indiscriminately scattered across the different religious communities of Lebanon. The message of Zalloua's study was one of unity not division to the Lebanese people. 'Their religions are just coats of paint over their much deeper genetic identity, which is common.' However, the claim that these men are descendants of Phoenicians based on this genetic trace is still a bit of a stretch, especially when it was been argued that the Phoenicians never really existed as a cohesive group at all.

In any case, Charbel is proud of the genes he carries. When the geneticists came to Tyre to do their tests, it was a major event in the sleepy seaside town. The Lebanese, so often distrustful of authority, of testing, and many of whom refused the Covid-19 vaccine, happily queued up to donate blood and cheek cells to the project. Charbel never learned to read or write at school, but nevertheless is passionate about history. His education was disrupted by the civil war, but he was born with a thirst to see and to understand the ruins scattered around his home town, and beneath the waves off the coast. 'Whenever I dive beneath the surface, I feel like I am going back in time,' he tells me. He has spent his days collecting priceless trinkets from the bottom of the sea, and before I leave he presses a clay oil lamp and pieces of silvered ancient glass into my hands, putting a finger to his lips and smiling. As he chats to me, he calls his wife over to join us. She smiles, a little embarrassed, as he shows us a pendant around her neck. It is a pure blue stone, set in gold. He found this stone on the sea floor and made it into a necklace for her. He owes her a lot; she taught him to read and write enough to run the café, not to mention sharing her life with him and giving him his children. Neither she nor the elder boys share his passion for the sea and for their history, but the youngest likes it 'a bit'. He swims a lot, and his father has taught him to look for artefacts after the rains, which churn up the ground and yield fresh treasures.

After feasting on calamari and tabbouleh in Charbel's café, I go out to swim in the spots to the south that he suggested. Just as he told me, the sand is filled with fragments of the past. This is not surprising, as the area he has directed me to is known to archaeologists as 'the submerged quarter' – a part of the island city that fell away under the waves. I don't find coins, but my fingers do close around a large amphora handle embedded in the sand, and I have just enough breath to unearth it before I resurface. Triumphantly I show Bachir, watching me lazily from a kayak. He smiles ruefully, and tells me to throw it back.

The old city of Tyre, now the Christian quarter, occupies the area that was once an island. This is the ancient heart of Tyre, the place where Roman roads intersected the island between colonnaded streets and the most magnificent temple to Heracles ancient writers ever saw. Archaeologists have industriously raised the ancient stones and reconstructed areas of the Roman metropolis. The marble columns are interspersed with mosaic fragments, and vibrant petals of the native oleander and bougainvillea cluster the roads which overlook the sea. They evoke hints of the splendour of ancient Tyre, an island city of white stone embraced by the waves.

In the evenings men drag tables up to the railings that separate the archaeological site from the main street. They gather to drink Lebanese coffee from ornate *requaes* and arak from delicate glasses, and to smoke hookah overlooking the columned Roman road.

There is a second archaeological site just south of the modern city.

This is where the most extensive excavations have taken place, revealing the necropolis, churches and the magnificent hippodrome. Directly adjacent stands the Palestinian refugee camp of Al-Bass. This ghetto is part of the city's identity, and as I walked through the necropolis, the ramshackle buildings and barbed-wire fences loomed over me. One forgotten people beside so many more. Some of them have less private space than the dead Romans in their sepulchres. I can't help wondering how it must feel to look down from those crowded windows at Beiruti weekenders and international tourists wafting around the ruins. The Al-Bass camp is considered dangerous for visitors. It is certainly true that machine-gun fire sometimes chatters out in the evening, but more often than not they are shooting in the air, either in celebration or frustration. This kind of thing is common across Lebanon.

In 2015, a British artist named Tom Young mounted a project in Tyre Hippodrome. He wanted to explore the history of the city through a collaborative collective painting that would be turned into a stop-motion film. Young chose the site of the hippodrome not only for its historical significance, but also because his five-metre canvas would be in plain view of the Al-Bass refugee camp. In the weeks that followed, tentatively at first, refugee families would visit out of curiosity, to see what the strange European in the straw hat was doing in their back yard. Little by little, they began to paint together. Word spread and before long members of other communities were joining too, painting Europa being carried away on the back of a bull, the arrival of the ancient Persians, and Alexander the Great. Lebanese soldiers were sketching alongside Palestine refugee children. Every so often, members of Hezbollah would arrive to inspect the goings on, and when they saw Young asking Muslim children to paint crusaders and Israeli gunboats, he had to reassure them that if they returned the next day they would find Saladin driving out the crusaders, and Hezbollah clashing with the Israelis.

During my time in Tyre, I speak to several Palestinians. One is a teacher at Cadmous College. He is quitting, though, and leaving Lebanon. 'My wages no longer cover the cost of food and transport, it's costing me money to work there, I can't keep it up.' Naively, I think his position as a teacher and a Palestinian is a good example of integration, and I put this to him. 'Integration?' he asks, almost spluttering in anger. 'My mother is Lebanese, but my father is Palestinian. That might look like integration, but where is my passport? My Lebanese citizenship? I was born and raised in Lebanon, so were both my parents. But because my father's family fled from Palestine, we have no rights. I can't vote. How is that integration?'

Many of the treasures from the Al-Bass site have been moved to the Museum of Beirut. A significant Egyptian influence can be seen in the Phoenician art discovered there. This is testament to the pivotal relationship between the Egyptians and the Phoenicians. For a thousand years, the King of Tyre and Pharaoh of Egypt were closely intertwined.

Egyptian records begin to mention the city of Tyre in the sixteenth century BC. By the seventeenth century BC strong Egyptian influence was present in Phoenician culture, and certainly by the fourteenth century BC the archaeological and written records attest that Tyre was firmly under the control of the Egyptian pharaoh.

Trade with the Phoenician city state was essential for Egypt, as nowhere in their domain did they have forests to rival the cedars of Mount Lebanon, which provided the long, tough and rot-resistant timbers prized among the mariners of the ancient world. The Lebanese mountains are dense with thick cedar forests, much decimated but still evident today. The oldest cedars in Lebanon have stood for over two thousand years, and have witnessed the many transitions of civilisations.

This period also marked the conflict between the Egyptian and Hittite civilisations, which warred for control of Syria. For centuries Tyre was caught in the middle of Egypt's wars with the Amorites and the Hittites. When the Amorites attacked Egyptian allies, Tyre was loyal to Egypt, while Sidon took the other side. Egypt often did little to support her Tyrian allies, showing the hierarchical nature of the relationship between the two civilisations.

Egyptian influence over Tyre would begin to diminish in earnest in the twelfth century BC, as they came under the attacks of the Sea Peoples. In turn, the Sea Peoples began to raid the Levantine coast and intermingle with the local Canaanite populations. Following this, the civilisation that has become known as the Phoenicians began to assert itself and clearly develop.

The Tyrians and inhabitants of other Phoenician cities, in addition to their valuable murex shells, purple cloth, cedar trees and unrivalled boats, had one other thing of great value in the eleventh to the ninth centuries: independence. The influence of Egypt dwindled, allowing them to pursue their own agendas. The Tyrians soon began to forge themselves a new reputation as masters of the sea. They traded and exchanged, rather than destroyed. A thousand years before Jesus Christ was born, the Tyrians had sailed past the pillars of Heracles and out into the Atlantic. Tyre soon earned the title Queen of Seas from the sweat of the brows of her sailing sons.

The moment that clearly shows that Tyre had risen and become superior to the other cities in the region was when the Assyrian King Tiglath-Pileser failed to capture Tyre when the other cities of the coast had capitulated. Tyre would reach its golden age under the rule of King Hiram (969–32 BC).

It was under King Hiram that the Tyrian Phoenicians would garner their reputation for fine craftsmanship and their prowess in seafaring. On the outskirts of modern Tyre is a monumental sarcophagus dating from the Persian period. It stands twenty-one feet high, and its situation is superb, commanding views of the sea and countryside all around. A traveller – W. M. Thomson writing in *The Land and the Book* about the landscapes of the Bible – wrote in the nineteenth century:

> As there is nothing in the monument itself inconsistent with the idea that it marks the final resting-place of that ancient king of Tyre, I am inclined to allow the claim to pass unquestioned. It bears about it unmistakable marks of extreme antiquity… There is nothing like it in this country, and it may well have stood, as it now does, since the days of Solomon.

Until recent decades it has indeed been unquestioningly assumed that this tomb, the largest in the region, must have belonged to the Phoenician King Hiram, as he is the most famous of all the Phoenician rulers, leading to the reasoning that the largest tomb must be his. It was Hiram who ruled over Tyre's golden age as a mercantile superpower, and it was Hiram who enjoyed a collaborative friendship with King Solomon. Biblical records attest that the pair struck a bargain to exchange grain and oil from Israel for cedar wood and master builders from Phoenicia to construct the Hebrew temple in Jerusalem. Hiram worshipped the Phoenician gods, of course, and in addition to constructing new temples he began the practice of celebrating the ritual of Melqart's *egersis*. The two were good friends it seems, with the Romano-Jewish historian Flavius Josephus claiming that they used to send each other riddles to solve. Solomon, being wiser, was of course better at this game. Hiram ruled Tyre for roughly thirty-four years in the tenth century BC.

Hiram was not the only Tyrian royal to earn significant mentions in the Old Testament. Another famous Tyrian described in the Bible is Jezebel, the daughter of King Ithobaal I of Tyre. He gave her as a bride to the King of Israel, Ahab, demonstrating the close diplomatic and familial relations between the kings of Tyre and Israel. The name Jezebel has become synonymous with manipulative and deceitful women. She was a Phoenician and worshipped Phoenician gods. Instead of converting to the religion of Israel, Jezebel, with her husband's co-operation it seems, created altars to Baal throughout Israel, and encouraged the Hebrews to convert. For this reason, she is reviled in biblical texts and presented as a villain associated with false prophets. She also stands accused of ordering the murder of Jewish priests. She was eventually killed for her actions, thrown from a window, but it seems she was coolly prepared for her end:

> And when Jehu was come to Jezreel, Jezebel heard of it; and she painted her face, and tired her head, and looked out at a window. And as Jehu entered in at the gate, she said, Had Zimri peace, who slew his master? And he lifted up his face to the window, and said, Who is on my side? who? And there looked out to him two or three eunuchs. And he said, Throw her down. So they threw her down: and some of her blood was sprinkled on the wall, and on the horses: and he trode her under foot.

Jezebel saw her death coming and put her make-up on: her mask, her beauty, her bravery. And then she was destroyed, body and all, her blood spattering the coats of the horses. This demonstrates the volatile relationship between the Tyrian kings and the kings of Israel: sometimes harmonious, trading, collaborative, other times descending into full-blown religious warfare. It is hard to get any real sense of Tyre's rulers and relationships with Israel at this time as the Bible is the main source, and it is unclear how familiar the writers of the Old Testament were with the political balance of the early Iron Age. What is known however is that Tyre certainly emerged as the foremost city of Phoenicia at this time, and began to dominate Mediterranean trade. It was during this period – that of Hiram and his successors – that Tyrian merchants founded the colonies of Carthage, Cadiz, Kition, Utica and more.

This expansion and settlement was not prompted only by a thirst for exploration and adventure, but also by necessity. Tyre had developed its independent identity in a slim window of opportunity between the waning influence of Egypt and the rising power of Assyria. Before long, the Tyrians found themselves obliged to pay hefty tributes to the Assyrian rulers. An inscription in the great Palace of Kalhu reads: 'I receive the tribute of the kings of the seacoast . . . the lands of the peoples of Tyre . . . silver, gold . . . multicoloured linen garments . . . They submitted to me.' Tyre had been successfully besieged by several Assyrian kings, and in return for peace at home, it paid them treasures from abroad.

During the eighth and seventh centuries, then, the people of Tyre found themselves under the jurisdiction of the Assyrians and forced to pay tributes which prevented them expanding their civilisation. When the Assyrian Empire crumbled in the wake of the advancing Babylonian Empire, and the Tyrians were no longer under the Assyrian yoke, the trade and seafaring activities of the citizens would begin to flourish. The city would become widely renowned for its beauty and its wealth, and it was at this time that Ezekiel prophesied the destruction of glorious Tyre, Queen of Seas.

With what seems remarkable prescience, in the sixth century BC the Hebrew prophet Ezekiel wrote:

> Thus saith the Lord God; O Tyrus, thou hast said, I am of perfect beauty. Thy borders are in the midst of the seas, thy builders have perfected thy beauty ... O Tyrus ... shall fall into the midst of the seas in the day of thy ruin ... What city is like Tyrus, like the destroyed in the midst of the sea? When thy wares went forth out of the seas, thou filledst many people; thou didst enrich the kings of the earth with the multitude of thy riches and of thy merchandise. In the time when thou shalt be broken by the seas in the depths of the waters thy merchandise and all thy company in the midst of thee shall fall.

He also prophesied the siege of Tyre by Nebuchadnezzar II of Babylon. This is not technically a prophecy, as it is quite possible Ezekiel was writing his book simultaneously with Nebuchadnezzar's siege:

> For thus saith the Lord GOD; Behold, I will bring upon Tyrus Nebuchadnezzar king of Babylon, a king of kings, from the north, with horses, and with chariots, and with horsemen, and companies, and much people. He shall slay with the sword thy daughters in the field ... And they shall make a spoil of thy riches, and make a prey of thy merchandise: and they shall break down thy walls, and destroy thy pleasant houses: and they shall lay thy stones and thy timber and thy dust in the midst of the water. And I will cause the noise of thy songs to cease; and the sound of thy harps shall be no more heard.

In the sixth century – from 585 to 573 – at least part of this prophecy would come true: Tyre would withstand a prolonged siege by Nebuchadnezzar II. This Babylonian conqueror, famed for his military prowess and indeed for conquering Tyre's neighbours, failed to conclusively defeat Tyre, despite constructing a temporary causeway linking the island to the mainland, in a military manoeuvre made more famous some centuries later by Alexander. However, despite his failure to 'break' the city, Nebuchadnezzar still triumphed in practice. Ithobaal II, the defending King of Tyre and father of the famous Jezebel, died around the ending of the siege, and while his son Baal succeeded him, he would rule as a vassal king. Many of the details surrounding this siege cannot be nailed down conclusively, as the sources err on the side of vagueness rather than clarity, however we can be sure that Nebuchadnezzar waged a long and persistent siege on Tyre, and no great victory was recorded.

Baal would rule for ten years before being overthrown and replaced by a Tyrian named Eknibaal who would take command, but ruling in the role of a judge, rather than as a king.

The Babylonian Empire was absorbed by the Persian Achaemenid Empire in 539 BC under the rule of Cyrus the Great, bringing Phoenicia and the city of Tyre under his control as well. Cyrus was the founder of the first Persian Empire, and under his rule all the states of the Near East were absorbed into his dominion and expanded in nearly every direction, eventually encompassing territories from the shores of the Mediterranean Sea to the banks of the Indus River. Thus Babylonian overlords gave way to Persian ones, marking the beginning of Persian dominion over Tyre, which would last more than two centuries, until the coming of Alexander the Great. Cyrus – known as one of history's more benevolent conquerors – never occupied Tyre or installed his own lord. Instead, he allowed the city to retain a certain amount of freedom in exchange for the use of its legendary fleet.

Cyrus and his heirs held Tyre successfully until Alexander of Macedon, the next Eurasian conqueror to earn the epithet of 'Great', arrived to rattle the city's gates.

THE COMING OF ALEXANDER

Persian influence in Tyre would come to a dramatic end with the arrival of Alexander of Macedon in Phoenicia. In the West, this conqueror is known as Alexander the Great, but he is not given this epithet of admiration in modern Lebanon, where instead he is known as 'the horned one' and other negative titles. Alexander had inherited the throne of Macedon from his father in 336 BC at the age of twenty, and he launched his invasion of Asia in 333 BC. His reign would last only twelve years, as he would die of illness at the age of thirty-two, in Nebuchadnezzar's former palace in Babylon. However, in that short time, he would decisively carve a sprawling empire out of Eurasia, subduing Egypt, Persia and eventually reaching northern India.

Alexander defeated the Persian King Darius III at the Battle of Issus – an area near Antioch – in 333 BC. From there he launched his attack on the Levant, marching his army of approximately 35,000 men down the Phoenician coast. He received the submission of the northern cities on the Phoenician coast with little difficulty; Arwad, Byblos and Sidon surrendered without bloodshed. Tyre, however, did not. The 'impregnable' island fortress liked its chances against the might of Macedonia, and thought to win favour from the Persians by buying them time, so put up fierce resistance. Alexander could have marched on past the city, but he was not a man to do things by halves, and feared that Tyre could be used as a rallying point for his enemies if he left it unconquered. He therefore settled in for what he knew would be a long siege.

This siege is certainly the most famous and best documented episode in Tyre's long and varied history, attested to in the writings of three important classical writers: Arrian, Diodorus and Quintus Curtius. It was in this siege also that Tyre's unique geography would be her strongest advantage.

Alexander must have eyed the island city with grim determination. It was small, but fortified, and taking it would be one of the great challenges of his career. Tyre was a fly he needed to swat if he was to neutralise Persian naval power. Additionally, the fabled Phoenician city would be a jewel in his crown, alongside the already capitulated Sidon, Arwad and Byblos, filled with magnificent buildings and great wealth. Geographers and historians wrote of the glory of Tyre, claiming the walls rose to a height of 150 feet, directly out of the churning surf. It was a wealthy, beautiful and powerful city, and Alexander wanted it.

Alexander presented an unprecedented challenge to Tyre's independence. He did not follow the example of Cyrus the Great and allow cities to retain autonomy, but instead conquered and incorporated. He wished to take control of the coast before moving deeper into the Persian heartland. The Phoenician cities had long lent military and naval support to the Persians, and if he was going to make any meaningful and decisive assault on Persia proper, he could not have these states harrying his rear.

A conventional siege would not be possible in Tyre. He could not surround the city, or cut it off from its trade routes: the Phoenicians had more naval power than the Macedonians. The Tyrians on the other hand did not want trouble with Alexander; they could not hope to defeat him in conflict, and merely wanted to retain their independence. To this end, they dispatched friendly envoys to makes co-operative noises to the great general – promising him friendship and sending him a golden crown to demonstrate their recognition of his rule.

In reply, Alexander proclaimed that he wished to make a sacrifice to Heracles, a figure he claimed as his own ancestor, at the famous Tyrian temple of Melqart. The leaders of Tyre suspected that this was a ploy to gain entry for him and his soldiers to their city. Furthermore, they believed it would be tantamount to a surrender of their sovereignty, as only the kings of Tyre were permitted to make sacrifices in that holy place. They denied his request, suggesting that he made his sacrifice on the mainland instead. Alexander read this response as a clear gesture of hostility, and potentially an indication that the Tyrians intended to ally with Persia against him. Quintus Curtius, one of our primary sources for the Macedonian siege of Tyre, wrote: 'Alexander could not restrain his anger, which as a rule he was unable to control. Accordingly, he said "You indeed, relying on your situation, because you live on an island, despise this army of foot-soldiers, but I will soon show you that you are on the mainland [...] I will either enter your city or besiege it." ' He sent a final mission of envoys to offer the Tyrians the chance to surrender, and when the proud men of Tyre slit the throats of these men, and cast their bodies from the high walls into the sea, Alexander declared war.

The Tyrians felt safe from Alexander's threats, and believed they only needed to buy time while the Persians rallied themselves. After all, their city was half a mile from the mainland, Alexander as yet had no fleet and so far seemed to have no means of procuring one. How could an army of infantry attack a city at sea with no ships?

Alexander made a rousing speech to his troops, declaring that they could not proceed into Persia until the entire Phoenician coast was under his dominion, and they could not continue with their campaign until Tyre was captured. He warned them that if they left the Persians in control of the coast with the strongest part of their navy – the Phoenician ships – intact, then they might attack Greece while Alexander was occupied in Persia. If this was not enough, he also told them of an auspicious dream he had had, of Heracles reaching out his hand to him from the walls of Tyre, and giving him safe entrance to the city.

This dream would have greater resonance still, as Heracles was a hero famous for his endless toils, and the siege of Tyre would require much toil. Given that a traditional siege was impossible, Alexander came up with one of the most ingenious strategic decisions of his career, and one which would change the geography and identity of Tyre forever.

Alexander lacked the ships to defeat the Tyrians at sea, but had ample troops to outnumber them on land. If Tyre was anything but an island his victory would have been a straightforward one. Thus, instead of lamenting the gulf of sea between his men and the towers of Tyre, he decided to fill it. He commanded his soldiers to pull down the ruins of Old Tyre, the decaying city on the mainland where the Tyrians had suggested he make his sacrifice to Heracles, and harvest stones from it. These he bid them cast down into the half-mile of sea separating the fortified island from the mainland, and thus construct a land bridge, or causeway, connecting Tyre to the mainland. This would allow his hordes to march on Tyre on their own terms, playing to their strength and superiority in numbers.

While at first the Tyrians watching from their high walls must have laughed and thought that Alexander was mad for what he was doing, their derision must soon have turned to trepidation as they saw his progress. And their mocking swiftly ceased when they realised this was a threat they would have to take seriously. Slowly but surely, Alexander was closing the gap between his army and the walls of Tyre.

This was no easy task however. While the first section of sea was relatively shallow, the second half was not, and required far more materials and technical skill. The further the builders got from the mainland, the deeper the water became, and the nearer they came to hostile Tyrian defenders, who were certainly not going to stand idly by while a road was built for the biggest army they had ever seen to reach the gates of their city. Rather, they pelted the toiling soldiers with missiles and arrows to prevent them carrying out their work. They also sent triremes to fire on the builders from the sea and disrupt their efforts. To defend the workers, Alexander constructed defensive siege towers at the tip of his causeway, from which arrows could be fired back at the defenders and which shielded the men working to fill the sea with stone. A palisade wall was also constructed from Lebanese cedars along the edges of the causeway.

The Tyrians tried still more strategies to impede the progress of the causeway. They filled an old horse transport ship with bracken and sulphur and set it alight, propelling it into the side of the mole. The Macedonians were powerless to stop the destruction this wrought, burning down their protective towers, their palisade wall, and undoing much of their progress. The sea also proved to be on the side of the Tyrians: a storm followed the attack of the fireship, churning up the water which destroyed much of the causeway. Alexander would not be deterred, and returned to the construction with gusto, and with changed strategies to increase the stability of the structure.

However, even with the completed land bridge, Alexander could not capture Tyre. He realised that he would need naval support if he was to defeat these masters of the sea. It was then that he turned to Sidon – the ancient sometime friend and sometime rival of Tyre. The Sidonians – somewhat shockingly, given their similarities with the men of Tyre – donated ships to Alexander's cause, and ships also came to his aid from Cyprus, Rhodes and even as far as Macedon itself.

When Sidon betrayed them, it seems the men of Tyre tasted defeat in the salty air. While they still refused to capitulate, they put their women and children on ships and evacuated them to their daughter city of Carthage, which had previously promised them aid but delivered none.

Morale reached an all-time low in the city when rumours of a dream, or perhaps even a mass hallucination, caused many of the citizens to believe that the god Apollo had deserted them to lend his support to Alexander. The desperate Tyrians attempted to literally restrain the deity, binding his statue with golden chains to the altar of Heracles-Melqart, Tyre's patron god.

Alexander's ships advanced, and while the Tyrians valiantly made every effort to rebuff them, blocked their own harbours and sabotaged them, with divers cutting anchor chains in the night, they could not check his advance. Alexander's battering rams were soon beleaguering the walls of Tyre, forcing literal cracks in their defences. The Tyrians fought on until the end – hanging bags of seaweed from their walls to soften the blows of stones hurled by the Macedonians, and throwing their fishing nets over the soldiers as they tried to breach the walls – but they could not repel the relentless force. Perhaps they knew that after all this trouble their surrender would not mean survival, and so they battled on. They prepared to be stormed by a force 30,000 strong. They made a last stand against the Macedonians, but the majority of the men were annihilated. Two thousand of those that survived would be crucified along the coast, and the remaining women and children were enslaved. Only those who took refuge in the temple of Melqart were spared.

Alexander untied the statue of Apollo and carried out splendid sacrifices to Heracles in the temple he had made such a fuss about entering. Azemilcus, the pro-Persian king who had reigned throughout the siege, was deposed and Alexander appointed a new King of Tyre, a man named Ballonymus, who was apparently poor but of royal stock, and would reign in deference to Alexander's overlordship.

Alexander was not destined to return to Tyre. He would go on to conquer Egypt, found Alexandria and expand his empire as far as India. On his death in June 323 BC in Babylon his empire would fragment, pulled into pieces by his greedy generals. Egypt passed to Ptolemy and originally Phoenicia went to Laomedon, but was quickly annexed by Ptolemy. In the wars of succession that followed Alexander's death, Phoenicia became a scrap of the empire over which the Ptolemies of Egypt, the Seleucids of Asia Minor and the Antigonids would fight. Tyre would change hands many times. The city rebuilt its prosperity and its fleet in the aftermath of Alexander's capture, but the permanent legacy of his conquest was the city's connection to the mainland. Ever since Alexander's siege, Tyre has existed as a peninsula on the Lebanese coast. Never again would it be an island.

Walking in Tyre today, it's hard to detect Alexander's mole, for it has become land in earnest, and the isthmus that connects the area that was once an island to the mainland is no longer narrow, but sprawling, and densely developed. One can still sense however when one reaches the 'island'. The old city – the *hara* – is built here. In this patch of Tyre, one enters a Mediterranean oasis. It is here, rather than further in or further along the coast, that one feels oneself to be in ancient Tyre. It is here the fishermen keep their boats in the same harbour once used by the Phoenicians, and here that old women sit in the streets and hang their washing, and men smoke hookah in little hidden coves and in neighbourhood cafés. The houses are painted bright colours, and everywhere flowers spill from window boxes. On three sides, there is the sea, and somehow the proximity still permeates people's lives. Tourism thrives here, and Old Tyre has become one of the most expensive places in modern Lebanon. People will pay to come here, because it feels like stepping back in time, or into another world.

ROMAN TYRE

Following the Alexandrine wars of succession, Tyre was taken over by the Seleucids and became swiftly Hellenised. The city briefly played host to Hannibal Barca, the legendary Carthaginian general, fleeing the Punic Wars and on his way to Antioch. Tyre managed to convince the Seleucid overlords to support Hannibal, and their daughter city of Carthage, in their wars against Rome.

In 126 BC Tyre declared independence from the Seleucid Empire and went so far as to mint its own currency as a symbol of this. However stability in the city decreased as the Seleucid Empire succumbed to internal power struggles, with rival heirs fighting one another for control. In 83 BC Tyre was among the vassal states that invited the king of the Armenian Empire, Tigranes the Great, to rule over them instead. This he did, until 64 BC when Rome swept into Syria and annexed the entire region, including Tyre, to their empire. Tyre would be given rights as a free city, allowing it to retain a certain degree of autonomy and to continue its trading activities unchecked. Originally, Antioch – the Seleucid capital – would be the capital of the newly formed province of Syria Phoenice, but in AD 198 that role would pass to Tyre.

In being absorbed into the Roman Empire, Tyre also found itself at the mercy of Roman politics. During the conflicts between Caesar and Pompey, Tyre was stripped of its riches. Caesar accused the people of fraternising with Pompey, and used this as a pretext to divest Heracles–Melqart's temple of its treasure. Furthermore, in the incessant struggles, Tyre's rule changed many times, with many governors being enthroned then deposed and sometimes executed in quick succession. In some cases, Tyre's strong fortifications mean that harried would-be conquerors of Syria bypassed it entirely, not having the energy or resources required to capture the city. For the most part, even when under Roman rule, the city had its freedoms preserved. When Mark Antony gave Phoenician cities as a gift to Cleopatra, Tyre was not among them, and – writing in the first century AD – the Greek geographer Strabo described Tyre as a sovereign city, indicating that of all the cities of the Levantine coast, it was the one to retain the most independence and preserve its identity as a city state.

Through all of this, Tyre never ceased to make and export its famous purple dye, celebrated and draping the bodies of royalty across the Mediterranean. This dye had been produced in Tyre since the earliest times, with evidence of its creation and trade as early as the second millennium BC. Mounds of the broken, discarded shells of murex snails have been found all over Tyre, demonstrating the scale of the enterprise. While it seems all of Phoenicia produced the purple dye, Tyrian purple was by far the best, richest in tint and never fading. When Hiram of Tyre sent gifts to Solomon of Israel, and skilled craftsmen to build his temple, he included among them purple cloths and a man skilled in dyeing. The purple hangings of the temple's inner sanctuary were among its most prized possessions. Pliny writes that purple mantles were as valuable and sought after as pearls. Indeed, the Romans recognised the international importance of Tyre's purple trade, and regulated it. In the Al-Mina archaeological site, perhaps the most beautiful artefact remaining is a marble sarcophagus from the Byzantine period, inscribed with the Greek epitaph 'Of Antipater, murex fisher' – demonstrating that the purple trade continued even after the fall of Rome, and brought wealth to those involved. Antipater was certainly no pauper, but likely owned a large-scale murex fishing operation, supplying the raw materials of the dye. His tomb is perched on the edge of the archaeological site. Like many of the tombs, it has been smashed open at one end, and only animal bones remain inside. Nevertheless, it is an object of wonder, the lid carved with overlapping fish scales and the head of Medusa carved on the side.

Under the Romans Tyre prospered, if not in the same ways as before. No longer the mother of Mediterranean trade, it found itself situated on a Roman trade route that ran from Antioch to Alexandria and other Egyptian cities. Its name was briefly changed to Claudiapolis under the reign of Claudius and it was an important strategic ally to Titus and Vespasian in suppressing the revolt of the Jews of Palestine in AD 66. The emperors invested in the city, and minted coins for all of Syria in the Tyrian mints. Phoenician ships no longer played a major role in Mediterranean trade routes, but under the Romans the coins bearing the images of Astarte and other Phoenician gods followed the routes previously taken by the ships, and have been found across the empire.

It was certainly a lively and wealthy city – the magnificent structures of both archaeological sites attest to this. In the site of the city centre, a remarkable rectangular arena with seats for 2,000, sunken into the earth, was in ancient times filled with water for the re-enactment of sea battles, or ancient water sports. At the Al-Bass site, the hippodrome has been revealed as one of the finest in the classical world. Dating to the second century BC, it is 480 metres long and 90 metres wide and could accommodate 40,000 spectators. Its entrance is flanked with white marble columns, and what is left is a field more than anything else. On windy days the wind tears through the grass and pampas, bending the palms, giving a sense of the speed and movement that once rushed through this space. You can just imagine it: ranks of cheering crowds, egging on the chariots and four-horse teams that thundered past the race markers.

CHRISTIANITY IN TYRE

The condition of Tyre would once again be attested to in the Bible during the Roman period. Jesus Christ would visit Tyre and Sidon and perform an important exorcism of a Phoenician woman's daughter. A Christian community would spring up in Tyre, and St Paul would spend a week there conversing with the faithful.

The Tyrian writer and orator Paulus gave a speech promoting his native land, which earned the city the title of Metropolis from the Emperor Hadrian; it became a rival to Antioch for importance in the region. However, the city would pick the wrong side in a conflict between Septimus Severus, governor of the region of Pannonia, and Niger, governor of the Roman Orient. Niger destroyed Tyre, but was eventually destroyed himself. Septimus Severus rewarded Tyre for its loyalty and rebuilt the city, consecrating it capital of Syrian Phoenicia. The Roman remains that ornament the modern city are largely those of the buildings and *polis* created and restored under Severus in AD 193.

In the following centuries, the Roman Empire would continue down a path of weakening and fragmentation – leading historians to by and large make a distinction, beginning in the year AD 395, between the former Roman Empire and the surviving Byzantine Empire. The Byzantine Empire is the part of the eastern empire that survived Goth and Vandal incursions, centred on Constantinople, although the emperors known by historians as Byzantine emperors certainly still thought of themselves as Roman emperors – they had simply adjusted their borders and the placement of their capital.

Culture in Tyre would tilt towards Christianity under the gaze of Byzantine emperors, a process arguably started by Paul during his week-long stay in the first century AD. The city would see gruesome persecutions – executions and torture – of the Christians in the third century, and the majority of its inhabitants would adhere to their pagan faith. This would gradually change as the capital moved east, and Constantine the Great converted to Christianity.

During the Byzantine period Tyre would become Christian, building some of the earliest churches and basilicas in the history of the religion. Mosaic floors, foundations and altar fragments of these building still remain. The archbishopric of Tyre was supreme over all other Christian communities in the Levant. This later history of Tyre now joins in broadly with the history of the wider Mediterranean region and the spread of Christianity, which shall be explored more fully in later chapters. Tyre's golden age came under King Hiram, not Justinian. For all this, Tyre continued to flourish commercially and architecturally in the Byzantine period.

Tyre was briefly wrested from Byzantine hands by the Sassanid Persian ruler Khusraw II, the same shah who would conquer Jerusalem. However, following the industrious campaigning of the Emperor Heraclius, arguably the father of the crusading movement and the notion of Byzantine holy war, the city was regained. The Sassanid conquests were only a warm-up however for what would follow.

Perhaps more significant in the history of Tyre than the word of Jesus Christ reaching the city were the teachings of the Prophet Muhammad. Muhammad was born in the sixth century in Mecca, in modern-day Saudi Arabia. He is believed in Islam to be the last great prophet of God, and he united the lands of the Arabian peninsula. The Islamic dynasties that followed in his wake would prove the undoing of the Byzantine Empire. The unified polity of Arabia would rapidly expand under the Rashidun and Umayyad caliphates. This led to a series of conquests known collectively in Western history as the Arab conquests. Among these victories for the Islamic caliphates was the capture of Tyre.

ARAB TYRE

In 634 the Rashidun armies defeated the Byzantine armies after a six-day conflict. This opened the path for the Arab conquest of Syria. In 635, Damascus fell, and the armies rushed down the Phoenician coast, conquering as they went. In the century that followed the Prophet Muhammad's death, the caliphates would take possession of lands stretching from the Pyrenees to the Himalayas, via North Africa and Arabia. Tyre became an Islamic territory ruled first by the Rashidun Caliphate until 661, then the Umayyad until 750, when it was taken over by the Abbasid Caliphate. While the inhabitants were allowed to retain their Christianity, many opted to convert to Islam to avoid paying the tax imposed on non-converts, somewhat to the annoyance of some rulers, who would have preferred the cash.

Tyre shows no sign of commercial or political decline in this period; however it did – superficially at least – lose its status as an independent city. Its splendour and wealth was remarked upon by Muslim travel writers, who refer to it as 'a beautiful and pleasant city' in which 'many artificers swell and ply their special trades'. It was described as pre-eminent among the coastal cities of Syria, and its ancient rivalry with Sidon seemed long forgotten. It was known as a producer of sugar and fine glass, as the naval base of the sultan, and the point from which he dispatched his ships for further conquests and wars with the Byzantine Empire. Perhaps during this period the production of the special purple dye decreased, as there is little mention of it in Islamic sources. The travel writers however marvel at the situation of Tyre, just as ancient

Greek and Romans did, and its monumental walls that rose so seamlessly from the waves.

Under the Umayyads the city became the port of Damascus, and the
regional centre of ship manufacturing, carrying on its ancient craft. It
was also clearly expertly restored so as to garner praise and admiration
from travel writers. Mosques were built, and hammams, although little
evidence of these structures survives today. While Tyre was not an Arab
capital under the various caliphates, it was clearly an important and
esteemed city – not only for its beauty and productivity but also for its
strategic location.

During the period of Fatimid control, a great uprising took place in
Tyre, resulting in one of the most remarkable rags to riches stories in
the city's history. An adventuring sailor of undistinguished rank, by the
name of Aalaka, whipped up the people into a revolt against the Fatimid
government. He succeeded in overthrowing the Fatimid officials and
installing himself as ruler, fortifying the city against recapture, styling
himself as prince and even going so far as to mint his own currency
bearing his name and the motto 'Glory after poverty is to prince Aalaka'.
However, his glory was short-lived, and in AD 998 the Fatimids succeeded in using their naval might to retake the city. The city would pass
briefly to the Seljuk Turks, an encroaching Turkic Empire from the east,
and then be recaptured and remain in Fatimid hands until the arrival
of crusading Europeans in the Levant.

That said – even under Fatimid jurisdiction – Tyre seemed to present
many of the qualities of an independent polity or city state in much the
way that the more well-known city states of Italy functioned – even if no
such formal status or acknowledgement was conferred. In 1070, a judge
– Ibn Abi Aqil – took over the rule of Tyre. This was not necessarily
unusual for a vassal city of the Fatimid Empire; he was a man of serious
wealth and social status, owning ships that traversed the Mediterranean,
and ruling Tyre until his son was able to succeed him, thus starting a
pattern of dynastic succession. Contemporary sources seem to suggest
that Ibn Abi Aqil acted as though he were the ruler of an independent
city state, rather than a steward or governor on behalf of the Caliphate.
He led military ventures and captured neighbouring lands, expanding
his territory as far as Acre to the south, and conducted diplomacy with
neighbouring lords.* However, this attempt at a dynasty and independence was short-lived: by 1084 the people were tired of Ibn Abi Aqil's
heirs and by 1089 the city had re-embraced Fatimid rule, but somewhat

---

* Patrick Lantschner, 'City States in the Later Medieval Mediterranean World'.

shakily. The Fatimid governor, Munir al-Dawla, clearly wanted to claim some of the autonomy and power enjoyed by his predecessors, and tried to declare Tyre's independence once again. However, the citizens did not give their support and he ultimately failed. Still, what this does prove is that through the many regime changes, the notion of Tyre as an independent polity lived on, and this would be seen again and again down the centuries.

THE CRUSADERS IN TYRE

The wheels of the First Crusade were set in motion when the Byzantine Empire suffered a major defeat in eastern Turkey, at the Battle of Manzikert in 1071. This triumph for the Seljuk Turks is still celebrated today in the republic of Turkey in Istanbul. The day is marked with concerts and parades. This decisive victory for the newly expanding Seljuk Empire opened Anatolia to them, resulting in the capture of crucial Byzantine cities, including Antioch and Jerusalem. The crusaders set out from Europe to reclaim these lands.

The most important source for understanding the politics and role of medieval Tyre is the chronicle of William of Tyre, sumptuously titled *A History of Deeds Done Beyond the Sea*. This text focuses on the challenges and achievements of the European crusaders, both as soldiers and as settlers and rulers in the Levant. The territories they carved out from Seljuk and Fatimid territories ran from Antioch and Edessa in southern Turkey to the Gaza Strip in modern Palestine. The crusaders came primarily from lands in France and Italy, and travelled east for a variety of reasons. The crusade was triggered by a plea for help from the Byzantine Emperor Alexius Komnenus, in the aftermath of the Seljuk invasion and capture of large swathes of Byzantine territory, upsetting the delicate power balance in Anatolia and the Middle East. The Pope called on the magnates of Europe to take the cross, to journey east and liberate the holy places from the clutches of the 'infidels'. Many agreed.

The reasons they agreed varied. Some were doubtless motivated by a thirst to be part of this spiritual adventure; others had the more mundane motivation of greed. Many crusaders were tempted more by the prospect of winning lands and wealth than spiritual salvation and furthering the Christian cause. It was a motley crew of knights that journeyed east, but they were led by some highly able commanders, and this – alongside the disunity of the Muslim forces across the

Levant – allowed the crusaders to take territory. From Seljuk and Fatimid lands along and around the Phoenician coast, the crusaders carved four distinct territories: the Kingdom of Jerusalem, the County of Tripoli, the Principality of Antioch, and the County of Edessa. Tyre came under the jurisdiction of the kings and queens of Jerusalem and was seen as a major trading centre and an important bishopric. Among other offices, which included chancellor of the Kingdom of Jerusalem, court historian and tutor to the Prince of Jerusalem, William of Tyre served as bishop of Tyre.

Even in the Middle Ages, the myths and history of Tyre were important to the invaders. William of Tyre, writing in his chronicle, called it 'the famous capital of that region and the ancient home of Agenor and Cadmus'. Tyre's reputation as tough to capture did not wane in the crusader period. Indeed, Jerusalem and Antioch had both fallen to the Christians long before Tyre could be captured. Jerusalem fell in 1099, and it took a full twenty-five years – with the aid of a Venetian fleet – for the crusaders to take Tyre. The governor called in the aid of Toghtekin, the Emir of Damascus, and attempted to send him the city's most valuable treasures for safe keeping, but the caravan was plundered en route – and thus the crusaders received the wealth of Tyre before they breached the walls. In 1111 the new King of Jerusalem, Baldwin I, tried to capture Tyre but was unsuccessful, in no small part because the crusaders had no navy. The Byzantine Empire might have provided one, and in general they provided a lot of conditional support for the crusaders, but the Byzantines enjoyed a friendly and functional relationship with the Fatimids at this time. Both were against the Seljuks, and thus Byzantium did not want to damage this relationship by sending ships to attack a Fatimid possession. The crusaders had instead to wait for a mercenary fleet from Venice, which would come over a decade later under the banner of 'The Venetian Crusade'. On 8 August 1122, a fleet in excess of 120 ships left the arsenal of Venice, carrying over 15,000 men, and many horses as well. They were led by the doge himself.

The fate of Tyre, and the decision of the Venetian Crusade to make its capture their goal, was not decided through careful consideration and meetings of military strategists, but rather through sheer chance. The crusaders had to make a decision: to attack Fatimid Ascalon, or Tyre. In the end, when a decision could not be reached through conventional methods, an orphan boy was summoned to choose between two scraps of parchment placed on an altar. The scrap he chose was inscribed with the word 'Tyrus'.

However even with Venetian assistance from the sea, the siege would not be a straightforward one. The city was defended now by a garrison installed by the Atabeg of Damascus, for although Tyre was still nominally a Fatimid city, and offered up prayers for the caliph, the citizens had been taken aback by how little support their overlord offered them during the crusaders' first attempted siege, and had appealed to Damascus for more effective aid, resulting in Toghtekin becoming defender of the city. The siege lasted nearly six months, and by the end the crusaders had lost their bloodlust and were willing to offer terms. The inhabitants of the city were spared for once. This must have seemed a divine reward for their perseverance and suffering, for before the siege was completed the Tyrians starved for months, with little food or water making it into the blockaded city, and continuous bombardment raining in from land and sea. The terms negotiated were some of the most favourable in the history of crusader sieges: those residents who wished to depart could take their wives and property with them, while those who wished to be remain would retain their rights as citizens and not be subjected to brutalisation or looting. This was naturally unpopular with the crusading army, who felt that after six months of besieging under all weathers they had earned the right to pillage, but the agreement was respected, and Tyre remained a multicultural and multi-devotional city. When the crusaders finally entered, they marvelled at the splendour, William of Tyre recording:

> They admired the fortifications of the city, the strength of the build-
> ings, the massive walls and lofty towers, the noble harbour so difficult
> of access. They had only praise for the resolute perseverance of the
> citizens, who, despite the pressure of terrible famine and the scarcity
> of supplies, had been able to ward off surrender for so long ... The city
> was now divided into three parts, two parts being assigned to the king
> and the third to the Venetians.

The Venetians would be granted special privileges in the newly won city of Tyre – under the *Pactum Warmundi* – and would play a key role in its defence and governance until their expulsion in 1258 by a rival Christian faction. Through this victory, the Venetians became a major power in the Latin East, were exempt from many taxes and owned vast sugar plantations surrounding Tyre and in Cyprus – making them rich indeed. The Pisans and Genoese, who had contributed ships to aid the states of Outremer, also were afforded property in the city.

It was not only Christian writers who praised Tyre in the crusader period, but Islamic and Jewish writers as well. Ibn Al Idrisi admired its production of glassware and linen, and the Jewish traveller Benjamin of Tudela from Spain remarked that its harbour was one of a kind, and the city was beautiful. He even took the time to climb the ramparts and look down into the sea to the ruins of ancient Tyre: 'A man can ascend the walls of Tyre and see ancient Tyre, which the sea has now covered ... and should one go forth by boat, one can see the castles, marketplaces, streets and palaces in the bed of the sea.' The same is possible today, except that alongside the ancient fragments of Tyre's Roman centre – cast beneath the waves by time and earthquakes – one can also see the traces of the walls that Benjamin of Tudela once stood upon and looked down from. Little of medieval Tyre still stands.

In 1187, a series of calamities befell the crusaders of Outremer in quick succession. Their army was annihilated at the Battle of Hattin, and the Muslim army – united under the command of Saladin, Islam's most famous defender – swept through Outremer. Acre fell, and Ascalon, and even Jerusalem itself. Tyre however held out, and became the foothold of the Christians in the east – defended valiantly against Saladin's siege by Conrad of Montferrat, a newly arrived crusader from northern Italy who had his eye on the throne of Jerusalem. From that point forward, the kings of Jerusalem were crowned in the Basilica of Tyre, rather than the Church of the Holy Sepulchre in Jerusalem. Following the fall of Jerusalem, Tyre's history was turbulent, eventually passing under the jurisdiction of the kings of Cyprus, who also styled themselves kings of Jerusalem.

MAMLUKS AND DESTRUCTION

In 1291 the Mamluks would arrive outside Tyre's gates, under the command of the eighth Mamluk sultan Al-Ashraf Khalil. The writing had been on the wall for some time by the time of his arrival: the neighbouring city of Acre had fallen two months previously, the inhabitants massacred and the city razed. Tyre was the last Christian possession in the east. As a result, the population had acted with pragmatism rather than pluck, and evacuated by ship. The city that the Mamluks took was a ghost town already. Nevertheless, they razed it.

The Mamluks were descended from nomads from the steppes. They were originally enslaved soldiers, conscripted into the armies of the various dynasties that ruled Egypt in the Middle Ages. Indeed, the word Mamluk is Arabic for slave. It was the Abbasid dynasty of Baghdad that first began the programme of purchasing young non-Islamic boys, separating them from their families and raising them in the Islamic faith into elite soldiers. Due to their particular skill and loyalty, they were more highly esteemed than other slaves, and in some cases enjoyed higher status than the average citizen. In time, they would form the backbone of the military forces. Their use spread beyond Baghdad and across the Islamic world. In 1250 these slave-soldiers – who had formed the mainstay of the Egyptian Ayyubid army, overthrew their leaders by usurping the succession and established the Mamluk Sultanate of Egypt. From here, they would expand their lands through conquest.

The Mamluks were thorough in their ruining of Tyre. The sultan ordered that the fortifications be roundly destroyed. Buildings were pulled down and dismantled, and the great cathedral, resting place of William of Tyre and many other nobles of the Latin East, was pulled to pieces. Today, its remains nobly moulder in an overgrown field a stone's throw from the site of the Roman city centre. Covered with grass and lined with barbed wire and Hezbollah flags, it has not been excavated as fully or carefully as the Roman site. Prior to 1870, much more of it indeed remained. While the Mamluks certainly destroyed large parts of the cathedral, they are not solely responsible for its current condition. In the nineteenth century a team of German archaeologists under the command of a retired cabinet minister – Johann Nepomuk Sepp – made efforts to find the tomb of Frederick Barbarossa – the Holy Roman Emperor who died in the Holy Land and was interred at Tyre – and while they did not succeed in finding it, they did succeed in turning over much of the archaeology and making a mess of the site, including damaging the remains of the cathedral. Sepp was a shoddy statesman as well as a shoddy archaeologist, with some of the motivation for his activities being blatant colonialism and a desire to claim Tyre for Germany. Today the red granite columns that held up the ceiling of the crusader cathedral stand once more; before they were part of the Christian church, it is likely they supported a Roman temple.

The site now is eerie, but one can still imagine the grandeur of William of Tyre's cathedral, suggested by the remains of the foundation of the triple apse basilica and the monumental columns – overlooking the Mediterranean Sea. Squeezing between the loosely chained gates, the interested traveller can enter the site, climb up to sit on the pillar bases and imagine the coronation of Isabella of Jerusalem. The faces of martyrs of the Hezbollah and Amal movements stare down from the sides, and a modern Islamic cemetery stands nearby.

From the point of Sultan Al-Ashraf Khalil's destruction of the central

Christian monuments of the city and its defences, Tyre would never again recover its former glory. The prophecy of Ezekiel was made true, and the city declined into a humble fishing village. The remains of the once mighty towers did indeed become rocks over which fishermen spread their nets. They still are today. The columns of ancient temples can be sat on by tourists drinking beers, or basked on by stray dogs soaking up the Mediterranean sunlight.

For centuries, the town only had a handful of inhabitants, and empires and regimes that fought over ownership of the Levant paid little heed to Tyre – no longer commercially or strategically useful, desolate as it was.

One thing made completely clear down the centuries, following the Mamluk destruction, is that the people of Tyre are a warm and hospitable people. And so they are. In the 1600s, the English writer and traveller George Sandys wrote in his book *A Relation of a Journey begun an. Dom. 1610* that the people of Tyre 'retaine the old worlds hospitalitie be the passenger Christian or whatsoever, they will house him, prepare him extraordinary fare, and looke to his mule, without taking of one Asper' (an asper being a silver Ottoman coin). He goes on to say that the Muslim inhabitants would not eat or drink with a Christian, but would look after a visitor nonetheless. He reflects on all that classical texts have told of the nature of the Tyrians, 'a people fierce in warre'. With weapon-bearing maidens 'the Tyrian virgins quiver use to beare; And purple buskins, ty'd with ribands', but he goes on to quote Lucan – 'Inconstant Tyrians – tyrians double-tongu'd'.

> But this once famous Tyris, is now no other than an heape of ruines; yet have they a reverent respect and do instruct the pensive beholder with their exemplary frailty. It hath 2 harbors, that on the North side the fairest and best throwout all the Levant … the other choked with the decays of the City.

The warmth of Tyrians is well attested down the centuries, and the same is true of the community today. My experience has been that they are – with strangers at least – faultlessly courteous, always hospitable and rich in spirit.

When Englishman John Carne visited the Holy Land in the nineteenth century, he preferred Tyre, in all its desolation, to the grander and better preserved city of Sidon further up the coast. In his book *Syria, the Holy Land, Asia Minor* he wrote:

It was a scene and hour that in after days it will be delightful to remember: the noon-day heat was tempered by the light sea-breeze ... a
few Tyrian boats were moored near the ruins: the voices of the fishermen, at intervals, came on the solitude like the voices of the past ...
The modern town of Tyre, that contains several good stone dwellings,
and a population of two thousand people, is situated at the extremity
of a sandy peninsula ... that has the appearance of having been once
an island; from its north-eastern end extends a range of fragments
of former buildings, beaten down and now broken over by the waves
of the sea. There are considerable remains of walls around the town,
and of fragments of towers ... The traveller finds little cause, in the
accommodations of modern Tyre, for thoughts or images of desolation:
there is comfort to be found in her homes, friendliness and kindness
in her people ... there are pleasant chambers still left, pleasant faces
and voices within ... Time need not hang intolerably heavy on [the
stranger's] hands, even should he linger a few days within the walls:
travellers in general take a hasty glance, and pass on to Sidon ... [T]he
streets were noiseless ... the bazaar was closed: a few Tyrian women
and an Armenian priest passed by; and one little group of tradesmen
and fishermen were idly enjoying the balmy evening. Tyre had no
Eastern luxuries or amusements; one bath only of the plainest kind;
no story-teller to enhance the joys of the pipe and coffee, no fountains:
no caravanserai for the stranger: he must trust to the hospitality of some
private family, and he will not be deceived.

Tyre was diminished but not destroyed. For centuries, the ancient capital
was destined to be just a fishing village, rich in spirit and natural beauty
rather than commercial wealth.

A new force would arrive in the historic lands of Phoenicia in 1517,
from a powerful empire of obscure Turkoman origins in Anatolia, the
dynastic descendants of one Osman. They had come a long way from
their origins in Söğüt, near Constantinople, and now commanded an
expansive empire, under the watchful eyes of Sultan Selim I – or Selim
the Grim. Selim's armies had two decisive victories over the Mamluk
Sultanate, allowing them to annex the entire territory – including the
Phoenician coast. Selim, and his magnificent son Suleiman, paid little
heed to the fishing village of Tyre that they had acquired alongside
more glorious territories, and the town would remain undeveloped and
obscure for yet another century. It was under the reign of the Druze
Emir Fakhr al-Din II that forlorn Tyre would be given a new lease of

life. It was during this time that George Sandys paid his visit to the quiet coastline.

Emir Fakhr al-Din is often considered to be the first founder of the modern state of Lebanon, uniting the various regions and religions under one banner – even succeeding in bringing the Druze and Maronites together. He was a Druze leader from Mount Lebanon, who maintained a surprising degree of authority under the Ottoman over-lordship. He went so far as to make secret allegiances with Europeans, most notably in Tyre's case with the dukes of Tuscany, with whom he schemed to refound the city and attempted to reopen the port to accommodate them to this end. His brother constructed a palace in the city in anticipation of its revival, but Fakhr al-Din II would fall from grace in 1613, and his plans for Tyre ground to a halt.

The town would remain modest until 1750, when a slow process of rebirth was initiated by Sheikh Abbas Al-Mohamad Al-Nassar. This leader, in the hope of attracting settlers to Tyre, began a building pro-gramme aimed at elevating the status of the city once again. The old mosque was built at this time, and the Church of St Thomas. He built trade partnerships with European nations, particularly France, which had already expressed interest in cultivating influence in Tyre. Despite the sheikh's political downfall, from this point forward Tyre has con-tinued to grow, and re-emerge from the sands of history. This has never been smooth; for all her changing fate from decline to resurgence, Tyre was still situated on a tectonic plate boundary and every so often a devastating earthquake would ravage the city.

From this point on, the history of Tyre bleeds into that of Lebanon. It came under French mandate in 1923. It experienced huge influxes of Armenian refugees following the Turkish genocide of the Armenians, who originally settled in the area of Al-Bass camp. These Armenians then resettled further north, as wave after wave of Palestinian refugees flooded into the country following the foundation of the state of Israel. Refugee camps sprang up, and the country played host to Yasser Arafat, the leader of the PLO, before eventually forcing him to flee to Tunisia. The city was embroiled in the civil war, and was a key location in the war of the camps. It became a political centre for the armed parties of Hezbollah and Amal. In 1978, UNIFIL moved in – not interim at all, it is now very much part of the furniture. In 1982 and 1983, Hezbollah blew up Israeli headquarters in Tyre in the midst of the Israeli occupa-tion. Tyre's recent history is as bloody as its ancient history. The people suffer and recover, and protest, and fight, and provoke, as they have done on this land for millennia. For all this, they welcome strangers.

*

The convent of St Joseph of the Apparition was founded in 1882, and stands on the sea road that runs around the coast of Tyre's old city, on the very tip of the peninsula. The execution is utilitarian, whitewashed and unadorned, but the layout is Ottoman, with courtyards, walkways overhung with vines, and a vegetable garden tended by the sisters. To the side is the small chapel where the sisters pray. Once a bustling place, run as a school, today just four nuns remain within the convent walls. In the summers, they host teams of archaeologists from Spain and Poland, who uncovered the Roman temple beside the cathedral, and with whom I was lucky enough to volunteer. The convent is situated in the small Christian quarter, in the *hara*. It is hard to say how many Christian families still live in Tyre. The Maronite church has 500 families registered, maybe upwards of 3,000 people, but many have left. More recent estimates suggest there may be as few as 500 Christians remaining among a population of 200,000. The two younger nuns are both called Soeur Christine and the two elder are Soeur Archangela and Soeur Catherine. They are in their eighties and nineties, and they are tiny. For sixty years, these women taught Tyrian children of all faiths. They taught throughout the Lebanese civil war, and only stopped teaching during the Israeli occupation when soldiers billeted themselves in the convent. It is strange to think that the cell in which I now write this book may once have hosted a member of the Israeli Defence Force, manning the security zone, intended to neutralise threats from the Palestinian Liberation Organisation.

I descend and encounter the elder Soeur Christine on the steps that lead down into a broad concrete courtyard. This is where the children used to play, and bright murals of birds and whales remain. Soeur Christine is hard at work, hosing away the night's dust, while Anushka scrapes the water away with a squeegee. Anushka – employed by the convent – is Sri Lankan. The nuns are kinder than her first employers in Lebanon, but the hours are long and the pay is low. She is married to a local man whom she met in a café in the fishing harbour.

I would not have found the convent had I not met Anushka's teenage daughter on the beach one morning. My morning swims were always solitary, except for the occasional fisherman, but that morning there were two girls, hand in hand, picking their way carefully between the sharp rocks and spiky shells. I was struck by the closeness of their friendship, and what they were wearing as they swam and basked in the sun. They were in their late teens, and giggled as much as they chattered. Thouraya could have stumbled from the pages of a fashion magazine, wearing a black bikini and with long talon nails painted on a gradient from pink to white. Celine wore full hijab – a burkini. There was easy harmony between them, of the kind I did not expect to find in the city known as a stronghold of Hezbollah and Amal. Even in Lebanon, Tyre is a misunderstood city; many of my Beiruti friends – regardless of religion – are scathing of the south, deeming it backward, hostile. In some ways, maybe, but in others, far from it. One morning while walking in a UNIFIL memorial park, I meet women from the Shīa community who meet every morning for somewhat haphazard aerobics and to share coffee. I ask them if they feel any tension between the different religious groups that live in their city. They tell me no. They are people first and foremost – and this is more important to them than religion or nationality. Of course there are extremists – but this is not the norm. Sometimes Celine joins Thouraya's family at church, and likewise Thouraya has visited the mosque. With the warmth common to nearly every Tyrian I meet, the girls offered to show me the town and take me sailing with them, and afterwards Thouraya took me to the convent to meet her mother. Both girls are ambitious – about to leave school, they want to study law and medicine, but the Lebanese financial crisis has hindered their plans abroad.

I have arranged to meet Soeur Archangela and Soeur Catherine in the sitting room in the *maison* of the convent. The younger Soeur Christine brings us orange juice and encourages me to speak '*très fort!*' – she laughs as she leaves us. The sisters are genteel. Both are Lebanese, but first took the veil in Palestine. Soeur Catherine tells me that she was in the last car out of Palestine into Jordan, with three other young novices. Their habits gave them a rare protection to cross the borders – not now though. During the occupation, the sisters hid refugees in the secret basement of the convent; they show me the trapdoor that leads underground.

I ask about the invasion, and the civil war. They tell me what I have heard already, but not yet quite believed, that the civilian Christians of Tyre were protected during the civil war. I ask if they ever felt worried for their lives. '*Jamais!*' they tell me: Muslim guards were stationed at the entrances to the Christian quarter to protect the citizens. Even as a tiny Christian minority, they have never felt threatened by their neighbours. To illustrate this, they tell me a story about Imam Musa al-Sadr from the civil war. When tensions began to rise, a Christian who ran a small ice cream shop went to the imam, who was a pillar of the community for both Muslims and Christians alike. He told him that the Shīas in the city were boycotting his shop on sectarian grounds, and it was putting him out of business. The imam said to leave it with him.

That week, after Friday prayers, Musa al-Sadr invited the congregation to march with him. The crowd followed him, muttering, not sure what was going to happen. Would it be violence at last? He led them to the ice cream shop they had been boycotting. Tensions were high as the crowd gathered outside, and to the anxious shopkeeper it might have looked menacing. Then the imam did a curious thing. He opened the door of the ice cream parlour, went in, greeted the owner, and ordered an ice cream. He paid for it, and then settled himself in a garden seat to enjoy it. Hesitantly at first, his congregation did the same, and the Christian owner could not serve his Muslim neighbours fast enough.

The sisters told me that during the Israeli occupation of the south, the occupiers would force the citizens to assemble on beaches in the hot sun and keep them there, just waiting, for hours, for no purpose other than humiliation. They turned the sisters' convent in Saida into a prison. When I ask them if they have forgiven the Israelis, they look at me strangely: '*Mais bien sûr*,' they say, almost incredulous at the question. People are people, they explain, their palms upturned.

Pondering their words, I return to my cell on the second floor of the inner courtyard. It is white and bare. I left the shutters half drawn to keep out the heat of the day, but the metal brackets are broken, and they rasp a little in the breeze. The light streaming in through the slanted gaps casts fiery streaks across the walls. Outside, I can hear the crash of the waves, and gulls circling. A motorbike revs its engine, and backfires a few times as it catches. An imam's voice swells from some distant point, quickly joined by more from other directions. Then the church bells come too and the sound crescendos.

Flinging wide the shutters, for a moment I am dazzled. Everything is white. Then after a moment the colours settle, and an expanse of diamond-strewn sea opens up before me with a bright sky overhead. I breathe deeply and stare across the waves, and wonder how far it is to Carthage. It must be more or less a straight shot from here. How long would it take a Phoenician ship to cross that vast expanse of blue?

CARTHAGE

The Decline of the Carthaginian Empire, J.M.W. Turner, 1817

Ships no longer sail from Tyre to Carthage. The waters around Tyre are strictly regulated, and ships cannot sail freely out into the Mediterranean and cross to the Tunisian coast. Instead, I have to fly.

I am staying walking distance from the ruins of ancient Carthage, in the picture-postcard village of Sidi Bou Said, next to the Basilica of St Cyprian and Hamilcar beach. Everywhere, antiquity displays itself. In Sidi Bou Said, every building is painted ocean blue and bright white. I am told it took ancient sailors a month to journey here from Tyre – stopping for supplies in Cyprus and Crete and Sicily, finally rounding the headland, and docking in the famous port of Carthage.

The sailors who made that journey – tossed and turned in the gusty Mediterranean winds – would have finally moored up in the first of the two fantastic harbours of Punic Carthage. They would have tumbled from their crafts, exhausted, to find themselves in a city greater and more splendid than the one that they had left behind. The horizon their eyes raked over would have been dominated by the 'Tyrian towers' eulogised by Virgil, and their gaze would have risen upwards to a glorious marble temple to Eshmun on the crest of Byrsa Hill. They would have found themselves in the heart of one of the most powerful and vibrant cultures of the ancient Mediterranean.

When the mythic Aeneas arrived, storm-tossed, on Carthaginian shores, fleeing the Trojan War and the wrath of Hera – queen of the Graeco-Roman gods – he found a hive of activity, and Tyrian settlers eagerly raising up their new city. Aeneas stared in wonder at the massive stone buildings that had risen out of mere huts, at the monumental gates and the walls of the citadel rising before his eyes. The Tyrians toiled with alacrity – an optimistic people building their own future. Doubtless he was contemplating the city that he himself would build, the city that one day would be Rome. He watched as the men dug their harbours, laid the foundations of their theatres and carved noble columns out of the white rock of the cliff face. He looked up to see that the roofs built by the new Carthaginians, on their multistorey houses, had already reached the shrouding clouds. He stared hungrily at this young city, as though he saw his destiny before his eyes. 'Happy they whose walls already rise!' he cried. This bustling scene captured the imagination of Turner too, who in 1815 made the painting *Dido Building Carthage*, which hangs in the National Gallery. The painting, with its flurry of activity bathed in buttery dawn light, captures the idealised splendour of the birth of a civilisation that would rise to become one of the greatest of its time.*

The city Aeneas stumbled into dazzled him, as ancient Carthage dazzled all visitors. For a century at least it was the grandest and most advanced Mediterranean city. The Carthaginians, like their Phoenician ancestors from Tyre, were inventive, curious, industrious. Excellent craftsmen and architects, the city they built, radiating out from Byrsa Hill, was elegant and sophisticated. They built two magnificent harbours,

---

* Ancient dates don't quite align, with most scholars dating the Trojan Wars to the eleventh century BC, when Carthage was not yet even an idea in a Phoenician mind, and also dating the foundation of Carthage even by the mythical Dido-Elissar to the ninth century. So the likelihood of Aeneas stumbling upon Dido raising up her capital was small.

one leading to another, the second of which was round with an island in the centre and designed for the construction of their warships. The remains of these harbours are visible today, overgrown and marshy. One can stand on the central island and imagine the flurry of activity that took place in ancient times, making out the circular plan of the area. The cultural authorities have added scale models of the ancient ports and ships, but few genuine artefacts survive of this centre of industry.

Carthage and her ruins today have been absorbed by the sprawl of modern Tunis. No longer an independent city, the glory of the Mediterranean, but a suburb of the Tunisian capital. It is a patch of earth that has lived three lives, each separated by a long sleep. The first phase is undoubtedly Carthage's most famous, as a Punic city and one of the great powers of the early Mediterranean, before meeting destruction at the hands of Rome. The second phase was as a Roman colony, and Christian centre, refounded after that Roman razing of Punic Carthage. The third is as the bougie district of Tunis, known for its large white houses, sandy beaches and archaeological sites.

When the Arabs took North Africa by force, they used the stones of Carthage to build Tunis, and thus the two cities are connected, if only by the stones that make up their very fabric. Citizens of Tunis cherish the legacy of the Carthaginians who once lived and breathed on the same patch of earth as them. They seem to know the names Hannibal and Dido better than they know the names of the Arab conquerors who founded Tunis. The legacy of one city has bled into the identity of the next, along with the stones. Images of Hannibal and Dido-Elissar decorate various dinar notes. Beyond this, though, their history is somewhat hazy in their minds. Tunisians do not identify with Phoenician or Punic culture the way many of the Lebanese do. Despite sharing some of their DNA with the men of Tyre, their fondness for the history is thin. Tunisians identify more as Berber and Arab, but nevertheless the myths remain popular as curios, if not as a foundation of national identity.

This is natural. Carthage was destroyed, and the sense of identity has not carried down the generations. During my time in Carthage, I do not meet a single Tunisian who describes themselves as Phoenician. Again, I am not surprised, but Pierre Zalloua's work revealed that Tunisians too carried a disproportionately high percentage of that Phoenician Y chromosome, and they have as much claim to Phoenician heritage as the Lebanese.

So, from the original Phoenician trading outpost, imaginatively named Qart Hadasht – ('New City') – Carthage would swiftly grow into a city with its own distinct identity, before swelling still further into an empire that nearly brought down Rome. Carthage is perhaps the most famous legacy of Tyre, and the foundation myth of Carthage comes in many forms. All start in Tyre. At some point in history, the Carthaginians would cease to be Phoenicians, developing their own distinct Punic culture, but to this day, the inhabitants of Carthage have not forgotten their roots across the sea.

The story goes that in the ninth century BC, the King of Tyre was a man named Matten. His wife gave him twin children: a son and a daughter named Pygmalion and Elissar. Elissar is better known under another name made eternal by Virgil: Dido.

Matten made both the children his heirs, leaving the Kingdom of Tyre to them jointly upon his death. But it was a decision the Tyrians did not accept. They did not want the kingdom divided, or to suffer a female ruler. They decided that Pygmalion would rule alone, and they sidelined Elissar. Neither history nor myth relates how the princess felt about this ousting, but the surviving record shows us that she was an ambitious woman, and thus it is likely to have rankled. Nevertheless, it seems she was quick to bounce back, marrying the most powerful man in the kingdom after the king himself. Her suitor was in fact her own uncle, her father's brother and the high priest of the Melqart. According to the Roman writer Justin, his name was Acerbas.

Acerbas was wealthy, in possession of more gold than even Pygmalion himself. Wary of thieves and aware that power and wealth attracted enemies, he concealed his riches under the earth in a secret place. Rumours of the hoard spread thick and fast among the Tyrians, and the gossip soon reached the ear of the king. Insecure on his throne, and doubtless worried by the threat posed by his wealthy uncle married to his sister, Pygmalion wanted the treasure for himself.

To this end, 'forgetful of the laws of humanity', he gave commands for Acerbas to be assassinated. His men succeeded in murdering the priest but failed to squeeze the secret of the treasure's whereabouts from him before he died. When they searched, they searched in vain. The myth relates that – murdered and unburied as he was – the ghost of Acerbas lingered on the earth, and paid a visit to his widow. Coming to Elissar in a dream, he told her who had killed him and warned her that she too was in danger. He revealed the location of the gold, and urged her to flee from Tyre as soon as she could.

This would not be simple. Chests of gold are bulky, and cannot be gathered by a lone woman into a carpet bag and smuggled away under the dark of night. Nor can princesses living in walled cities guarded by jealous brothers take to the sea and make their escape without someone sounding the alarm. Pygmalion's men were searching high and low for Acerbas's wealth, and they were watching the princess. Any indication she gave of a planned journey would arouse suspicion, and a full-on escape attempt was likely to be foiled. Slowly and quietly therefore, Elissar hatched her plan.

With sisterly tenderness and honeyed words, she asked her brother if she might come back to live at the royal palace. She sighed that her husband's memory in their marital home made her sad, and she wanted a change. Pygmalion's ears pricked up at this request, as he thought she might bring with her the wealth of her dead husband. He granted her request, and rooms were made ready.

Elissar then did a curious thing. She instructed her attendants, with a flamboyant display of would-be secrecy and loud stage whispers, to take some sacks and chests out to sea, and throw their contents into the water. As they did this, she mournfully invoked the spirit of her husband, wishing him to happily receive his wealth in the abyss.

After she had emptied these sacks into the water, Elissar fled with her attendants on the swiftest ships, joined by some of the great men of Tyre who had heard of her intentions to flee. They resented the rule of Pygmalion, and his murder of Acerbas, and they wished to strike out for new lands with her. As we have seen, the ancient Tyrians lived and breathed adventure.

The king soon also learned of his sister's flight, and set to chase her. His mother and his priests tried to restrain him, pleading that were he to catch her, he would halt the founding of a city that would be the richest in the world. How they knew this we are not sure, but queens and priests in ancient times were prone to prophesying. Fuming as he was, the king was dissuaded, believing that the wealth of Acerbas was already lost and at the bottom of the sea. He would waste no more time on his treacherous sister.

Secretly, Elissar had stored a second set of sacks in the hold of her ship. The treasure had not been sent into the depths – only rocks and sand. If Pygmalion ever learned of her deception, it was long after she had escaped beyond his reach.

How mythical Elissar felt as she sailed away from her home cannot be known, but she must have been conflicted. She had a great destiny ahead of her, had finally found true freedom and achieved some power over her own fate – but she had left behind the kingdom of her ancestors, and her childhood home. To this day, the Lebanese coast surrounding Tyre is one of the most beautiful places in the world, and there is great sorrow for anyone forced to sail away from such a homeland, knowing that they will never return.

First and foremost, Elissar's mind must have focused on practicalities. Long sea voyages and ancient urban planning were logistically challenging, even for mythic princesses. If she were to undertake such a journey, Elissar would need to stop to gather provisions, and if she wished to found a new city then she would need to gather women. Only men had joined her on her ship to escape, and men need wives. Her first stop was Cyprus, the mythical birthplace of Aphrodite, and a Mediterranean paradise in its own right. But the island of Cyprus, lying only a handful of miles from Tyre, could not be Elissar's refuge and final destination. She stopped only long enough to entice or coerce eighty women onto her ship, and then set sail once again. At some point during her meandering journey across the Mediterranean, she earned the nickname Dido, which is supposedly a Phoenician word for 'wanderer'. And so she wandered.

Her ship would berth for the last time on the coast of North Africa, a stone's throw from Sicily, on the coastline of what is now Tunisia.

The locals were pleased at the arrival of friendly visitors, whom they saw as potential trading partners. The Phoenicians were widely famed for their commercial activities, but the Berber population seem to have been taken aback by the princess's desire to settle, rather than to sail back to Cyprus or Tyre laden with African goods to sell. Eventually, following hard-wrung negotiations with the fugitive princess, the local king agreed to give Elissar a piece of land – a hollow gesture, as he stipulated she could only have the amount that she could cover with one oxhide, maybe about four metres squared. But to be fair, he did provide the oxhide. Instead of accepting this as defeat and humiliation, Elissar sat down with the dedication of Penelope, and painstakingly shredded the pelt, cutting it into one long, continuous ribbon.

She laid this ribbon on the ground, encircling a well-positioned hill on the coast. In the morning she showed her handiwork to the king, who – although doubtless incredulous at first – laughed at being tricked and allowed her to keep the hill. That hill is Byrsa Hill – the name of which is derived from Elissar's oxhide – still a landmark in modern Tunis, and the heart of the city that would grow to become Carthage. From this small patch of sloping land radiated one of the greatest empires of antiquity. Little by little Carthage was founded. Various animal skulls were found during the digging of the foundations, which the ancients interpreted as signs that the city would be wealthy, and its people warlike.

It is here that the myths of Carthage and its plucky queen diverge. Elissar, or Dido as she is better known in the West, splits into two personalities. She becomes either a doomed love slave or a powerful female ruler determined to live single.

Justin, a Roman writer dating from around the second century AD, gives a version of Elissar's story that continues with Hiarbus, King of Mauritania, demanding her hand in marriage, and threatening war if she refused. Her male entourage, knowing that she would be unlikely to take kindly to such a request, particularly when offered in this style, phrased the matter another way when they put it to her. They told her that Hiarbus had requested someone from Carthage to go and live among his people and teach them a more civilised life, but that no one could be found who was willing to go. Elissar robustly condemned this selfishness, declaring that people should act in the interest of their city. Her advisors said they quite agreed and then revealed to her the real nature of Hiarbus's request. She was caught in her own logic, and felt compelled to agree.

She shed many tears, and – as if to appease the ghost of her husband – ordered the construction of a monumental funeral pyre on the edge of the city. She made numerous animal sacrifices, and then, while her people watched aghast, ascended the pyre herself. Standing amid the flames, she declared that she would do as her people demanded, and go to her husband, before plunging a sword into her breast and flinging herself into the fire. This began a longstanding Tunisian tradition of self-immolation: it is a nation with fire in its blood.

Virgil tells a different story, but one that likewise ends in fire.

His version, famous across Europe and America, holds little interest for the citizens of Carthage today. I am surprised when speaking to Tunisian master's students studying various parts of history that they are unfamiliar with the story of Dido and Aeneas, despite being very aware of Elissar.

Virgil did Dido a disservice. He made her a passionate woman who fell so deeply in love with the fugitive Trojan Prince Aeneas that she laid her city at his feet. When pious Aeneas left her to continue his quest to found Rome, she threw herself on a funeral pyre in despair. Virgil's Dido likewise died in flames, but for very different reasons to Elissar.

Virgil's characterisation of Dido is often praised as being searingly human: 'Dido, changing with all the course of circumstance, has that vital growth which is the master-test of a lifelike character. She rises to such heights of noble achievement, she sinks to such depths of shame and humiliation, she is now so weak, now so strong, that she seems one of us.'* Perhaps she does seem human, but weak and mercurial too. The Dido of the *Aeneid* is not the greatest queen ever conjured by mythology, a woman of such perseverance, such loyalty, such personal power, that Penelope, Hecuba and Clytemnestra pale in comparison. The Carthaginian conception of their ancient queen does not have her prostrate herself at the feet of the founder of Rome. The love story of Dido and Aeneas, epic as it is, is part of a cycle of Roman propaganda that explains and justifies the enmity between the two great empires which jostled furiously for control of the Mediterranean. In Virgil's version of Dido's demise, she curses Rome and Aeneas as she throws herself into the flames, and swears that Carthaginians will always war with Rome:

> let him die before his time, and lie unburied on the sand.
> This I pray, these last words I pour out with my blood.
> Then, O Tyrians, pursue my hatred against his whole line
> and the race to come, and offer it as a tribute to my ashes.
> Let there be no love or treaties between our peoples.
> Rise, some unknown avenger, from my dust, who will pursue
> the Trojan colonists with fire and sword, now, or in time
> to come, whenever the strength is granted him.
> I pray that shore be opposed to shore, water to wave,
> weapon to weapon: let them fight, them and their descendants.

Whatever the fate of Elissar – if she existed at all – Carthage grew, and it grew to know great enmity with Rome. It grew from the patch of ground encircled by Elissar's oxhide ribbon into one of the great powers of the Mediterranean. How much of the story of Elissar is true is anybody's guess. The name Elissar is certainly Phoenician, and there are records of a king called Pygmalion ruling at an appropriate time. Archaeological findings similarly seem to tally roughly with the mythic date of foundation. Given the Trojan War is usually dated many centuries before the ninth-century foundation of Carthage, Aeneas's visit is perhaps the most unlikely element of the tale, and is certainly a Roman invention. What is certain is that Carthage began life as a Phoenician trading colony and expanded in size and influence. Furthermore, while previous archaeologists had rubbished the claim of an 814 settlement, recent results provided by radiocarbon dating do indeed put the foundation of the city sometime between 835 and 800. Whether it was founded by a fugitive

* J. Raleigh Nelson, 'Dido: A Character Study'.

queen cannot be proved or disproved, but it is not the most far-fetched foundation myth of ancient times, and could well have been based in truth. Carthage is unique both in mythology and reality as a city founded by a woman in the ancient world, and so it is certainly no trope that lazy chroniclers might have fallen back on.

The name New City, Qart Hadasht, morphed into Carthāgō in Latin and Karkhēdōn (*Καρχηδών*) in Greek, and eventually into Carthage in modern English. At some point after the Phoenician settlers founded their new city, it took on an identity shift, breaking from the cultural mores and identity of the mother city of Tyre. The people became distinctly Carthaginian, or Punic, rather than Phoenician (although the name Punic is derived from the Greek word *Φοινίκη*, meaning Phoenicia). Punic, generally, means western Phoenicians – and they did develop a different culture. The original Levantine Phoenicians never had imperial ambitions. Their cities were not linked to a magnificent ruling centre, but formed distinct city states. The cities they founded were trading posts rather than points of invasive colonisation. The Carthaginians in contrast were a warlike people, interested in expansion and territorial gain as much as they were interested in trade. Their religious practices also developed differently to those of Tyre, although they clung to the old gods – Tanit and Baal Hammon.

In the early days of the city, Diodorus Siculus – a Sicilian-Greek chronicler – asserts that the settlers at Carthage sent one-tenth of all they produced to Tyre, to offer to the god Heracles-Melqart, to appease him and retain his favour. However, after some time, while the city became more and more Punic and less and less Tyrian, they sent less and less, until the offering was next to nothing.

Carthage prospered and eventually outstripped its mother city of Tyre for influence, but Carthage has not survived in the same way as Tyre. Their two histories are inextricably linked, but the great difference is that after many twists and turns of fate, Tyre has retained its name and exists as a relatively prosperous city on the south coast of Lebanon. Carthage's legacy is more modest: a nostalgically named suburb of another city, filled with fragrant jasmine, bougainvillea and whitewashed houses.

The remnants of the once-great capital are hard to discern. Of all the great archaeological sites of Carthage, most are Roman rather than Punic remains. The Romans wrought their destruction well, and the most impressive legacies of the ancient city date from the Roman period. However, vestiges of the Punic people remain. Byrsa Hill rises gracefully above the Carthaginian coast, and perhaps commands the most beautiful view in the Mediterranean, across the ruins of ancient Carthage and the bay of Tunis, out to the horizon. From the summit, one looks out over Roman columns, Carthaginian harbours and modern Tunis, to the mountains beyond. A heat haze hovers over it all, giving the scene an otherworldly quality, and the sea's profound turquoise beguiles. It is clear in an instant why Dido looped her oxhide around this hill to claim it for her people. If one can wrench one's eyes from the sea and the mountains and turn the gaze inwards, one will see that Byrsa Hill is now topped with the Carthage Museum and the Cathedral of St Louis, the ill-fated crusader King of France, who mysteriously led his fleet to Carthage, only to die there.

The museum contains the surviving treasures of the Carthaginian people, those that have not been appropriated by other museums – the Louvre and British Museum of course being the greatest culprits. While the Romans did a good job when they laid Carthage low, many traces of the splendid past have survived under layers of earth, and have been excavated and preserved in this museum. Grinning masks used at the theatre leer out from cases, showing crescent eyes and curved teeth. Wide-eyed talismans with blue ringlets and yellow-painted lips stare out beside them. Sculptures of Baal Hammon and sculptures made in honour of Tanit are well preserved.

It's a schlep to the top of Byrsa Hill today to visit this museum, but in ancient times Byrsa was much higher. The summit reached to the tip of the steeple of St Louis's cathedral, standing to one side of the museum, which occupies the cloisters and halls of a former monastery. The library and archive are still managed by the monastic order of Les Pères Blancs. When they captured Carthage in 146, the Roman conquerors essentially sliced off the top of Byrsa Hill, removing the evidence of the great Punic buildings and the temple of Eshmun on top. This rubble and dirt, they poured down the sides of the hill and buttressed with thick stone walls that stand to this day. Then they constructed a much larger space on the hilltop with a flat plateau, which would in time become the Roman forum and house the temple of Asclepius, the god of medicine.

Around the site of the temple have been excavated the remains of the Punic dwellings that once stood atop this hill. The red walls of a network of modest houses can be seen, laid out on a grid system and commanding views of the sea. Ironically, these building were preserved by the Romans, who covered them with earth, meaning that they were protected and undisturbed for millennia.

However, perhaps the most famous and controversial of the Punic sites is not under the earth of Byrsa Hill, but nearer the coast, the place that has become known as the tophet of Carthage.

When I arrive in Tunis, despite my plane landing at dusk and archaeological sites being theoretically closed, I head straight to the remains of the ancient city, hoping to catch the sun slipping down behind the ruins. It is not difficult to find your way into the old city at night. Tunis is more prosperous than Tyre, but that still doesn't quite equate to watertight security, and it is possible (if not encouraged), to climb over the low wall and enter. Short on time and courage, I do not stay long. The first and only place I visit is the tophet, and there in the twilight I wander among the Punic stelae, the engraved stones that are perhaps the most iconic remains of the Carthaginian Empire.

The shadowy grounds are eerie and unnerving. In many places, the rows of stelae are overgrown. Branches crack underfoot, and a sea breeze stirs the leaves of pomegranate trees, adding whispering to my rustling. Moonlight scatters through the branches, the leaves, through cracks in ancient buildings, the shafts falling on the ancient stelae that seem like tiny headstones. They are in fact little more than this: the tophet is a burial ground for Punic babies offered to the gods. Carved on the stones are the signs of the Phoenician god Baal Hammon and the goddess Tanit. The Phoenician settlers who founded and built Carthage brought their religion with them, and showed a remarkable dedication to the old ways, honouring Melqart and sending tribute back to their mother city for centuries. However, in time, they began to develop their own distinct culture. The thing most conspicuously different between the religious archaeological sites of Carthage and Tyre is the presence of this tophet.

The practice of child sacrifice happened in the Levant in the Bronze Age. It was not only Phoenician, and there is strong evidence that it took place in Judah too. The kings of Judea purportedly sacrificed their sons, Jephthah his daughter, and Abraham was on the brink of sacrificing Isaac when God reprieved him. For all this, passages in the Old Testament clearly condemn the practice of child sacrifice and charged followers to give up this ritual. Across the region, the practice quickly faded, and no tophets have been found in the Levant. In Carthage in the 1920s, two Frenchmen, suspicious of an antiquities dealer who seemed to have an everlasting supply of Punic stelae, planned a stake-out to see where he got his stock. At night, they found him digging in one of the oldest parts of Punic Carthage. They had found the tophet of Carthage. When they investigated further, they found that each stela was accompanied by a clay urn, inside of which were the charred and calcified remains of hundreds of babies, sometimes mixed with animal bones and amulets.

The name tophet is taken from the Hebrew bible, and is traditionally believed to be the site of child sacrifice. Rumours of the Carthaginians sacrificing babies were for centuries dismissed by sympathetic modern historians as part of the smear campaign mounted by the Romans against their greatest rivals, a smear campaign that followed the destruction and massacre of an entire civilisation and destruction of their written history. Although it was not called such, this was a thorough act of historic genocide.

Scholarly feelings on accounts of the sacrifice of children have come in waves. Originally dismissed, the discovery of infant remains mixed with animal bones at the tophet did indeed seem to back up the Roman assertions, but recent studies have argued relatively convincingly that in fact the tophet represents a cemetery for stillborn and premature infants, and the animal bones are an offering to the gods to go up with the soul of the lost child.

People have been quick to accept this argument, seeing it as part of a wider trend of rehabilitating oppressed and maligned people and civilisations from history. However it is perhaps worth considering that if the Carthaginians did indeed sacrifice their infants, which the evidence certainly suggests, then they did not see it as something shameful. Perhaps the most important thing to bear in mind when considering long-dead civilisations is the fact that they functioned differently, and with a different moral code. For millennia, Romans and Greeks abandoned infants they deemed unlucky or deformed; the sense of the innate value of an infant's life is relatively modern, and it is not 'slanderous' or 'insulting' to assert that there is evidence of child sacrifice in a society many millennia back.

The most graphic description of the Punic ritual of the infant sacrifice is to be found in the writings of Diodorus Siculus. Diodorus lived in Sicily in the first century BC, and wrote a brief history of time from mythic beginnings to his own lifetime. He dedicated a good deal of time to the Greek and Carthaginian wars, as the 'tyrants' of Syracuse struggled against the Carthaginians for control of Sicily. One of the greatest threats to Carthaginian security, before the true rise of Rome, came in 308–07 BC in the form of the Syracusan tyrant Agathocles, who drove the Carthaginians out of Sicily and took the skirmishes between Greeks and Carthaginians onto African soil. The Carthaginians defeated him repeatedly in Sicily, and terrified the Syracusans, only then to be pushed back all the way to Carthage itself. Agathocles of Syracuse landed his fleet at Cape Bon, defeated the Carthaginian soldiers lying in wait for him on the shore and set up a military camp near Lake Tunis. For two years he rampaged around Carthage, forging alliances with local rulers and chipping away at Carthaginian territory.

The Carthaginians were rightly terrified. Normally, their wars with Sicilian tyrants took place on the island of Sicily – this was the first time that they were truly threatened at home by a Syracusan warlord. The reaction, according to Diodorus, was shocking and barbaric. The priest declared that the gods were being unfavourable to Carthage in this conflict on the grounds of impiety. Noble families, meant to sacrifice their own children, had been giving up slave children instead, or even purchasing street children from poor mothers. Fearing for their community, according to Diodorus Siculus in *The Library of History*, 500 noble babies were demanded and taken from their mothers' arms. They were sacrificed in one day. Diodorus writes:

> They also alleged that Kronos [Baal] had turned against them inasmuch as in former times they had been accustomed to sacrifice to this god the noblest of their sons, but more recently, secretly buying and nurturing children, they had sent these to sacrifice ... In their zeal to make amends for this omission, they selected two hundred of the noblest children and sacrificed them publicly; and others who were under suspicion sacrificed themselves voluntarily, in a number not less than three hundred. There was in the city a bronze image of Kronos, extending its hands, palms up and sloping towards the ground, so that each of the children when placed thereon rolled down and fell into a sort of gaping pit filled with fire.

Kronos is the equivalent name for Baal Hammon – the highest god in the Punic pantheon. What must be remembered in assessing the validity of this account is that Diodorus was a deeply anti-Carthaginian writer, whose accounts of Carthage and the Punic Wars must be seen as a victor writing about a defeated enemy, and an exercise in anti-Carthaginian propaganda. Sicilian Greeks were constantly at war with Carthage, and Diodorus naturally inherited prejudices and enmities towards their enemy across the sea. He is not, however, the only writer to leave descriptions of ritual sacrifice among the Carthaginians, and there is sufficient archaeological evidence to support the belief that this did in fact take place *in extremis*. Nevertheless, Diodorus's graphic and sadistic description must be exaggerated.

No tophets have been identified with any certainty in Phoenicia. That said, there is textual evidence of child sacrifice being practised in the Levant, not least in the Bible, with Abraham's near-sacrifice of his son Isaac. It should also be remembered that Quintus Curtius Rufus claimed the Tyrians considered child sacrifice in an attempt to appease Baal during Alexander's siege, although the proposition was benched by the city's elders.

The Carthaginians brought their religion from Phoenicia, and kept it. Their main gods were Baal Hammon and Tanit, the equivalents of Baal and Astarte in Tyre, and Melqart and Eshmun as well.

Whatever the truth of their religious practices and devotions, the city prospered. Carthage was a natural stopping point and policing point for Mediterranean trade route from east to west and back again. The Carthaginians were well placed to control all the trade that passed through the straits between North Africa and Sicily, and furthermore had access to an extensive agricultural hinterland. In spite of the Elissar myth, it seems the first government was made of judges sent by Tyre, but gradually this gave way to kings.

True to their Phoenician roots, many explorers set out from Carthage, notably Hanno and Himilco. The Carthaginian Empire started on an informal basis, of trading posts like those of Tyre. But soon, as their wealth grew, the Carthaginians became aggressive and imperially minded. Before long, they had taken over Sardinia and large chunks of Sicily, and they were advancing along the African coast towards Spain. When Tyre signed its devastating peace treaty with Nebuchadnezzar in 573, which heralded its demise as the great mercantile power, the fall of the mother city created an opportunity for the daughter city to rise, and Carthage used its prime positioning at the centre of the Mediterranean to establish itself as a trading power. Carthaginian culture spread widely around the Mediterranean: some of the best examples of Punic art and architecture are found in Sicily and Sardinia. Perhaps the most famous instance is known as the Motya charioteer, an astoundingly advanced and nuanced carved marble statue of a youth wearing a finely pleated garment that clings to the curves of his body, as though blown by the wind of a moving chariot. Debate surrounds his origins.

Sicily was the natural battleground of Mediterranean superpowers. It is the centre of the Mediterranean and would become a crossing place for Greek, Carthaginian and Roman cultures. Greeks and Phoenicians both settled the island. The first major cycle of wars which the Carthaginians would face for control over Sicily and the sea around their city was with

Sicilian Greeks. Their two great rivals were the cities of Acragas and Syracuse.

By 265 BC Carthage had grown to become the most powerful city state in the Mediterranean region. But the power of Rome was growing too, and soon the city would enter into the power struggle with Rome that would define its apogee and its demise.

PUNIC WARS

The Punic Wars simultaneously signify the most glorious and disastrous moments in Carthage's history. This is of course in no small part because – as Carthage was ultimately defeated – the ways in which the wars were written about were entirely controlled by the Romans. The historiography of the Punic Wars is perhaps the best example of history being written by the winners. Roman victors, and their sympathisers, took complete control of the narrative. These protracted conflicts also marked the most frightening and embarrassing moments in Rome's rise to Mediterranean domination. Roman historians could not simply dismiss Carthage as feeble, but had to glorify her as a worthy adversary that indeed managed to threaten Rome but was ultimately defeated. Like the life cycles of Carthage itself, the wars came in three waves, known as the First, Second and Third Punic Wars. Each of these phases of brutal fighting left a lasting impact on the economy and culture of Carthaginian society, and the times between the wars were almost as devastating for the city as the wars themselves.

The First Punic War lasted twenty-three years – a series of bitter and bloody battles fought on land and sea around Sicily, the largest island in the Mediterranean, and the stepping stone between Carthage and Roman Italy. It was the natural battleground for the warring empires.

Carthage's mercantile reputation may have been waning in the third century BC, but its navy was stronger than ever. Rome might have perceived herself to be the equal of Carthage militarily, but only so far as land battles went; there was no real contest when it came to the sea. The Carthaginians were the successors of the Phoenician master craftsmen and seafarers, inheritors of centuries of perfected knowledge; the Romans were relatively new to the game. Where Tyre was founded in roughly 2750 BC, and Carthage in roughly 815 BC, Rome was only founded in 753 BC – and not as the colony of an already powerful city.

The *Marsala* wreck – a sunken Carthaginian warship found off the west coast of Sicily – testifies to the advanced and efficient nature of

Carthaginian vessels at this time. Made of carefully designed, individual pieces that could be collapsed, moved and reassembled repeatedly, it also incorporated an iron ram, space for cargo and space for oarsmen. The ship itself reads like an instruction booklet for ancient shipwrights, with letters from the ancient Phoenician alphabet demarking where sections joined another, and which piece went where. The craft was approximately thirty metres long. The skeleton of the hull is slim and light, suggesting speed and manoeuvrability were the priorities of the Carthaginian shipwright. It is possible that this vessel was sunk by Romans during the First Punic War. It was the same Honor Frost – the eminent marine archaeologist who excavated the Phoenician harbour at Tyre – who excavated the *Marsala* wreck in the 1970s. Among the ballast stones were found human remains, perhaps of a sailor who went down with the ship.

The city of Acragas, a historic rival of Carthage but now under Carthaginian control, was chosen as the Carthaginian nerve centre on Sicily, and the Romans besieged it nearly straight away. The Carthaginians sent a bulky army to support the besieged, comprising foot soldiers, cavalry and sixty war elephants under the command of the general Hanno. While this army was large enough to achieve its goal, it was not experienced, and Hanno was fainthearted. He did not strike swiftly, but dithered and then executed a poor strategy that saw his elephants stampede his own men and his force routed. Acragas was quickly taken by the Romans in 262, and while the Carthaginian defence force escaped, led by the general Hannibal Gisco, the ordinary inhabitants were taken as slaves. This event – the loss of Acragas – would prove to be the catalyst for the First Punic War. It showed the Romans that they could decisively beat Carthage, and lit the idea in their minds that they could drive their Carthaginian foes from Sicily.

Our main source for this period is Polybius, a high-ranking Greek, born in Arcadia, who was held hostage in Rome and integrated into its aristocracy, becoming a counsellor of the general Scipio Aemilianus. He is highly prejudiced against Carthage, but does provide a detailed account of the war from a Roman perspective.

Polybius asserts that the Carthaginians could only be defeated if Rome could also muster the strength to beat them at sea, where the Carthaginians were certainly masters. To this end, Rome built a fleet. By 260, they had commissioned a hundred quinquereme warships and twenty triremes, following the design of a captured Carthaginian vessel. The first test came when the newly appointed naval commander, Cornelius Scipio, rushed some ships to try to take the city of Lipara

(Lipari) in the Aeolian Islands, just north of Sicily. There they clashed with Carthaginians, also eager to take the town, and many of the inexperienced Roman sailors panicked, jumping overboard and heading to shore, where they were captured and enslaved. Scipio was captured too, but swiftly ransomed. A good PR campaign ensured that this defeat was not his downfall, and he continued to enjoy favour and public honours and high office.

The next major sea battle would take place off the northern coast of Sicily, known to history as the Battle of Mylae, the first major naval conflict of the Punic Wars. The Romans had a secret weapon up their sleeves. Aware of the poor manoeuvrability and lack of responsiveness of their ships, together with the general ineptitude of their seamanship compared to the Carthaginians, they had taken steps to compensate for these shortcomings. They had attached ingeniously designed gangplanks to their vessels that would be dropped when the ships came within reaching distance of a Carthaginian vessel, linking the two ships and anchoring them together with a spike. They called these gangways corvi, or crows. When their ships came together in the waters outside Mylae, the Carthaginians sped towards the Roman ships with alacrity, eager for what they supposed would be an easy victory. They were blindsided by the corvi, which the Romans deployed to great effect, using them to board the Carthaginian ships and bring the fight back to their comfort zone: hand-to-hand combat. Panicked by this unexpected tactic, the Carthaginians retreated and attempted to strike the Roman fleet from the side or behind, but the corvi pivoted, and in the turmoil the Carthaginians lost fifty of their hundred and thirty ships.

The Roman commander Gaius Duilius was rewarded for this victory, the senate granting him the crowning glory of military achievements. He processed in state in a four-horse chariot through the streets of Rome, at the head of a triumph, crowned with a laurel wreath and draped in purple robes. Following him were the Carthaginian sailors taken captive following the defeat – these were his war prizes. His final destination was the temple of Jupiter, where he would offer up a sacrifice in thanks for his victory. Duilius must have felt like a king indeed. They also constructed a monumental column recording his victories, the *columna rostrata*, in the Roman forum. It was decorated with the metal prows of ships. The Carthaginian general Hannibal Gisco (not Hannibal Barca, who would come later to the Roman struggle) who had led the disastrous Carthaginian mission received no such accolades at home, but miraculously escaped public punishment.

The Romans would ride the wave of this victory to take their ambitions still further, turning their attention to Sardinia and Corsica. The Carthaginians suffered an even greater defeat in Sardinia, at the Battle of Sulco in 258, and this time Hannibal Gisco did not escape recriminations. His troops were furious and attributed the defeat to his incompetence. He was arrested by his own troops and executed.

While Carthaginian ships floundered in sea battles in the Mediterranean, the foot soldiers were meeting with more success on land. The war continued here in the form of sieges and raids. Carthage managed to hold her own on land, with her most significant victory being the Battle of Thermae Himerae, where 4,000 Syracusans were ambushed and killed.

After many gruelling sea battles – including the largest naval battle of antiquity, which was fought off the Cape of Ecnomus in southern Sicily – Rome would emerge victorious from this conflict. At Ecnomus, over 700 vessels and 300,000 men joined the fray, the result of which was a Roman victory and landing in North Africa. Carthage asked to negotiate a surrender, but the terms Rome offered through their leader Regulus were draconian.

Carthage was ordered to release all Roman prisoners and pay Rome's war expenses, while ransoming their own prisoners at the market price. In addition to an annual tribute, Regulus stipulated that Carthage would only be allowed to go to war with Roman consent and would be expected to supply fifty ships to Rome's navy whenever they requested it. The final affront was the demand that the Carthaginian navy be reduced to a symbolic single warship, and that the Carthaginians surrender all claim to Sicily and Sardinia. This was clearly meant as an insult rather than a serious offer, and instead of brokering a wary peace that might have spared both armies decades of conflicts and hundreds of thousands of lives, Carthage was forced to fight on. They had some successes under the command of a skilled Spartan mercenary commander and a rising general named Hamilcar Barca, but were ultimately beaten by Rome in a devastating defeat. The might of Carthage was broken, and once again, they were forced to sue for peace.

The Roman consuls they dealt with were harsh but fair. They were not cruel in the way Regulus had been, and while the terms of the resulting 241 BC Treaty of Lutatius were tough, they were manageable. The Carthaginians were allowed to keep Sardinia, but they had to pull out of Sicily completely. For the defenders on land in Sicily – defending the important settlement of Lilybaeum under the command of the undefeated Hamilcar Barca – it must have been particularly harrowing to be forced to abandon their posts and their shrines. They had held on through twenty years of war, before being suddenly ordered to surrender. Additionally, a fine of 2,200 silver talents (the equivalent of 56 tonnes of silver) was issued, and Carthage had to disarm, handing over their weapons, along with any prisoners of war, to the Romans. Additionally, they were forbidden from making war on Syracuse – which had allied with Rome during the long years of conflict. Reportedly, the treaty was negotiated by Hannibal Gisco, because Hamilcar Barca refused to participate. He claimed surrender was unnecessary.

This was a resounding defeat. However, as has been seen, Carthage had not poured their all into Sicily, fighting concurrently in North Africa on their southern and western fronts. They may have been making provision for an empire that did not hinge so greatly on Sicily.

The result of the First Punic War was Carthaginian exit from Sicily, humiliation and a grave war debt. However the Romans had suffered too, investing much in the struggle and sustaining heavy losses. The worst hit of course were the Sicilian people; their island had become a battlefield for two rival factions, and only Hieron of Syracuse had managed to keep his citizens safe. In the aftermath of this First Punic War, Carthage retreated, licking its wounds.

Carthage faced another problem: the fact that Hamilcar Barca's army at Lilybaeum had not been decisively defeated by the time the war was ended. The army could not be shamed for defeat, and was still of a significant size, and because the men were successful – and, therefore, alive – they had to be paid. Hamilcar Barca gracefully withdrew as soon as peace was negotiated, and before this problem had time to rear its ugly head. Carthage was in the grip of an unprecedented financial recession. The war had been ruinous, lost them key territories and revenue streams, and disrupted farming and trade, and they had to pay their fines to boot. Thousands of well-trained, fierce mercenaries suddenly with no war to fight and clamouring for payment was the last thing the government of Carthage needed in the aftermath of their defeat.

The ruling class decided that in order to tackle this problem, they needed to break it up. So, they started transporting the mercenaries home from Sicily in small groups, and giving them small down payments – the hope being that in bringing them home in separate convoys, it gave them time between each payment to gather the next, and also stopped the troops conspiring together and uniting to claim their dues. However, the governors waited until all the men had arrived to announce that they wished to negotiate a lower rate of payment. Furthermore, the men were billeted in the city of Carthage itself, which proved chaotic. And so they sent them all together to a town outside Carthage to await the rest of their payments.

A bored army is a dangerous one, and a bored, unpaid one 20,000 strong all the more so. Carthage learned this the hard way. Instead of patiently twiddling their thumbs and queuing up in an orderly fashion, the soldiers – realising the government was trying to stall and evade paying them – reassembled as an army and began baying for blood and gold. The army was diverse, made of men following different religions and speaking different languages, making it impossible to deal effectively with them as a collective. The soldiers did not listen therefore and instead marched towards Carthage, occupying the town of Tunes, the same place the Roman army had reached under Regulus.

Hannibal Gisco and another general who had overseen the evacuation of the force from Sicily were sent to negotiate and brought gold with them to make a settlement. However, some members of the mercenary force – fearing the repercussions of peace – stirred up resistance to the offer. Two of them – a Libyan named Spendius and a runaway Roman slave named Mathos – appointed themselves generals of the army, and ordered the arrest of the Carthaginian generals who had come to negotiate. They allied themselves with the native Libyan population who, like the Sicilians, had been hard pressed by the war, having their crops seized and taxes doubled to meet the skyrocketing costs. They were easily persuaded to join the rebel cause against Carthage. Polybius estimated that 70,000 Libyans joined the force, and that their women donated their jewellery to the cause.

The most interesting facet of this uprising is what the rebels did with the coins they took from Gisco. Instead of merely paying the men, they restruck the coins into a new currency. In ancient times, coinage was a key conduit of propaganda, and in minting their own money the rebel army showed far more menacing intent than claiming withheld money. They planned to conquer Carthage themselves, and demonstrated that they might be organised enough to do so. They were certainly a force to be reckoned with.

What ensued was dubbed by Polybius 'the Truceless War'. Others have called it 'the Mercenaries' War'. Really it was both, characterised by such extreme brutality that a better name might be 'the Merciless War'. This conflict was as great a threat to Carthage as either the Syracusan tyrant Agathocles, or Rome's invasion under Regulus. They were cut off from the rest of Africa, barred from Sicily, and they had a reputation for not paying their soldiers. The very men they would have called upon to fight for them were the ones trying to destroy them. So chaotic was this war that it is difficult to give a precise chronology, but what follows is roughly what happened.

In response to this crisis, the general Hanno was put in command of what was left of the Carthaginian army, and the city then attempted to raise and train a civilian force to join with these remnants to take on the mercenaries and Libyans. But this force, and its commander, was not equal to the challenge that faced it. It was in large part a hastily brought together, ragtag group of relatively untrained soldiers, marching against a professional army that had spent over a decade fighting together in a real and bitter war – they were practised and battle hardened. Moreover, Hanno was not as skilled a general as would be required to make a success of such an operation.

While the rebels besieged Utica, a city near Carthage, Hanno attacked. Although the element of surprise briefly gained him the upper hand, he quickly fell victim to his own complacency. As he celebrated a partial victory, the rebels attacked again, killing many soldiers and seizing the siege equipment.

Mathos – one of the rebel generals – pressed his advantage, and his armies swept across Carthaginian territory, occupying towns and cutting Carthage off from the rest of Africa. In the midst of this crisis, Hamilcar Barca was recalled from his judicious retirement and put in charge of a force of 10,000 hastily assembled troops. He was successful at first, managing to wipe out 8,000 men in a swift victory. However, he quickly found himself victim of the tactics he himself had taught the mercenaries in Sicily: guerrilla warfare and raids from the mountains.

Hamilcar would soon find his camp surrounded, with death and defeat imminent. One of the rival Numidian generals, Navaras, leading a contingent of 2,000 cavalry in the rebel army, liked Hamilcar Barca. He had long admired the general's skill and tenacity, and perhaps seeing his hero cornered, snapping like a hound, moved something in him. Whatever it was that happened, Navaras changed sides without warning. He screamed at his men to kill the mercenaries instead, and to defend Hamilcar. It seems, under the cloak of darkness, he had presented himself unarmed in Hamilcar's tent, and told him that he wanted to offer his loyalty. Hamilcar, desperate as he was, must have been incredulous. An easy victory was at hand for the rebels. If they defeated Hamilcar now, as it was in their power to do, they could succeed in destroying Carthage. History does not relate how Navaras persuaded Hamilcar that he was serious, but it does show the general's gratitude – Hamilcar gave his daughter in marriage to the Libyan chief. It is unclear whether this was part of the price of his loyalty, or a reward for loyalty freely given.

This covert diplomatic meeting, conducted in the tent of a war camp on the eve of battle, changed the face of Carthaginian history. With the aid of Navaras's men, Hamilcar would win the day. Instead of punishing the 4,000 prisoners he captured, he dealt generously with them, in the hope of inspiring more desertions from the enemy army. His skill and honour had won him important loyalty before, and he wanted to see if he could do it again. He executed none of the prisoners, but instead offered them the option of joining his army – recrimination free – or being freed and allowed to return to their homelands.

This was sly indeed, and Mathos and Spendius were having none of it. Their troops could not perceive Hamilcar as a benevolent lord who could offer the soldiers more than the rebels could. In order to provoke harshness from Hamilcar – a harshness that would deter any soldiers from deserting to join him – they committed a war crime of gross brutality. Desperate men do desperate things.

They ordered that Hannibal Gisco, the captive general who had been sent to carry out the initial negotiations over pay, should be put to death alongside the 700 other Carthaginian prisoners. Not only that, but they were to be tortured – hands cut off, castrated, legs broken – then buried alive and in agony in a mass grave. News of these horrific executions were reported to Hamilcar, and after this, there could be no mercy. No forgiveness, no reintegration, no freedom for any rebel captured. Hamilcar swiftly killed his remaining prisoners. The rebels now had no option of changing sides; they were fighting for their lives.

The good fortune of Navaras's defection was the only piece of luck Carthage was to enjoy for some time. They would receive news that many of their shipments of supplies were lost at sea, that their allies in Africa were turning against them, and that Sardinia was in revolt. Hamilcar held the fort as best he could, attacking the countryside and rebel-held Tunes. He managed to corner the part of the rebel army led by Spendius along a steep mountain ridge. They did their best to resist, eating their animals, then their prisoners of war and their slaves to avoid capitulation, but help never arrived, and eventually they were starved into submission. Hamilcar massacred the entire army of 40,000 men except the ten highest ranking officers, including Spendius, who he marched back to Tunes and crucified on a hill in sight of Mathos and the rest of the rebel army. Anxious to avenge his comrade, Mathos launched a retaliation mission and succeeded in capturing one of Hamilcar's generals, crucifying him on the same spot where Spendius had died.

During these years of war, the Romans had conspicuously not taken advantage of Carthage's desperate position. Had they sent an army now, they might have destroyed Carthage once and for all, but as yet this was not their goal. They preferred a defeated and domesticated Carthage to a rabble-rousing rebel kingdom. They went a step further and released their Carthaginian prisoners without ransom so that they could return to their country's army. Likewise, Hieron II of Syracuse supplied the wheat that Carthage needed to feed its men. This was crucial, as the rebel forces were short of supplies, and it was this that forced them to lift their siege at Tunes and withdraw south to Leptis Parva.

Hanno – who had been forced out of the army due to perceived incompetence – received an envoy recalling him to lead alongside Hamilcar once again. Co-operation and respect was encouraged between the two men. While previously enemies and contemptuous of one another, they agreed to put their differences aside for the sake of the greater good. Together they marshalled an army of 40,000 men, comprising more or less every man able to bear arms. With this army, the two generals met with Mathos and his army on the coast near Leptis Minor and, in a great turn of the tide, destroyed them in a final battle. This spelled the end of the Truceless (or Mercenaries') War, and it was seen as a great victory for Hamilcar. He received the honour of the final win and on the back of this triumph, he and his family would remain at the forefront of Carthaginian politics over the coming decades.

However, Hamilcar's fame today is not for this victory but as the father of the most famous Carthaginian of all time: Hannibal Barca.

THE RISE OF HANNIBAL BARCA

Perhaps taking advantage of Carthage's weakness in the immediate aftermath of its repression of the Truceless War, the Romans demanded Sardinia from them and additional payments of silver talents. Rome had not wanted to see the Carthaginians fully destroyed, but perhaps it had no qualms about kicking them while they were down. Hard pressed and short of troops and resources as they were, Carthage had little choice but to yield. But the insult was not forgotten.

Hamilcar Barca took his son-in-law, Hasdrubal the Fair, and his nine-year-old son Hannibal with him to Spain, where he intended to conquer new territory. The child's eyes would have drunk in the changing landscape from the arid terrain of North Africa to the coast of Andalusia, where the trio of Barcid men made their mark – establishing the territory known as Barcid Spain. He would have travelled with his father, the celebrated general of the First Punic War, and had grit and military strategy hammered into his bones. By 221 BC, Hannibal was twenty-five and had come of age amid the Spanish wars, learning his trade as future general supreme of the Carthaginian military. The new lands stretched from Cartagena – New Carthage – near Malaga, the old Phoenician outpost, all the way to Cadiz.

The key to their success was as much diplomacy as force. As Hamilcar had already demonstrated when he won over the Numidian Prince Navaras at the eleventh hour, he was a man of remarkable charisma, able to build rapport quickly with strangers. This was a skill, an aura, he imparted to his son and son-in-law. Hasdrubal and Hannibal would both take Spanish brides, and the Spanish accepted Hasdrubal as their leader. In 221 Hannibal would be elected the high commander of the Carthaginian armies – armies tirelessly built up by both his father and brother-in-law. They revived the might of Carthage on land, if not at sea. They paid little attention to rebuilding the navy.

Hannibal had begged his father to include him in that childhood expedition to the Iberian Peninsula. Hamilcar agreed but on the condition that the boy swear never to be a friend of Rome. According to some sources, he even went so far as to hold the nine-year-old child over a sacrificial fire while he made the oath. Legend has it that from that day forward, the fate of Hannibal was pitched against that of Rome.

At first, Rome paid little attention to the expansion of the Carthaginian Empire into mainland Europe. They were busy fighting the Gauls, and had taken an assurance from Hamilcar that Carthage would not push their possessions beyond the Ebro river, Spain's longest, which bisects the north of the Iberian Peninsula, a good way south of the Pyrenees. However, when Hannibal, now a fully fledged general, marched his substantial army to the very banks of the Ebro, Rome's hackles began to rise.

The Second Punic War started with Saguntum, a small city that was allied with Rome, some 125 miles south of the river. Rome commanded Carthage not to touch Saguntum, and Hannibal responded to this perceived cheek by sacking the city in 219. Rome offered no help to the citizens, but nevertheless saw the attack as a provocation, which it undoubtedly was. Roman ambassadors were dispatched to Carthage, demanding punishment for Hannibal, but were rebuffed by the lords of the city. This interaction was the symbolic catalyst for the Roman declaration of war.

The siege of Saguntum was but a tiny factor in the outbreak of war, rather than the issue which caused it. This war had been brewing for some time, with many historians arguing that it was a war of revenge for the desolation caused by the First Punic War and the snatching of Sardinia, and others suggesting that it was a case of Rome wishing to slap down a former adversary that had begun to rise again. In any case, Rome did not lift a finger to aid Saguntum against Hannibal. Similarly, Carthage did not seem to have a coherent war plan in place. While its army had expanded impressively, its navy had been neglected. If Carthage had been truly planning to start a long war against Rome, it would have built up its navy in advance, given the important role sea battles had played in the First Punic War.

Famously, the second war would not be fought in the sea but on land. Hannibal marched his armies through Spain, over the Pyrenees, through France, and over the Alps to challenge the Romans on home soil. Not only did he march men and horses through the mountains, but war elephants as well. To date, this is the only known time in history that elephants have crossed the Alps, and Hannibal crossed in winter. Even without the elephants, it was a remarkable victory in itself.

Hannibal proceeded to hammer Rome. He defeated their legions time and time again in battle across Italy. In the two years between 218 and 216 Carthaginian forces slaughtered over 100,000 Roman soldiers in a series of spectacular and unexpected victories, the most famous of which was perhaps the Battle of Lake Trasimene. Ambushing the Roman legions on the banks of this lake in northern Italy, Carthage destroyed the entire Roman army. Fifteen thousand men were killed, and the remaining 10,000 were injured or else fled. This defeat made very clear to Rome the reality of the Carthaginian threat and created panic. Following the battle, Hannibal released all non-Roman prisoners, asserting that his war was only with Rome and encouraging non-Romans to join him.

His next great victory was the Battle of Cannae. Here, he executed envelopment strategy so perfectly that his tactics are still studied by generals to this day. Within hours, as many as 47,000 highly trained Roman soldiers were dead. The Carthaginians, glutted as they were, must have felt invincible. Among the 14,000 troops that escaped was one Scipio, who would go on to take his vengeance against Carthage.

Hannibal's mistake following his victories in the north was to not march on Rome. Had he done so, he might have broken his old enemy, and entirely changed the future of European and potentially world order. That said, he had his reasons for staying away from the capital, and it cannot be known if he really would have been victorious. The result in any case was another fifteen years of prolonged conflict between the two great Mediterranean powers. The war spread across the Mediterranean, being fought from Spain to eastern Greece. Rome levied army after army, recruiting and training thousands of men, rejecting peace talks, and fighting on.

A new commander rose to prominence in the Roman army, and respecting Hannibal's superior skill and numbers, avoided meeting him in a pitched battle. Nevertheless, he marshalled an effective defence by targeting his supply chains. But Fabius's command, and his strategy of scorched earth and playing the waiting game, eventually gave way to the policies of the more aggressive general Claudius Marcellus – a man who would also play a key role in the fate of Syracuse. Hannibal would before long be forced onto the back foot, losing ground, and asking his brother-in-law Hasdrubal to send reinforcements from Spain.

Outside Italy, Carthage's luck was mixed. Syracuse allied with them, but as we shall see, did not prove an effective ally.

Ultimately, despite the aid that Hasdrubal brought from Spain, Rome would be victorious under the command of that same Scipio who struggled off the battlefield at Cannae. Not only would Scipio drive Hannibal from Italy, and seize Carthage's possessions in Spain, but he beat him back to North Africa and attacked him on home soil. But before they reached this point, Hannibal's efforts were hit by another disaster. While he was encamped in Italy, Roman soldiers rode up to his camp and tossed a sack to the commanders. Inside was the head of Hasdrubal Barca, Hannibal's brother. On receiving this grisly symbol of his brother's defeat, Hannibal reportedly lamented that he 'saw the fate of Carthage'.

The armies converged near Bulla Regis, 108 miles west of Carthage. Hannibal's great allies Hasdrubal Gisco and his son-in-law the Numidian King Syphax were defeated, with Syphax captured and Gisco committing suicide to avoid capture. Gisco's daughter, the now legendary Ṣap̄anbaʿal or Sophonisba, drank poison to avoid the humiliation of being paraded in a Roman triumph as the spoils of war. Her life has been the focus of various plays, paintings and poems, perhaps most notably featuring in Petrarch's *Africa*. Sources attest that before she died, the Carthaginian princess made a new marriage to another Numidian king, Masinissa, who was allied with Rome. She had been betrothed to him before her forced marriage to Syphax, for although he was a Numidian king and now a Roman ally, he had been raised and educated in Carthage. Perhaps there was genuine love between the couple – the man was described as attractive with good manners – but perhaps more likely is that Ṣapanbaʿal hoped a hasty marriage to a Roman ally might spare her defeat and shame. Whatever the motivations for the quick marriage, it was not destined to be a long one. Scipio refused to accept the Carthaginian princess as the bride of his ally, as he feared she would turn her second husband against him, just as 'arguably' she had turned her first. Following this news from Scipio, and the demand that he surrender his bride, it was Masinissa who brought his new wife the cup of poison that she would drink. Following her death, Masinissa dutifully delivered his wife's remains to Scipio.

Carthage sued for peace, and was granted a ruinous treaty – but it did not hold. Hannibal was still alive, and although he and his army had been recalled by Carthage, as long as he lived he would be an enemy of Rome. Following provocation from Hannibal's troops in Italy, Scipio rode to another battle 125 miles from Carthage. The Carthaginians were soundly defeated, but Hannibal escaped with perhaps 6,000 others, and he returned to Carthage, this time to assist in the peace negotiations, and a new treaty was made in 201. Carthage remained sovereign, and lord of its Libyan territories, but a heavy fine of 10,000 talents was imposed, and Carthage was forbidden to ever wage war outside Africa, and only within Africa with the express permission of Rome. In a symbolic end of Carthage's greatness, the remaining 500 ships of the navy were burned in the water.

In the first half of the Second Punic War, Hannibal's incredible victories and feats of generalship made Carthage the supreme power of the Mediterranean, and the hammer of Rome, but by its close, it was a wounded and hobbled nation. From a human perspective, perhaps the most interesting element of the war is the reported relationship between Scipio and Hannibal. Scipio – for all that he had defeated, and been defeated by, the great Carthaginian general – held a wary respect for his arch nemesis. He used his influence to ensure that Hannibal received no punishment for his failings in the long years of the latter period of the Second Punic War, and at first Hannibal's political career seemed set to continue – albeit on the back foot. Meanwhile, for his defeat of the North African leader, Scipio was given the epithet 'Africanus'.

With Hannibal's perceived failure in the wars, and his brothers and allies slain or dead by their own hand, the Barcid supremacy in Carthaginian politics was certainly at an end. In 196 he was elected *suffete* or 'judge', and he brought about a series of reforms that seem to the modern eye beneficial. Misappropriated funds were tracked and restored, and judges were no longer elected for life but had to be re-elected – all things that might have earned him the esteem of fellow citizens. For all this, he was banished after a year in this position, and it was then that he fled to the ancient mother city of Tyre, arriving there in 195. Part of the reason for his banishment was an accusation in Rome that he had been conspiring with Antiochus III, current lord of the Seleucid Empire, against Rome. Hannibal roamed in exile for several years, before this great leader, still commemorated to this day on Tunisian currency, took his own life in Bithynia in 183.

Five decades of comparative peace would then follow, during which the city of Carthage licked its wounds and was harried by Ṣapanbaʿal's widower Masinissa, who would live to almost ninety. Hamstrung as it was, Carthage appealed to Rome for help against this aggressive neighbour, but the city's pleas fell on deaf ears. Carthage was disarmed, vulnerable and weak, and while it was no longer actively at war with Rome, it still had to defend its borders. Carthage could not relax and rebuild. Despite its humbled state, there were many in Rome who still wished to see their great enemy destroyed once and for all. Carthage had come too close, had threatened Rome's security, and even weakened as the city was, many Romans did not sleep easy while it existed.

Chief among these was Cato the Elder, who has earned historical recognition through his alleged dogged repetition of the phrase '*Carthago delenda est!*' – Carthage must be destroyed! – during meetings of the senate. When Carthage appealed for help standing up to Masinissa, a delegation was sent to the city led by Cato the Elder, now in his eighties but tenacious till the end, who was appalled at the recovery Carthage appeared to have made. He had fought in the Second Punic War sixty years earlier, and had expected a lowly and despairing provincial city that had barely raised itself from the dust of defeat. Instead, he found a city cautiously prosperous, with the ports that had once built and launched Carthage's navy undergoing restoration. His embassy declined to assist Carthage's defence, and what's more he returned to Rome bent on the city's destruction.

Standing in front of the Roman Senate, he allowed a handful of figs to fall from the folds of his toga. So large, juicy and delicious-looking were they that his colleagues immediately remarked upon this unusually abundant produce. Cato asserted they were from Carthage, and had been picked only three days ago. The symbolism was obvious – Carthage was mighty, growing, and too close to the capital for comfort. Cato, as ever, rounded off his announcement by asserting yet again that he believed Carthage should be destroyed. This time it seems, the senate was persuaded.

The figs also demonstrated to the Roman Senate the agricultural resources and wealth that would be in their hands if they succeeded in dealing the final blow to their old enemy. Not only would acquiescing to Cato's demands potentially buy them increased security, but it would also funnel gold into the coffers. With this in mind, they decided to act.

Meanwhile, Carthage was still entangled with Masinissa. Two outspoken nobles had established control in the city, Hamilcar the Samnite and Carthalo. They played on the frustration of the citizens at the lack of aid from Rome in the face of the Numidian invasions, and asserted that Carthage needed to defend herself. They began to build an army, and expelled any politicians sympathetic to Masinissa. Outraged, Masinissa dispatched two of his sons to negotiate, but they found the gates of the city shut against them, and Carthaginian soldiers attempted to ambush them as they were leaving. Although both sons escaped, Masinissa was provoked to declare war, and despite the popular general Hasdrubal leading the Carthaginian forces against him, they were surrounded, starved and massacred. Only the general and a handful of men escaped the disaster and made it back to Carthage.

In going to war with Masinissa, Carthage had violated one of the terms of peace following the Second Punic War, and Rome now had the legal right to attack their rival city once again. In 150, Rome sent an army to Utica. Carthage responded with panic, quickly re-electing the more moderate political party led by Hanno, ousting Hamilcar the Samnite and Carthalo and their faction. They also sentenced Hasdrubal to death. They sent an envoy to meet the Roman host in an attempt to broker peace, but it was too late; by the time they arrived the Roman troops had already begun their journey towards North Africa. In a bid to fend off the Roman legions, the Carthaginians gave 300 children of high-ranking citizens as hostages, to demonstrate they intended no aggression. On top of this, they surrendered all their weapons. Rome eventually agreed to negotiate. They agreed that Carthage could enjoy self-rule, and continue to exist unmolested, on one gruelling condition. The Roman senators declared that they believed Carthage to be a body of people, not a place. They promised Carthaginians their freedom on the condition they allow their city, the glittering capital Carthage, to be utterly destroyed. The aghast Carthaginian envoys were asked to agree that their entire population be displaced, and resettled inland in northern Libya, at least seventeen miles from the sea. For a Phoenician colony and former naval superpower, this was unthinkable and humiliating.

The Carthaginians spluttered their protests. One man named Banno stood up to talk for his country. He tried to make Rome see that it was both wrong and not in Rome's interest to raze Carthage thus. The brilliant display of rhetoric fell on deaf ears – the Roman decision was made. They wanted the city of Carthage gone, and it did not matter hugely to them whether they massacred the Carthaginians into the bargain. If they didn't, it saved them a military expedition; if they did, they wiped out their enemies and seized their wealth. In any case, destroying the site on Byrsa Hill was tantamount to a death sentence to Carthaginian culture as well. Their identity was so linked to their capital and the sea, to force them out of it and destroy their temples, their tophets and their harbours would probably destroy the people too. It would certainly break their spirit. Carthage would be destroyed.

Crestfallen, frightened, plagued with anxiety, the Carthaginian envoys returned home, bearing the worst of news. When they announced their message, panic reigned. Those leaders who were in favour of peacefully surrendering their city and making the best of things in Libya, were swiftly murdered. Once the initial pandemonium subsided, the city threw itself into indefatigable preparation for war. Every inch of public land was taken over for the production of weapons and defences. Even the sacred halls of the temples rang with the sound of hammers on metal. At an unprecedented rate swords, shields and spears were produced. Slaves were freed and conscripted, women toiled alongside the men. According to Appian of Alexandria, the women cut off their long hair to use as ropes for catapults. The city was preparing for its last stand. The Carthaginians were a proud people; miracles had happened for them before, they had withstood sieges before, and even if it was the end, they would go down fighting. The Third (and final) Punic War had begun.

Hasdrubal, the disgraced general who had been sentenced to death, was reinstated to his former rank and began to marshal the city's defences. The Roman siege began in 149.

Rome had expected a quick and easy victory. After all, they had hobbled Carthage, and what's more, the city had willingly given up its entire stockpile of weapons to Rome as part of the initial negotiations. They expected to find a bent and broken, unarmed civilisation, floundering in despair. What they found was a galvanised population willing to defend itself until its last breath, and the Third Punic War would prove to be anything but simple.

For all that Carthage was disarmed, it was still a city with formidable defences, its walls built by the same civilisation that had built the walls of Tyre. Chroniclers offer differing accounts of Carthage's defensive structures in this period. Appian of Alexandria described walls, towers and capacity for thousands of horses and hundreds of elephants. The reality was likely more modest, but nevertheless the city certainly had three levels of defences: broad ditches, steep banks and high walls. It is likely the walls were punctuated by watchtowers and could be manned by archers. Other parts were defended by the sea and palisades. Today these legendary defences are all but gone.

Two Roman consuls, Marcius Censorinus and Manius Manilius, were in charge of the siege, and were met with more serious resistance than they expected. For a year, they got nowhere. The besieged Carthaginians managed to burn the Roman ships in their port, sending fireships into their midst, and repelled numerous attacks. Meanwhile in the hinterland, Carthaginian cavalry harried Roman foraging missions and skirmished with the troops. During this time a young Roman officer, another Scipio – Scipio Aemilianus, the adopted grandson of Scipio Africanus – began to differentiate himself from the rest of the Roman command. While the two leading consuls made a series of bad decisions, and rushed headlong into traps, throwing away their obvious advantages, Scipio played the situation well, prevented numerous disasters for the Romans and won over Numidian allies to the Roman cause.

The fighting would continue for three long years. Both sides would suffer heavy losses, and disease would beset the Roman troops encamped in marshy land around the city walls. By 147, Rome waived the age requirements for consuls and promoted the young Scipio Aemilianus to commander of the Roman forces in North Africa. Later that year, Scipio organised his men to build a large mole to block the harbour, and thereby cut off Carthaginian access to the sea. The mole not only prevented supplies being brought into the city but also provided a crucial platform from which the Roman attackers could launch direct assaults on the Carthaginian defences. The Carthaginians were fearless in their attempts to destroy the Roman siege engines, but eventually were forced to retreat. With this crucial new advantage, Scipio could smell victory. Eventually he broke through the defences.

The Roman soldiers entered Carthage in the red mist of battle and hungry for human slaughter. Rome's aim had been to destroy Carthage, and after three years of siege warfare, the Roman soldiers were only too happy to oblige. Carthage was a second Troy. There are reasons for the comparisons drawn between the sacking Romans and the Greeks. They tore apart a civilisation, slaughtered men, women and children. The women they did spare were enslaved. The city was razed. The scene does not bear description. People were killed and burned and injured. Dead and half-dead Carthaginians lay in the street. Those still living whimpered in pain and shock and despair. The Romans did their work well; the city was destroyed, the citizens were slaughtered. For six days the invaders savaged the civilians and fires raged in the streets. Scipio may have wept at the violence he unleashed, but his tears did nothing to quench the fires burning Carthaginians alive. He rotated the men in shifts to make sure they were fresh as they annihilated.

As the seventh day of the week of slaughter dawned, a group of elders ventured out from their hiding places, bearing olives branches and begging for peace. Fifty thousand men, women and children had managed to stay safe behind the defensive walls of Byrsa Hill, and following their negotiations, they were allowed to leave with their lives but not their freedom. They had become slaves.

Hasdrubal, his wife and children, and a handful of 900 Roman deserters were all that was left inside the city, refusing to beg for mercy, and expecting none. Eventually however, Hasdrubal's courage and stamina failed him. He is described unsympathetically as red-faced, round-bellied and swathed in rich purple even as his city burned. Rumours had also circulated that he had continued to feast in the citadel while the population starved during the final stages of the siege. He secretly made the Romans an offer of surrender. His wife, on hearing this, drew herself up with all the pride of Carthage's first queen. She did not fear the fire. Like Jezebel, she dressed herself in what finery she could muster, and went proudly to her death. Appian wrote in *The Foreign Wars* that with her last breath she condemned her husband's cowardice and declared:

> Upon this Hasdrubal, betrayer of his country and her temples, of me and his children, may the gods of Carthage take vengeance, and you be their instrument ... Wretch, traitor, most effeminate of men, this fire will entomb me and my children. Will you, the leader of great Carthage, decorate a Roman triumph? Ah, what punishment will you not receive from him at whose feet you are now sitting.

After these words, she slew her children and leapt with them into the fire of the burning temple of Eshmun. Many observed that this remarkable death would have been more fitting for Hasdrubal, who indeed went in chains to Rome to decorate Scipio's triumph. Appian wrote:

> Scipio, beholding this city, which had flourished 700 years from its foundation and had ruled over so many lands, islands, and seas, rich with arms and fleets, elephants and money, equal to the mightiest

monarchies but far surpassing them in bravery and high spirit (since without ships or arms, and in the face of famine, it had sustained continuous war for three years), now come to its end in total destruction – Scipio, beholding this spectacle, is said to have shed tears and publicly lamented the fortune of the enemy.

Rome did not salt the plains of Carthage – this myth is an invention of later centuries – but they did destroy the city, and curse the land and anyone that settled there. Their enmity was so great that they left its site – one of the most strategically important in the Mediterranean and famously possessed of excellent harbours – desolate. What the survivors, if there were any, crawling out from their shelters and hiding places must have thought as they emerged once the fires had passed is hard to imagine. A city that had seemed untouchable was destroyed beyond recognition. Stones were blackened, roofs collapsed. Doors and floorboards consumed completely, human remains littering streets and what had once been homes and shops. Precious amulets with their blue curls and wide eyes were broken and desecrated underfoot. The temple they had looked up to see every day of their lives was no more; a charred shell only stood on the summit of Byrsa Hill, likely with the smoke still rising. They would have beheld the death of their civilisation.

The destruction of the city and annihilation of the army did not spell the end of the Carthaginian people and culture however, for survivors there were. Refugees would have escaped, and some trickled back, it seems, to live among the ruins. The Punic language would survive in the wider region for centuries.

One of the things the Romans won when they stormed the city was control over the history that would be written. They would dictate the written legacy of Carthage, and as such, it is murkier than ever.

It is ironic then, for all this hatred and slander of the people and their land, that the next phase in Carthage's history was indeed Roman resettlement. Scipio watched the burning city with a strange sense of foreboding and confided to Polybius, his Greek friend who would one day write the history of his deeds in Africa, that he was troubled by thoughts that the same might happen to Rome. Little did he know that revenge indeed would sail from Carthage's shores some centuries later to hammer Rome.

The destruction of Carthage made little sense economically, but it made great sense politically. Elissar had chosen the location of her city well. Of all Mediterranean cities, Carthage was perhaps best situated for trade, commerce, expansion and control. Destroying and abandoning the site would have been a waste. For all that, Rome was ecstatic about the annihilation of her ancient foe. The celebrations were frenzied and fervid in the capital. Just months later, Rome carried out a similar destruction of Greek Corinth in punishment for allying with various city states against them. The barbarity seems gratuitous and counterproductive, but it certainly sent a powerful message to would-be resisters of Rome.

With Carthage, however, the fervour for destruction lasted decades. Twenty-five years after the sack, proposals were made to create a Roman colony amid the ruins of the city which hitherto had lain desolate. However, the only Roman thought to have inhabited Carthage in the following century was the disgraced consul Marius, who in exile made a home among the ruins and spent his days meditating on failure. The once great city served as a romantic and forlorn refuge for the former leader. He made a sorry spectacle among the charred buildings, and he inspired numerous works of art and literature, a metaphor for the fragility of greatness.

Meanwhile the Carthaginians were dispersed across North Africa and Roman territories. The civilisation was not wiped out completely; the Carthaginians were not an extinct people. Not only had 50,000 survived, albeit as slaves, but many thousands more had fled the city during the long siege, and in the build-up to it. People practising Carthaginian culture still lived, and loyalty to the old gods and knowledge of the Punic language did not die. True, the city was destroyed and much of its library burnt, but the Romans liked their plunder and took Carthaginian artworks home with them. More than this, they put the word out to their Sicilian allies that they could come and reclaim the artefacts that Carthage had looted from them. The contents of Carthage's great library were not completely burnt; the texts that survived were given to the Numidians who had been loyal to Rome, among whom were scholars, and Mago's seminal 28-volume tract on agriculture was not only taken to Rome but translated from Punic to Latin.

For all this, the city was left fire-blackened and empty. It was a hundred years before any true revitalisation took place, although the surrounding region had been settled and Utica was functioning as a Roman regional capital. It was the triumph of Julius Caesar in the civil war against Pompey that led eventually to Carthage's resettlement. To ease overcrowding, he decreed that 80,000 Roman citizens be sent to settle abroad and designated the ruined city of Carthage as a place for one such settler colony. It was named Colonia Iulia Concordia Carthago.

At least 3,000 Roman settlers struck out to settle the remains of the ancient capital, and build it up again, this time as a beacon of Rome's glory rather than a threat to her existence, and inhabitants of the surrounding area came doubtless with mixed feelings to join the colony. Among them would have been Numidians and the descendants of the Carthaginians forced from the city during its destruction, decades previously.

Little by little, Roman Carthage grew from the ashes of Punic Carthage. The city they built was on a Roman grid system, centred on Byrsa Hill. It comprised walls, gates, broad streets, small houses and – of course – the revival of the two harbours.

Around the time of the new colony's settlement, the Romans made their calculated decision to level the top of Byrsa Hill, lowering the summit, creating a broader space and erasing the spiritual centre of Punic Carthage. Here they constructed the prime symbols of a Roman city: a forum and triumphal arch and a monumental Roman temple on an area of around 100,000 square feet. The settlers began to glorify and legitimise their new settlement through imperial architecture.

Following this initial settlement and investment, Roman Carthage boomed, overtaking Utica as the Roman capital of Africa. Soon it was the largest city in the western Roman Empire and by the second century BC was an intellectual centre as well. Its central Mediterranean position led naturally to the return of trade ships and colonisers. The ruins we see in Carthage today almost exclusively date to the Roman colony, and it is clear that the new Roman settlement at Carthage was a lively place. An amphitheatre was built for gladiatorial contests and other public spectacles, a theatre too, and the colossal baths of Antoninus. These *thermae* comprised the largest bath complex in the Roman world, and arguably were second only to the baths of Diocletian in Rome for size and grandeur. Today, it is easy to get lost in the winding, symmetrical arched passages that make up the archaeological site of the baths. The roofs of the chambers are long gone, but the ancient brickwork of the lower levels and channels remains, open to sky and the Carthaginian sun. Columns and fallen capitals litter the dusty floor, hinting at the architectural complexity that once existed here. When first constructed, the baths boasted the traditional facilities of *frigidarium*, octagonal *caldarium*, and *tepidarium* and *gymnasium*, as well as an open-air seawater swimming pool, which would have commanded a spectacular view of the sea. These baths were an important cultural centre in the Roman world and after, built just a short walk from the major Roman villas and fed with water by a newly constructed aqueduct.

The practice of public bathing has never gone out of fashion in Tunisia, in which Arabian hammam culture thrives. In Tunis's medina, and in the Carthaginian suburb of Sidi Bou Said, a stone's throw from the Antonine baths, one is never far from a hammam, though they vary drastically in quality, cleanliness and atmosphere.

CHRISTIAN CARTHAGE

The Roman temple atop Byrsa Hill replaced the Punic temple of Eshmun, into the flames of which Hasdrubal's proud wife flung herself. Dedicated to Caesar and Augustus, this monumental building would have dominated the skyline of Roman Carthage. However, a leaning towards the old Punic ways still lingered in the Roman city. Preference was given to the worship of Saturn and Caelestis – the Latin equivalents of Baal and Tanit, the Phoenician gods of old. It was into this world that a baby girl named Perpetua was born in around the year 182. She was a Roman but a product of Roman Carthage, a city with a history of stubbornness and sacrifice.

Perpetua's early life may have been unremarkable for a woman of her middle rank. She grew up, was married, and had a son. But in the year 203 there was a great commotion. Perpetua declared herself a Christian and refused to make an animal sacrifice to the Roman Emperor, believing the practice sacrilegious.

Christianity had been slowly spreading throughout the Roman Empire, both covertly and brazenly, from the fledgling communities in the areas around Jerusalem. By the time Perpetua was in her teens, there was a significant Christian population within Roman Carthage in addition to the Jewish community, many members of which had migrated to Carthage following wars in Judea.

The then Roman Emperor, Septimus Severus, had forbidden conversion to Christianity and Judaism in 201, meaning that Perpetua's actions broke the law. She was not born a Christian, but had been drawn to the teachings of the growing Christian community in Carthage.

Perpetua's family begged her to change her mind and recant her faith. She refused, and Roman soldiers, doubtless bemused, arrested her. She was not alone; an enslaved, pregnant woman named Felicity was arrested alongside her, as well as a handful of others. They were a motley crew of converts, slaves and freemen, rich and poor, pregnant women, nursing mothers, young men.

Perpetua's time in the Roman prison in Carthage was grim. She recorded her experiences in a diary. This in itself is remarkable, all the more so given that the work has survived. It sheds rare light on the level of education available to a Roman woman in Carthage, and on her own sense of identity, not to mention her relationship with her Christian faith.

During the early days of her imprisonment, Perpetua was separated from her son, and her breasts ached with the need to breastfeed. She described the prison as 'a dark hole', writing that she was crowded in with others in stifling heat, bullied by jeering soldiers, and worried for her baby. Her pagan family was shocked that she would endanger her life and potentially that of her child for such a cause. Her testimony relates that her father implored her again and again to reconsider, coming to visit her when he heard there was a hearing and perhaps a chance of a reprieve. He is recorded as saying:

Daughter... have pity... I have favoured you above all your brothers... raised you to reach this prime of your life. Do not abandon me to be the reproach of men. Think of your brothers, think of your mother and your aunt, think of your child, who will not be able to live... Give up your pride! You will destroy all of us!

Once again, Perpetua ignored his entreaties, resolute in her resolve and her faith. After some weeks in prison, Perpetua and her fellow Christian prisoners were marched from their cells to the Roman forum atop Byrsa Hill, there to stand trial. As Perpetua was dragged forward for questioning by the governor Hilarianus, her father once again begged her to pity him and her baby and perform the sacrifice the emperor demanded. Still she would not.

Hilarianus asked Perpetua just one question: 'Are you a Christian?'

She replied that she was, and she was sentenced to death. Not just any death, but being thrown to the beasts in the arena. That amphitheatre built to house gladiatorial contests now also played host to the execution of Christian martyrs. Perpetua's reaction to this, and to watching her father be beaten to the ground for remonstrating, was a little sociopathic but admirably brave. She wrote that she pitied her father, but following her condemnation she and her fellows returned to prison 'in high spirits'.

These high spirits were followed by prophetic visions while she awaited her execution. Perpetua was now finally and completely separated from her son, whom her father refused to bring to the prison again, and her role shifted from mother to martyr. As she reflected on her fate, she experienced four visions. The first was of her entry to heaven, two of her dead brother, and the fourth – just before her execution – was of her own fight and death in the arena. In this dream she became a man and fought with various adversaries including an Egyptian man, over whom she triumphed before standing on his head. A dream like this is not surprising in an imaginative young woman the day before she is scheduled to walk into an arena, where previously she might have watched gladiatorial contests.

In the days leading up to the execution, Felicity the slave experienced premature labour and was delivered of a baby girl, given to another covert member of the Christian community to raise. Felicity was now eligible for execution as well: according to Roman law a pregnant woman could not be put to death, but it had no such sanctions for a new mother. Thus together, Perpetua and Felicity walked into Carthage's amphitheatre.

The field inside was large and round and the amphitheatre had seating for thousands of spectators. Many Roman Carthaginians had turned out to watch the slaughter of the Christians. The ruins of the amphitheatre are still visible today, overgrown with grass. One can walk in the subterranean passages where Perpetua would once have waited, listening to the deaths of the men who went before her, in the sand of the arena above her head. Visitors can walk through the same tunnels she walked through as she approached her death. A single white pillar has been erected by Les Pères Blancs, standing in the centre of the arena, marking the spot where Perpetua and Felicity met their end.

Perpetua sought to take control of her execution and claim agency over it. She did not see it as her murder but rather as her sacrifice, her suicide in the name of Christ. She was proud to make this sacrifice, which meant so much to her, rather than an animal sacrifice to the emperor. Throughout her diary, she writes of her impending death as a decision freely taken, rather than a punishment foisted upon her. On the day, the prisoners marched joyously to their place of execution, firm in their belief that they were on their way to heaven. For all this, it is hard to imagine that they were not terrified. They had likely seen the wild beasts make kills before in this very same arena. One of the prisoners knew enough to hope that he would be killed by a leopard rather than a bear, probably from having seen that leopards killed more quickly and more cleanly.

Perpetua's diary ended with her final vision, at which point, as she prepared for death, she entrusted the document to a member of the Christian community. Other witnesses recorded the events in the arena, which of course Perpetua never had the opportunity to set down.

The slaughter of the Christians was timed to coincide with the emperor's birthday, and thus the proceedings seemed to be held in honour of the occasion. The organisers tried to make the Christians dress in festive costumes, as gods and goddesses. To do so would be to take solemnity out of their sacrifice, and the Christians firmly refused.

The men in the party were killed first, facing leopards and wild boars. The women the organisers thought should be killed by a female beast, and they were paired with a 'mad heifer' – an enraged cow. Anyone who has seen cows knows that heifers can have horns quite as lethal as a bull's. In what must have been an attempt to humiliate Perpetua and Felicity, the two were stripped naked before being forced into the ring. Unexpectedly, the crowd were horrified, seeing the vulnerable femininity of the pair – a young woman not long out of girlhood, and a woman fresh from childbirth. Quickly, they were dressed again and sent back out.

Perpetua was tossed first by the beast, which then charged Felicity and crushed her to the ground. Perpetua, scrambling to her feet amid the dust and blood, staggered to give Felicity her hand and raised her up as well. The experience must have been overwhelming – choking in dust and shock, under the hot sun, while thousands of jeering Romans heckled from the sidelines, all the while trying to think of the divine and hold their nerve.

The heifer did not kill them. Indeed, the beasts were inefficient executioners, and before long a scaffold was constructed so that the martyrs could be killed by having their throats cut in full view of the crowd. They went silently to their ends. The executioner failed to kill Perpetua with his first blow, which bit into one of her bones and glanced awry, causing her to scream in pain. She then guided his hand to her throat so he might cut it. In the end, it was very nearly an act of suicide. Perpetua became the third legendary Carthaginian woman to kill herself for pride in her convictions.

Perpetua was not the first Christian to become a martyr in Carthage, nor would she be the last. The Christian community would continue to grow, and face persecution, until Constantine converted to Christianity in 313 and kick-started the wider Christianisation of the Roman Empire. Before long in Carthage the tables had turned, and the pagans found themselves persecuted by the Christians.

Christianity became the dominant religion in Roman Africa, and much of our understanding of it comes from such venerable African-born Christians as Tertullien of Carthage and Augustine of Hippo. Tertullien was born and raised in Carthage and witnessed Perpetua's martyrdom, which he wrote about extensively. Augustine of Hippo, later St Augustine, was sent to Carthage from Numidia at the age of seventeen to continue his education at this burgeoning centre of African Christianity. He learned about more than theology in Carthage, beginning an affair with a local woman which lasted several years and resulted in a child. It was only after this that he decided to become a celibate priest. Augustine would go on to play a key role in encouraging the persecution of pagans and the destruction of the pagan temples.

This phenomenon unrolled across the Christian world. In 385, perhaps the greatest symbolic act of destruction by the Christians took place in the Syrian city of Palmyra. They stormed the temple of Athena, bursting in and tearing down the stately statue of the Graeco-Roman goddess of war and wisdom. They decapitated the goddess, struck the nose off the lovingly sculpted marble head and hacked off the ancient helmet, smashing the arms as well. Acts of such destruction of pagan art took place across the empire, with some statues even having crosses carved into their foreheads in an attempt to 'baptise' them – and took place in Carthage at the express instruction of Augustine.

In 401 Augustine commanded the Christians of Carthage to smash pagan objects as it was God's will. He used Psalm 83 to motivate them: 'May they ever be ashamed and dismayed; may they perish in disgrace.' Augustine explicitly ordered the community to sack the temple of Caelestis – the Romanised form of Tanit. Not only did the Christians smash the interior, but they levelled the temple complex and surrounding sanctuaries – almost a mile of buildings. On hearing reports of this, Augustine gloated with satisfaction. 'Consider what power this Caelestis used to enjoy here at Carthage. But where is the kingdom of this Caelestis now?' he crowed.

Where indeed? It was the triumph of Christianity, not Rome, that finally destroyed the cult of Tanit in Carthage. Still, this was not enough. At the time of the annual ceremony at which the devotees of Carthage re-gilded the beard of the statue of Heracles-Melqart, this year the Christians mockingly 'shaved' the statue, striking off the beard, to the despair of the pagans. At last, Christianity was victorious in Carthage. This cry to arms was an eerie forerunner of the medieval crusades, as across the Mediterranean frenzied Christians jumped to action to destroy the statues and places of worship of their pagan neighbours.

Christianity continued to grow in Carthage, and the city gained fame as an important early Christian centre. A series of important Church synods were held there, known as the Councils of Carthage, between the third and fifth centuries, and it became a hub of debate and dissension over various early controversies within the Church, such as Donatism and Arianism. Indeed, the Donatist movement began in Carthage, surrounding the controversial and allegedly illegal appointment of a new bishop.

However, by the time of St Augustine and the Donatist controversy, the power of Rome in North Africa was on the wane. Barbarian tribes were besieging the fringes of the empire, and North Africa was no exception. While Goths and Huns did not attempt to cross to Africa, the Vandals – a Germanic tribe originally from the area now comprising southern Poland – did so cheerfully. They swept across North Africa, first successfully besieging Hippo, before moving on to Carthage. St Augustine died of illness during the siege of Hippo, and while the barbarian conquerors ransacked the town, they left Augustine's library and cathedral intact.

Following this, the barbarian armies occupied and conquered Carthage itself, under the command of their King Geiseric on 19 October 439. Geiseric was an experienced commander aged around fifty at the time of this triumph. The Roman historian Jordanes described him as 'of moderate height and lame in consequence of a fall from his horse. He was a man of deep thought and few words, holding luxury in disdain, furious in his anger, greedy for gain, shrewd in winning over the barbarians and skilled in sowing the seeds of dissension to arouse enmity.' Not only did he capture the city, but a sizeable chunk of the Roman imperial fleet, which was docked in the port of Carthage. Geiseric did not destroy the city, but rather settled it and far from withholding Africa's wheat supplies from Rome, he proceeded to profit from them.

The Vandals were a Christian tribe, but they followed the alternate doctrine of Arianism which rejected the idea of the Holy Trinity, that Jesus was eternal and one with God. This branch of Christianity, which had originated in Alexandria, was loathed by the Catholic Church. The Arians loathed the Catholics somewhat less however, and were moderately tolerant, expelling Catholics from leading positions but not persecuting the general populace or forcing conversion. Under Vandal rule, Carthage continued to prosper, as did Christianity in North Africa.

Under Geiseric, the Vandals exploited the central location of their new city to attack and plunder ships as they traversed the Mediterranean, and they raided coastal cities of Sicily and the surrounding region. While at first Rome tried to reclaim the lands taken by Geiseric, eventually they accepted defeat and negotiated a temporary peace. In 442 the Roman Emperor Valentinian III signed a peace treaty with Geiseric, and agreed that his son Huneric would be betrothed to a Roman princess. When internal strife at the Roman court led to this betrothal being cancelled,

Geiseric sent his ships to Italy and sacked Rome, carrying off the princess. By all accounts she and her mother were complicit in this scheme, for reasons that will be discussed in the chapter on Ravenna.

Culture in Vandal Carthage naturally marked a departure from what had gone before. Changes were made to buildings across the city, and the Antonine baths fell into disuse. Geiseric was somewhat tolerant of the Orthodox religion: he expelled leading churchmen, but he did not kill them, and they were offered the chance to convert. His son took things further, murdering some Orthodox clergy, and eventually enslaving all those who refused to convert. Education and scholarship however continued to thrive in Vandal Carthage – the word barbarian has completely inappropriate connotations nowadays for these Germanic tribes that were indeed devout Christians and set great store by learning. Under Vandal rule Carthage produced not only Christian religious texts but also secular works of literature. The sixth-century African poet Florentius waxed lyrical about the literary and scholastic environment in Vandal Carthage. He wrote:

> Carthage preserves her glory over the heights:
> Carthage triumphs; the ruler, victorious Carthage
> Carthage the mother of the Hasding, Carthage shines;
> Carthage pre-eminent over Libya's shores,
> Carthage flourishes with learning, and Carthage with teachers.

It seems that in addition to a love of learning, Vandal society also had a predilection for more indulgent pastimes. Procopius, the prolific Byzantine historian of the sixth century, gave a slightly different portrait of the capital of the Vandal kingdom of Africa and wrote:

> For the Vandals, since the time when they gained possession of Libya, used to indulge in baths, all of them, every day, and enjoyed a table abounding in all things, the sweetest and best that the earth and sea could produce. And they wore gold very generally ... and passed their time, thus dressed, in theatre and hippodromes and in other pleasurable pursuits, and above all else in hunting. And they had dancers and mimes and all other things to hear and see which are of a musical nature or otherwise merit attention among men. And the most of them dwelt in parks, which were well supplied with water and trees; and they had a great number of banquets, and all manner of sexual pleasures were in great vogue among them.

It is certainly true that the Vandals built more baths, and profited hugely from their conquest of Carthage. The capture of the city and Rome's merchant fleet had served to make the Vandal nobility wealthy men overnight. It is not such a stretch to think that they profited from the pleasurable pastimes of the Roman-African elite and embraced some of the more indulgent traditions of Roman culture.

Procopius is disdainful, of course. He was writing at a time when the Vandals were no longer the great power in northern Africa. Procopius's master, the celebrated Emperor Justinian, had finally put an end to nearly a century of Vandal supremacy in Carthage. His extraordinary general Belisarius steamed into North Africa with a relatively small force of 15,000 men. Geiseric had died in 477 after thirty-eight years ruling in Carthage, and the throne had passed first to his vicious son Huneric and then through the hands of various other family members until it reached one of his great-grandsons, Gelimer. Gelimer was taken completely by surprise by Belisarius's invasion and was unprepared to repel the attack, the bulk of his army being at that time occupied subduing a revolt in Sardinia.

In only weeks Belisarius had clashed with and beaten Gelimer and taken Carthage. The citizens welcomed the Byzantine general with open arms, keen (superficially at least) to be brought back into the imperial fold. It also may have occurred to them that if they presented themselves as Romans, welcoming their emperor, then the conquest of their city might be viewed as a liberation rather than a conquest, and they might be spared the brutalities of a sacking. Belisarius certainly spared the inhabitants, in no small part because the victory had been easy. Had his men had to commit months to a long and gruelling siege, he may have had to reward them with rape and plunder; but as it was, they were content with their pay, and the city suffered minimal disruption as the Byzantines reclaimed North Africa for the eastern Roman Empire. Gelimer was not yet defeated however, and after three months of recovery and consolidation in Carthage, Belisarius rode out to meet him in open battle, and defeated the last Vandal King of Africa once and for all.

Gelimer fled to a remote and defensible mountaintop on the border with Numidia. Here he passed a desolate winter, living in small huts and comparative squalor. When he received a letter urging him to end the hardship he endured and surrender honourably, the Vandal king wept, and asked for such small comforts as a lyre, a sponge and a loaf of bread, so deprived was he. This is surely an exaggeration on the part of Procopius, but Gelimer did indeed surrender at the end of winter, and it cannot be imagined that his time in the mountains was pleasant.

With the conquest of Carthage, Byzantine imperial authority was secure in North Africa. The vestiges of the Vandal state quickly disintegrated and dissipated. The new masters set to work restoring the splendours of Roman Carthage that had fallen into disrepair and neglect under the Vandals. Byrsa was revamped, as were the Antonine baths and the impressive circular port, which bizarrely the Vandals had preferred to use for burials rather than shipbuilding. They also, crucially, reverted from Arian Christianity to Catholic Orthodoxy.

Despite initial success, the Byzantine grip on Carthage would prove tenuous. Belisarius was quickly called away to lead campaigns in Italy, and Moors from Numidia would busy themselves harrying the borders. And it was during this period that Justinianic plague swept the empire, wiping out almost a quarter of the population in the eastern Mediterranean.

Some two decades after Justinian's death, around 587, under the reign of Emperor Maurice North Africa became an exarchate, with Carthage serving as its capital. From here, a viceroy ruled this satellite territory of the Byzantine Empire, much shrunk since the time of Belisarius's conquest. The exarchates, ruled by exarchs, were subject to less direct control from the emperor at Constantinople, and had both civil and military authority. The creation of two exarchates at Carthage and Ravenna was a serious delegation of authority, and was a sign of an empire under immense strain.

This would come to a head in the form of a Carthaginian revolt against the emperor in 608. The exarch at this time was a former general named Heraclius, and this man – together with his son and leading nobles of the city – refused to accept the authority of the new Emperor Phocas, who had murdered the last Emperor Maurice and seized the throne. Together these men planned to overthrow Phocas. The senators of Carthage decided their leaders Heraclius the Elder and his son Heraclius the Younger would be better emperors, and went so far as to mint gold coins with their likeness, presenting them to all intents and purposes as new emperors. The pair sailed for Constantinople and swiftly deposed and executed Phocas. The younger Heraclius was crowned the new emperor, while his father sailed back to attend to matters in Carthage. The dynasty this pair had formed and inserted at the heart of Byzantine government would last nearly a century, and Heraclius demonstrated himself to be one of the most capable Byzantine emperors. During his reign, the holy city of Jerusalem would fall to Sassanid Persians, and Heraclius would launch a successful campaign to retake it. He is credited by medieval historians as the father of the crusading movement, and was the first emperor to cast the image of Golgotha on Byzantine coinage, a major moment in the narrative of religious warfare.

Heraclius's Persian wars would be the defining struggle of his reign. So perilous was the conflict that in 615, with the relentless warlord Khusraw II at the very gates of Constantinople, Heraclius seriously considered abandoning the golden capital and setting sail for Carthage to establish the new capital there. He was however dissuaded, which was to prove a blessing over subsequent decades.

Carthage for much of Heraclius's reign seemed immune from the conflicts shaking the rest of the diminishing empire. The Avars and the Persians did not spread that far, and their relationships with their neighbours were more peaceful than previously. For all this, peace was not destined to remain, and nor was the Byzantine exarchate of Africa.

Islam had begun to spread in the lands to the east of the Byzantine Empire, and in the seventh-century Islamic regimes also began to push westwards. The ever-shrinking and more beleaguered remains of the Roman Empire were no match for them, certainly at their outer borders. Byzantine Egypt was conquered in 641, and in 695 the Umayyad Caliphate captured Carthage under the command of Hassan ibn al-Numan. Here, years later, a Byzantine fleet managed to retake the city, but was swiftly beaten off again, and by the close of the seventh century the Byzantine Empire had completely withdrawn from Africa, with the exception of a small garrison and population at Ceuta.

The Umayyads adopted a similar but less extensive policy to that of the Romans themselves when they wrested Carthage from the original Carthaginians. They certainly destroyed large portions of the city, wishing to prevent the Byzantine armies returning and re-inhabiting it and using it as a base to launch offensives against them across North Africa. With this in mind they burned sections, pulled down its walls and cut off its water supply. Glorious Carthage was once again laid low. The citizens were variously slaughtered, enslaved or driven out, and the city 'destroyed and dismantled'. Dismantled is the key word here: the city was not wantonly burned and destroyed for the sake of vengeance and spite but rather turned into a monumental stone quarry for the building of their new capital – Tunis.

The stones of the Roman amphitheatre were used to construct mosques in Tunis. Churches were pulled down, and the building materials used to pave roads and embellish dwellings. The physical material of Roman Carthage became the fabric of Arab Tunis. The Umayyad thinking was sound – Carthage was too exposed to attacks from Sicily, which was still held by Byzantines, and they were not yet in a position to take that island, so instead they moved their urban centre to the other side of Lake Tunis. The medina – still standing at the centre of the old city – is the oldest section of Tunis and dates to the Arab conquests.

At the heart of the medina is Al Zaytuna Mosque, the construction of which began shortly after the Umayyad conquest, although the exact date is hazy. Its dome is likely built with stones of Christian Carthage, and the Christian Basilica of St Olicia which stood on that site before. Maybe even marble from the temple of Eshmun, dragged first to build Roman structures and then Christian shrines, has survived in the oldest parts of the walls and foundations of this monumental edifice, the dome of which floats above the crooked alleyways of the medina. Much of the structure of the present-day mosque was completed by the Aghlabids, who made extensive use of spoil from the nearby ruins of Carthage. They cut nearly 160 columns at the base and rolled them to the centre of Tunis, where they were erected inside the glorious mosque that was slowly rising. The result is majestic. The mosque consists of the columned prayer room, with fifteen rows of columns creating distinct, arched aisles, the grand courtyard visible through the great gates that open onto the medina, the cloisters, galleries, university, and many other rooms and outbuildings. The dome and the ornate square minarets are landmarks of the city.

Entering from the street, one is struck by the contrast and the calm inside the courtyard of paved white marble. The prayer hall is calmer still. The stone floor is muffled with what feels like hundreds of rugs, which are also wrapped around the base of the salvaged columns that – like all *spolia* – vary in colour and shape, some topped with acanthus leaf capitals and others not. The ancient marble columns support the arched ceiling of yellow brick, interspersed with crystal chandeliers.

Today, Tunis is home to nearly three million inhabitants, and is the capital city of Tunisia. It has seen as bloody and turbulent a history as its ancient neighbour, being the birthplace of the Arab Spring in 2012, and for centuries before that a centre of the Barbary pirates and slave trade and the Barbary Wars. In the nineteenth century, American ships from Boston fired their cannons into the walls of Tunis. The city still feels some connection to its Carthaginian past, but it is more abstract than the sense of connection felt by the Lebanese for the Phoenicians. In 1985, the mayors of Carthage and Rome finally signed a peace treaty, officially ending the Third Punic War, which otherwise had lasted 2,131 years.

The destruction of Carthage was one of the seismic turning points in Mediterranean history. It marked Rome out as the major power of the Mediterranean, and the shockwaves would be felt across the ancient world. If Hannibal had struck Rome when he had the chance, the face of Europe would look inestimably different today.

Prior to their sacking of Carthage, indeed as part of their campaign against that city, the Romans had attacked another great Mediterranean rival. This city had been the enemy of Carthage as well, but in the midst of the Punic Wars changed sides, allying with the Carthaginians against the Romans. This city was the Greek metropolis of Syracuse.

SYRACUSE

You will often have been told that Syracuse is the largest of
Greek Cities, and the loveliest of all cities. Gentlemen, what
you have been told is true. Its position is not only a strong
one, but beautiful to behold.

– Cicero, *In Verrem*

Duomo of Syracuse, 1840

So spoke Cicero in the first century BC, and still his words ring true.
Irresistibly situated off the south-east coast of Sicily, the island of Ortygia
hovers above the sea, connected to the Sicilian mainland by two narrow
bridges. It is the historic heart of Syracuse, the ancient city at the centre

of the Mediterranean. It is steeped in history that has blurred with legend. The mythic birthplace of Artemis and an old stomping ground of Plato, in its time the city has played host to Aeschylus, Archimedes, Cicero, Caravaggio and more. Over its 3,000-year history, conquerors and the conquered have mingled in its streets, and the language has shifted gradually from Siculi, to Greek, to Latin, to Arabic, to French, to Spanish and – finally – to a rich blend of Sicilian and Italian. Since before historians put pen to paper, Syracuse has occupied the minds of men. Its name has rolled on the tongues of travellers. Touched with light and intrigue, and lying at the centre of the Mediterranean, it is the beating heart of that ancient sea. For millennia, Sicily has been the battleground of empires – most devastatingly the battleground of the First Punic War, the arena in which Carthage and Rome clashed, and thousands upon thousands of lives were lost.

Throughout antiquity, Syracuse was the foremost city of Sicily – and for a time it was the foremost city of the Mediterranean, surpassing Athens, Rome and Carthage. The Middle Ages of Syracuse were dictated by the struggles between what was left of the Roman Empire and the threat of her enemies: first Ostrogoths, then Egyptian Arabs. The Arabs shifted Sicily's capital from Syracuse to Palermo, and so while Palermo is awash with minarets and mosques, Islamic architecture has scarcely left a mark on Syracuse. The Arabs were not destined to stay long in Sicily, and in the eleventh century Italian Normans came, under the command of Robert Guiscard, to drive them out, and long would the Sicilian Arabs miss their homeland as they wandered across the Maghreb and Al-Andalus.

Much of this history of conflict is down to geography. Beginning life as an island, Syracuse had natural protection on all sides and, like Tyre, had two remarkable natural harbours. It is also this gorgeous natural location, and the beautiful appearance of the bright stone buildings rising over the sea, that has guaranteed the city's survival. No man who approached the city could bear to order its destruction; while Carthage and Corinth were razed by their Roman conquerors, Syracuse was spared.

My first glimpse of Syracuse was across the waves, with full sails behind me. The engine on the sailboat was broken and our mainsail was torn, so the spinnaker carried us in to port. Approaching Syracuse by sea, the breath caught in my throat. My journey to reach the city had been difficult and unplanned. We were heading to the port of Ragusa, having just passed the Strait of Messina, and I had no idea what to expect of Syracuse. I had never even heard of the ancient city, and my main priorities were finding pasta and a sail mender. I also wanted to get away from my crewmates, who were irritating.

Arriving through the mouth of the Great Harbour, storm-tossed on a rickety sailboat with a torn mainsail and feeling battered, I found myself in ancient company. I did not yet know it, but Syracuse has a history of being a safe haven for weary travellers. I was twenty-one when we moored up, and watching the golden city come into focus on the horizon is a sight I will never forget. The last rays of the sun fell soft over the water, gilding the city's aspect of honey-coloured stone. This deceptively calm curve of water, the skyline of which is cluttered with the masts of many yachts and the domes of many churches, has witnessed some of history's most legendary battles, battles that decided the fate of the Mediterranean region. The Syracusan scuppering of the Athenian fleet paved the way for Roman dominance of the Mediterranean. It was here too that the defences of Greek Syracuse fell, stormed by the Romans, but valiantly defended by Archimedes' war machines. Reaching the harbour is an achievement in itself. As the Carthaginians and Romans learned, and as I experienced as well, the waters around Sicily are treacherous. The Ancient Greeks had a helpful habit of situating gods and monsters exactly where geographical dangers were, and between the fury of Aeolus, Stromboli, Scylla and Charybdis, the journey to Syracuse has never been an easy one. Sicily is a land of smouldering volcanoes, plunging gorges, and record-breaking summer heat. Even to the uninitiated, something of this weighty past is detectable – the evening air hangs heavy with myth. The sea is filled with bioluminescent plankton that make it sparkle even at night, and the sky dances with bright stars.

Approaching the walled city from the harbour, visitors can fill their lungs with heady, citrus-scented air. As I make my way into the city, last night's cigarette butts and wine bottles litter the doorsteps of narrow, angled *vias* gently rising to the central Piazza of Ortygia. A film of hot dust covers everything. Sounds of lives being lived crowd around: music wafts from windows and terraces, donnas smoke and call out to each other across baroque balconies, laundry is reeled in overhead. In the main piazza, dark-haired children screech past on mountain bikes, and the notes of an accordion fill the square as a musician plays idly to his dog. Well-turned-out tourists clutching bags of souvenirs crunch cannoli at wrought-iron tables. They wear crisp white dresses, embroidered with lemons and fish.

Sicily has always been a land of abundance, but not always for weary travellers. Today, migrants to Italy from North Africa break their journey here, and they do not always find a warm welcome. A Senegalese man I meet named Moussa sells African bangles to tourists in the streets of Syracuse. He commutes every day from Catania, and he hates it here. 'The Syracusans are rotten,' he tells me. 'I was a pharmacist, I speak many languages, but here this is all I can do. They won't even look at me. When I first arrived, before they knew I was a migrant, people were friendly. But now, now they know, they won't talk to me. You think it's beautiful, but it's a rotten city.'

Some three thousand years ago, another journeyman washed up on these shores, before Syracuse was even an idea in a Corinthian's mind. He was a Greek with a mighty history, and he kept his name to himself. He was returning home rather than setting out to build a new life, and he never meant to stay. According to Homer, Odysseus came when the land was owned by the Cyclopes and their flocks of sheep, and perforated with many caves, and then made his way on to Ithaca.

The ancient Greek geographer-historian Strabo situated the land of the Cyclopes on the south-east coast of Sicily, right about where Syracuse is today. In the archaeological museum in Syracuse there can be found the skeleton of what looks like a curious one-eyed creature, a dwarf elephant. In 1914 the palaeontologist Othenio Abel suggested that the presence of these seemingly one-eyed skeletons in Sicily gave rise to the legend of Polyphemus – the furious one-eyed son of Poseidon who cursed Odysseus on his journey home.

Myth would have it that three nymphs founded Sicily, collecting the best of the world – earth, fruit and stones – and planting them in the middle of 'the Middle Sea'. From the crystalline waters rose three peaks, which merged to form the triangular island of Sicily. A rocky oasis of green and gold, and a stepping stone between Italy and Africa. Today the culture and food reflects this heady blend of cultures, and the many empires that have fought for control of the island. Spanish architecture jostles with the remains of Greek temples, Carthaginian sculptures stand alongside Roman ones. Aubergines, originally from North Africa, are cooked with pasta. The people have olive skin, strong features, curly hair, and ooze Arabian and Mediterranean hospitality. Willingly or not, the island has hosted strangers for years, and the practice of hosting and of sharing has become second nature to the locals. Today the main industry of the island is tourism.

The story of Syracuse begins with the Greeks, and for the Greeks it began with the sea. Five hundred years after Odysseus made it home, and twenty years before Aeneas founded Rome, Corinthian Greeks founded Syracuse, just as colonists from Tyre founded Carthage. They sailed from their city in mainland Greece and built a new city that for fifteen hundred years would be one of the great capitals of the Mediterranean. The Greek heritage is celebrated in the city. One of the first Sicilians I meet is a man named Francesco Pusateri, who proudly introduces himself as a descendant of Archimedes: a DNA test revealed that his genes were mostly Greek, despite his family living in Sicily as far back as records go. For all its relative obscurity today, Syracuse was once the great power of that region. Even in later centuries it would boast a glimmer of importance: for five years in the seventh century, the eccentric and ill-fated Roman Emperor Constans II made his court in Syracuse, trying to make it the imperial capital.

Like Sicily, Syracuse was born as a result of a nymph – a by-product of an escape from an attempted rape. The city grew around a natural phenomenon: a spring of fresh water on an island a little way from the main island of Sicily. This fresh water ran through a secret channel under the sea, bringing a vital supply of drinking water to Ortygia. Tour guides leading groups around the city will take them to lean over the metal railings around the font of Arethusa. They will tell them that this spring is the beginning of Syracuse, and relate the story of how the river nymph was caught bathing in a river by the river god Alphus, who determined to rape her. The terrified nymph, a favourite of Artemis, fled hysterically, and to aid her escape, Artemis transformed her into a spring of water, so she could speed away underground, under the sea from the mainland of Sicily, and reach the island just off the shore. Here she emerged into the clear air of Ortygia, safe she thought, at last. What Artemis didn't reckon on was Alphus throwing himself after her and mingling his waters with hers. In the end she was forced to submit, but one must hope that over the millennia Stockholm syndrome has finally made the nymph fond of her pursuer whom she has been bonded with for three thousand years.

These stories, these foundation myths, were conjured by the Greeks to link them to the island and give them the 'right' of settlement, and domination, over the people who lived there before. These people were known as the Sicels, an Italic tribe that thrived in the Iron Age in Sicily.

After Arethusa's fountain, the next port of call for tourists taking a speedy walking tour of Ortygia is the Piazza Duomo. Unlike most Italian squares, it's not a square at all, but a monumental open space leading down to the fountain and the sea beyond. Occupying one side is the duomo itself, a giant of glowing limestone rising seamlessly from the white paving. Parts of the building seem much older than others, and visitors passing through the Piazza Minerva into the central square can run their hands over the ridges of age-worn Doric columns, half sunk in the tufa wall. In ancient times, this building was not a Christian church but a temple to Athena, goddess of war and wisdom. Consecrated under the first tyrant of Syracuse, it has never ceased to be a place of worship, although the god it honours has changed many times. The Doric columns built by the early Greeks have been absorbed by the extravagant baroque adornments favoured by Sicily's eighteenth-century Spanish rulers, and there are traces of every architectural style that has happened in between.

The facade, decorated profusely in high-Sicilian baroque carvings, is at odds with the simplicity of the wall. Complete with Corinthian columns, acanthus leaves, a superfluous eagle and frozen saints preaching in perpetuity, the face of this great church dominates the central piazza. This facade and all its dramatic sculptures adorn what was once the back of the Greek temple, which was built to face the sun, on what was the highest point of Ortygia. Around its base in the smooth, worn piazza are curious black lines, drawn to demarcate the original foundations of the temple. To understand the true magnificence of this building in ancient times, one has to imagine the island empty of other buildings, and this temple rising in the centre to salute the sun, topped with Athena's golden shield, and imagine everything else sinking away.

This was not the first temple built in Syracuse. The oldest is the temple of Apollo, the august remains of which dominate the northern part of Ortygia. This was built in around 734 BC. The first settlers were known as Gamoroi, and were oppressive towards the indigenous people and disdainful of the later settlers.

THE FIRST TYRANTS

Syracuse in the earliest part of its history was ruled by a series of tyrants.

The first tyrant of Syracuse was Gelon, a man we can be certain was energetic, pragmatic and a skilled general. He solidified his power in Syracuse by crushing the Carthaginians at the Battle of Himera. Before Gelon ruled Syracuse, the city showed promise: settled by industrious Corinthians, temples were beginning to spring up, and of course the city occupied an excellent strategic position, and the island of Ortygia was blessed with Arethusa's fountain. It was not, however, important. We know this because it is hard to find mention of its role in the struggles for Sicily that took place between its foundation and the rise of Gelon, indicating that in this stage in its history, the Syracusans were not movers and shakers.

Gelon changed things. His rise to power was quick. Beginning as an aristocrat and elite soldier in the retinue of Hippocrates of Gela, Syracuse's more powerful neighbour, he managed to manoeuvre himself to usurp Hippocrates' two sons on the ruler's death. One of his first acts as ruler of Gela was to finally take control of Syracuse, something in which his predecessor had failed, through diplomacy rather than by the sword. While Hippocrates had reigned, civil unrest was rife in Syracuse, and something akin to a revolution had taken place in the 490s BC with the result that the city's elite – the Gamoroi – had been expelled, and attempts were made to install an elected government. This strife gave Gelon the opportunity he needed to absorb the city into his dominion. How exactly he did this is unclear; perhaps he allied himself with the dispossessed elite, or perhaps he made a deal with the disorganised new government; perhaps he simply threatened them with his armies during a moment of transition, but in any case his next move took all parties by surprise.

Maybe for its beautiful and well-defended position, Gelon preferred Syracuse to Gela, and in a radical move relocated his centre of operations to Ortygia. It was under his rule, from 485–478 BC, that Syracuse began to come into its own as a power in Sicily and the wider Mediterranean.

Gelon enlarged Syracuse, quarrying more limestone from the city's now infamous *latomie*,* and drafted citizens from other settlements to live there, thus increasing the population to fill the new buildings he was commissioning. These people made this move variously due to Gelon's conquest, insistence or incentives. Few voluntarily made the move, and thus it was a programme of cruel displacement and sometimes enslavement that began Syracuse's rise. Gelon built a new agora, and crucially the city's ports and dockyards, which sowed the seed of Syracuse's naval power that would play such a great part in deciding the fate of Greek civilisations in the Mediterranean. The city was divided into five districts: the island of Ortygia, the Acradina, the Tyche, the Neapolis and the Epipolae. Ortygia was the centre of religious and political life; the Acradina was where the market was held; the Tyche was largely residential; the Neapolis was where the theatre would be built; and the Epipolae was the defensive hinterland.

* These quarries were infamous because in later centuries they became used as inhumane camps for prisoners of war.

We know little of Gelon's early life before his rise to power, except for two anecdotes from his childhood, related in the now fragmented history of Diodorus. The first describes a nightmare experienced by young Gelon, in which he dreamed of being struck by lightning. He cried out, frightening the dog that slept by him, who in turn woke Gelon with his cries. This dream could be interpreted as a warning of downfall, but in the context of Diodorus's narrative, it is more likely that the dream was a device to show that Gelon was selected by Zeus the cloud gatherer himself. The second story carries a similar message. A young Gelon, practising his writing in school, had his wax tablet stolen by a wolf who ran off with it. Gelon gave chase, and while he was gone in pursuit of the wolf his school was razed by an earthquake, killing both the teacher and his classmates. While charming, it does not quite have the ring of truth to it, but what it does show us is that Gelon had the reputation of a preordained leader, spared for a great future.

While Gelon ruled in Syracuse, Xerxes ruled in Persia. This was the same Xerxes who would be held at bay by, but ultimately vanquish, the famed 300 Spartans at the Battle of Thermopylae. Xerxes and his Persian Empire represented the greatest threat to Greek civilisation thus seen in the Mediterranean, but while Xerxes advanced towards the mainland, Gelon's mind was focused on troubles in Sicily, namely, his Carthaginian neighbours under the command of Hamilcar.

As has been seen, during this period Carthage was a serious force in the Mediterranean, and given its proximity to Sicily was a constant thorn in the side of the Sicilian tyrants. Gelon was no exception to this, and in 480 matters came to a head in an almighty clash at the Battle of Himera. Hamilcar had threatened Syracuse; the Carthaginians were keen to expand their territory and solidify their position in the eastern Mediterranean, and Sicily with its position at the heart of the Mediterranean was key to this. In 480, the time was also right, as Xerxes was harassing the peoples of mainland Greece, meaning the likelihood of reinforcements from Corinth coming to the aid of Syracuse against a Carthaginian invasion force was low.

As Xerxes geared himself to cross the Hellespont, mainland Greek envoys made their way to Gelon's court and implored him to lend the strength of his army and navy to a common Greek cause to resist the Persian invasion. Gelon first displayed the strength of his forces, then toyed with the idea, asked for command of the navy, was rejected in this, and thus refused to supply any help at all.

Soon after the Athenians and Spartans were sent home empty handed,

Hamilcar marshalled his troops to march on Syracuse, and Xerxes his to march on Thermopylae. Legend has it the Greeks of Syracuse clashed with Hamilcar on the same day of 480 BC that the Spartans clashed with Xerxes. Both armies of Greek soldiers were outnumbered and fought gloriously in both battles; even in defeat the deeds of legendary King Leonidas of Sparta and his men have echoed down the millennia, and Gelon's troops – allied with Theron of Agrigentum – were victorious against Hamilcar's Carthaginians, whose casualties included Hamilcar himself.

It was in thanksgiving for this victory that Gelon commanded the construction of Syracuse's, and arguably the Mediterranean's, most iconic building – the temple of Athena, now styled as the Duomo of Syracuse and dominating the central Piazza of Ortygia.

The building would have been clearly visible from the sea, and the golden Athena acted as a beacon to Syracusan sailors coming home. Views to the sea can today only be seen from this point by churchmen, and a lucky few who are granted access to the roof.

More surprising than Gelon's decision to erect monuments in honour of his victory was his treatment of the defeated Carthaginians. Instead of putting them to death, enslaving them or ransoming them, he was surprisingly lenient. This was at the request of his wife, Demarete. Gelon clearly held Demarete in great esteem: he honoured her, building a great and 'many towered' monument to both of them near the temple of Zeus – the Olympieion – now reduced to a couple of columns. Demarete played a strong role in politics. Following the victory at Himera, she urged Gelon to spare the captives, and he did not humiliate them. He exacted from them only reparations for the cost of the war and the construction of two temples. In gratitude to Demarete who had interceded for them, they gave her a golden crown, and some of the most beautiful coins in the history of Sicily were struck, the *Demareteion Tetradrachm*. These feature on one side a profile portrait of the nymph Arethusa, crowned with an olive wreath and wearing dangling earrings, and with her wavy hair tied away from her face, surrounded by gambolling dolphins. The reverse features an intricate image of a charioteer wearing a long chiton and driving a team of walking horses. Above them, Nike, goddess of victory, hovers, waiting to crown the horses, and below a lion paces.

Gelon was not destined to rule long in Syracuse – only seven years – but his reign was a turning point in Sicilian history, and the beginning of the pre-eminence of Syracuse. Herodotus wrote that once Gelon had taken charge 'the city like a sapling shot up and burst into a bud'. The other great surviving monument of ancient Syracuse – the Greek theatre, one of the largest in Europe – was likewise constructed under Gelon's leadership.

The theatre today forms the heart of Syracuse's archaeological park, a stone's throw from the echoing cave now known as the Ear of Dionysius. It was once the largest theatre of the ancient world, with seating for up to 15,000 spectators. It is an awe-inspiring space, the vastness of which always takes visitors by surprise and demonstrates Syracuse's ancient status as an important centre for the dramatic arts.

Gelon was succeeded by his brother Hieron, and under Hieron the city began to flourish culturally as well as militarily. A great sea battle saw off the Etruscans from Cumae, and Pindar, Aeschylus, Simonides and Bacchylides all lived and wrote there. Aeschylus is likely to have written *Prometheus Bound* and *Prometheus Released* at his quarters in Syracuse, and his plays are performed to this day, in Syracuse's ancient theatre. There was of course, a hiatus, and after millennia of inactivity the Istituto Nazionale del Dramma Antico (INDA) staged Aeschylus's *Agamemnon* in 1914.

Today still there is something in Syracuse that draws artists here. Actors and dancers converge on the city in the summer months to take part in performances at the theatre, which, 3,000 years after its construction, still functions as an artistic space. There is magic in the stones, instilled by centuries of ancient incantations in many languages. For the actors, performing in the Greek theatre is a moving experience, and a culmination of many years of training and aspiration. I speak to one actress, Alice Canzonieri, who recalls the first time she performed on that ancient stage, as part of the Greek chorus. She wept at the end. The audience rose to applaud her and she felt the impact of the experience in which she had just partaken. She had communed so directly with the ancient actors. The history of Syracuse had thudded in her blood, and she had been overwhelmed.

The Greek theatre of Syracuse is its cultural heart. It is the only world-class cultural venue in the city, and during my time in the city it is headed by Antonio Calbi, director of INDA. He has a vision for Syracuse, which he would like to see as the cultural capital of Europe in the coming years.

The ancient stones carry something like enchantment. They have been alive with the voices of actors, and the hooves of goats, for thousands of years. When I attend, I see *The Bacchantes* performed, widely hailed as the greatest Greek tragedy. The play has moved with the times, and bare-breasted women beat their chests and scamper around the stone-carved seats, wailing and gnashing their teeth at scandalised spectators, made up both of local Syracusans, and visiting Americans, who are somewhat mortified. When Pentheus disguises himself as a bacchante, he transforms also into something feminine in form. Speaking to the actor, Ivan, after the show, he reveals he was inspired for his role of conservative autocrat by none other than Margaret Thatcher.

The Greeks brought democracy as well as drama to Syracuse, but it ebbed and flowed. After Hieron's twelve-year reign, the tyrant who succeeded him was overthrown, and Syracuse enjoyed some forty years of prosperity during a period of stable democracy. This peaceful increase would have unpeaceful consequences. Across the Ionian Sea, the two great powers of fourth century BC Greece, Athens and Sparta, were fighting. Greece had seen off Xerxes's Persian invasion at long last at the Battle of Plataea in 479 BC, and had now fallen to wars between the separate city states – in a series of conflicts that would become known to history as the Peloponnesian Wars. Athens and her allies were known as the Delian League, and Sparta and hers constituted the Peloponnesian League. These wars would last twenty-seven years. The result was decided not in Athens or Sparta, but in the Great Harbour of Syracuse.

THE ATHENIAN EXPEDITION

In 415 BC Athens, Syracuse's great rival among the Greek city states, decided to act against the growing threat posed by Syracuse's expansion. This took the form of a great naval expedition: a fleet of 134 triremes and 30,000 men sent to besiege Syracuse from the sea and capture and sack the city. Two leaders sailed with the fleet, one more decisive and daring than the other. Alcibiades was the risk taker, who might have led the Athenians to victory, but he was summoned home to stand trial for domestic crimes before fighting could commence, leaving the expedition under the command of Nicias, a less experienced and more anxious leader.

This huge force, far superior to the army of Syracuse, was intended to aid the people of nearby Leontini in their struggle against the city. To begin with, they acted effectively, luring the Syracusan army away from their city overland towards Catania, then sailing forcefully into the city's Great Harbour and setting up their siege camp by the Olympieion.

However, sieges mounted by Greeks against walled foreign cities on the sea are rarely a swift affair, and for all the anticipation and power of the forces involved the siege would be slow and long-drawn-out. In the end it lasted for two years from 415 to 413 BC, and was the deciding moment of the Peloponnesian Wars.

Shortly after making camp, Alcibiades left for home and Nicias assumed sole control. Alcibiades' departure, and Nicias's squeamishness, paved the way for the gradual erosion of Athenian power in the Mediterranean, and laid the groundwork for Sulla's sack of the city and the assault on Greek culture that that battle represented.

Nicias did not disgrace himself at first, and after an arguably unnecessary withdrawal during the winter season, launched a surprise attack in the spring that allowed his troops to occupy the east of one of Syracuse's districts, the Epipolae.

His progress was checked by the commander of the Syracusan army – Hermocrates – who had with admirable foresight fortified the east of the city and hastily constructed a new wall defending the shrine of Apollo Temenites and the side of the city that bordered Epipolae. Although the wall was a work in progress when the Athenians moved in, it did the job and managed to keep the Athenian soldiers at bay, while further defences were built and provisions gathered inside the city.

The Athenians responded in kind with their own wall, this one running from their position in Epipolae to the Great Harbour. And so, something as magnificent and noble sounding as the Athenian expedition against Syracuse really depended less on Greek heroes and the red mist of battle than on the ability to schlep chunks of limestone to various locations, lay it there solidly and hope that one's commanders had chosen the right place. These new walls were pivotal in dictating the course of the action. In the first year, the bulk of the fighting was not hand-to-hand combat and feats of heroism but rather rival building works. The Athenians attempted to build two more walls, but the Syracusans cut them off by building their own walls in their path. One imagines beleaguered but zealous slaves waving mallets at one another and hurling chunks of rock across foundations at each other. It is not quite the glorious warfare of the *Iliad*.

Defeat was spelled for the Athenian fleet when Athens failed to send reinforcements to Nicias as quickly as he needed them. The result was that Gylippos managed to eject the Athenians from their land base by the Plemmyrion promontory and forced the entirety of the Athenian force onto the water in the Great Harbour. The reinforcements did arrive, but failed to make a strong enough impact to aid the plight of the ships. Nicias decided the best course was to retreat, and he would have done so and saved the lives of many thousands of men, had it not been for religion.

On 27 August 413 BC, the moon turned blood red in the sky, the result of a lunar eclipse, and to the pagan Athenians this was interpreted as a sign from the gods, an omen. The Athenian chronicler and general Thucydides wrote that:

> All was at last ready, and they were on the point of sailing away, when an eclipse of the moon, which was then at the full, took place. Most of the Athenians, deeply impressed by this occurrence, now urged the generals to wait; and Nicias, who was somewhat over-addicted to divination and practices of that kind, refused from that moment even to take the question of departure into consideration, until they had waited the thrice nine days prescribed by the soothsayers.

Never was a celestial sign so fateful as that eclipse of the moon in the summer of 413 BC. It was that eclipse, as much as the dedication of the Syracusans, that crushed the Athenians and heralded the final decline of Athenian power in the Mediterranean.

Pressing their advantage on land and sea, the Syracusans set to closing the mouth of the harbour. Their priority was no longer simply defending Syracuse from the aggression of Athens, but now also to crush the Athenian armada, and in so doing demonstrate across Hellas that Syracuse was master of the middle sea.

To this end, they cut off the means of escape for the Athenian ships, mooring their own ships broadside, bow to stern, across the entryway and lashing their vessels together with chains. As Thucydides put it 'There was, in fact, nothing little either in their plans or their ideas.'

Nicias made a rousing speech to his men (how exactly he did this, arrayed as they were across many vessels, I'm not sure, but so the chronicles report) imploring them to fight for their lives and for their homelands, that each man might once again return to the city of his birth.

He concluded his speech with these words to the Athenians in his army:

> For the Athenians among you I add once more this reflection: You left behind you no more such ships in your docks as these, no more heavy infantry in their flower; if you do aught but conquer, our enemies here will immediately sail thither, and those that are left of us at Athens will become unable to repel their home assailants, reinforced by these new

allies. Here you will fall at once into the hands of the Syracusans – I need not remind you of the intentions with which you attacked them [...] Since the fate of both thus hangs upon this single battle – now, if ever, stand firm, and remember, each and all, that you who are now going on board are the army and navy of the Athenians, and all that is left of the state and the great name of Athens, in whose defence if any man has any advantage in skill or courage, now is the time for him to show it, and thus serve himself and save all.

Nicias's fine words came too late to change his bad decisions, and the Syracusans were triumphant, routing the Athenian fleet and taking all the survivors captive. The Syracusan general Gylippos made his own speech to his men, to put fire in the blood to deal the mortal blow to their Athenian enemies. Thucydides recorded his words as follows:

Syracusans [...] The Athenians came to this country first to effect the conquest of Sicily, and after that, if successful, of Peloponnese and the rest of Hellas, possessing already the greatest empire yet known [...] for the first time they found in you men who faced their navy which made them masters everywhere; you have already defeated them [...] let us engage in anger, convinced that, as between adversaries, nothing is more legitimate than to claim to sate the whole wrath of one's soul in punishing the aggressor, and nothing more sweet [...] than the vengeance upon the enemy, which it will now be ours to take. That enemies they are and mortal enemies you all know, since they came here to enslave our country, and if successful had in reserve for our men all that is dreadful, and for our children and wives all that is most dishonorable, and for the whole city the name which conveys the greatest reproach. [...] if we succeed [...] in handing down to all Sicily her ancient freedom strengthened and confirmed, we shall have achieved no mean triumph. And the rarest dangers are those in which failure brings little loss and success the greatest advantage.

The Athenian expedition to Syracuse would usher in the final phase of the Peloponnesian Wars, which had lasted for twenty-seven years between Sparta and Athens, and marked a decisive shift of power from Athens to Sparta in the Mediterranean. While a resounding victory for Syracuse at the time, this military triumph would ultimately prove the undoing of Greek Syracuse, and the beginning of the city's decline from one of the foremost cities of the Mediterranean to what it is today.

Athens had always fought strongly against Rome for Greek interests in the region, and with the destruction of Athens's fleet and the beginning of Athens's decline, so too was the fate of Greek Syracuse marked. The fate of Syracuse was inextricably linked with the fates of her greatest rivals, Athens and Carthage.

More than this, the defeat was a human tragedy. The Syracusans showed no mercy to their Athenian captives. Thucydides recounted their experiences with much pathos:

> The prisoners in the quarries were at first hardly treated by the Syracusans. Crowded in a narrow hole, without any roof to cover them, the heat of the sun and the stifling closeness of the air tormented them during the day, and then the nights which came on autumnal and chilly, made them ill by the violence of the change; besides, as they had to do everything in the same place for want of room, and the bodies of those who died of their wounds or from the variation in the temperature, or from similar causes, were left heaped together one upon another, intolerable stenches arose; while hunger and thirst never ceased to afflict them, each man during eight months having only half a pint of water and a pint of corn given him daily. In short, no single suffering to be apprehended by men thrust into such a place was spared them. For some seventy days they thus lived all together, after which all, except the Athenians and any Siceliots or Italiots who had joined in the expedition, were sold. The total number of prisoners taken it would be difficult to state exactly, but it could not have been less than seven thousand.

Thucydides' account is harrowing, and the treatment of the prisoners of war was worse.

The youth of Athens, those that survived the sea battle, perished in some of the harshest conditions recorded by ancient chroniclers, and these makeshift camps made by the Syracusans for their enemies can be called nothing except proto-concentration camps. In an act of mercy that seems almost cruel in its selectiveness and puppetry, sources have handed down that those Athenians who could recite Euripides for their tormentors were allowed their freedom. Whether any of them made it home is another matter.

Thucydides concluded his writings on this event with the sobering words:

> This was the greatest Hellenic achievement of any in this war, or, in my opinion, in Hellenic history; at once most glorious to the victors, and

most calamitous to the conquered. They were beaten at all points and altogether; all that they suffered was great; they were destroyed, as the saying is, with a total destruction, their fleet, their army – everything was destroyed, and few out of many returned home. Such were the events in Sicily.

One might think that the man who had led the Syracusan defence would spend the rest of his life as one of the great and the good of the city, but this was not so for General Hermocrates. Two years after his great victory at home, he led the Syracusan navy to defeat at the Battle of Cyzicus. He was banished for this perceived failure, and spent the next few years planning a coup to seize control of the city and presumably install himself as tyrant. This failed, and he was killed ignominiously in a street fight.

This death, and the ensuing political turmoil, paved the way for the next tyrant to seize control.

DIONYSIUS AND THE AGE OF IDEAS

On a hot day in 406 BC, in the aftermath of Hermocrates' death and the Athenian defeat, in the agora of Syracuse an assembly of irate citizens clamoured for change. A young man, a petty official named Dionysius, raised his voice among the hubbub. He criticised the generals, he called for action and he spoke with such vigour and charisma that soon the assembly was convinced. He whipped them up into a riotous passion and won their admiration. Before long, when requests for soldiers came from Gela, he was given command of the army to face down the steadily encroaching forces of Carthage, who were capitalising on Syracusan instability and pressing their advantage. By 405, he had managed to use his new-found military position to impose himself as the new tyrant of Syracuse. He made efforts to legitimise his rule in the eyes of the people by allying himself through marriage with Hermocrates' family – himself marrying Hermocrates' daughter, and his sister marrying his brother-in-law.

History has not been kind to the memory of Dionysius I of Syracuse. Dante portrays him dwelling in hell for all eternity, languishing in a river of boiling blood, a comeuppance for his brutality as tyrant, but from an impartial perspective he was a successful ruler. He kept the Carthaginians at bay in Sicily, at times succeeding in driving them back to their own soil. He conquered lands in Italy, and ruled over the most expansive territories of any European ruler until Alexander the Great. Under his rule, Syracuse surpassed Athens and Sparta for wealth, power and position, and only Carthage rivalled her for prominence in the Mediterranean.

Dionysius ruled in Syracuse for thirty-eight years. He was as unpopular a tyrant as it is possible to come by in history books – a cruel man, with a vindictive sense of humour. For all this, he was undeniably an effective ruler, subduing all the Greek cities around him, as well as a good many Carthaginian ones. He ruled with an iron fist and, as Diodorus said, when he died he left an empire 'bound fast by adamantine chains'. He strengthened Syracuse considerably, undertaking a huge construction programme and improving the city's defences and infrastructure. Ortygia was turned almost into a private fortress, so impregnable was it, and outside of the changes on the island he also built the Castle of Euryalus, the impressive ruins of which still stand today, commanding breathtaking views over the coastline, and the walls of the Epipolae. This site is important for giving a sense of the scale and sophistication of warring in Greek Syracuse. Ancient Greek civilisations were famous for their temples, but their fortresses were equally dramatic. Euryalus sprawls over a wide site, with lightless, subterranean tunnels linking different parts of the structure and providing secret means of supply and escape.

Dionysius I clashed repeatedly with the Carthaginians, waging four wars against them, but never quite succeeding in ousting them from Sicily. These wars were risky, and in 397 the Carthaginians reached the very gates of Syracuse, despoiled the temples of Kore and Demeter and destroyed the tomb of Gelon and Demarete. They besieged the city, but were unsuccessful, defeated as much by disease as the strength of the Syracusans, and retreated to their territory in the east of Sicily.

Dionysius married twice – on the same day, in fact, which raised almost as many eyebrows in ancient times as it would in modern ones. Both wives gave him two children, and the eldest son was named Dionysius as well. Dionysius I kept his family around him, and his brother-in-law Dion was given a position in his household. However, we know that in around 387 BC, Dion went to study across the sea in Calabria, in the city of Taras,* because while he was there he made the acquaintance of a forty-year-old Athenian who had grown up amid the furore of the Peloponnesian Wars, in an Athens under siege by Sparta. This man would have known of Syracuse from his earliest days, and

* Modern day Taranto.

regarded it for most of his life as a place of tragedy, for he was fourteen years old when the Athenian navy was so definitely defeated in the Great Harbour of Syracuse. They struck up an instant friendship, with Dion eager to learn all he could from his new Athenian friend, and he convinced him to return with him to Syracuse. The friend had been named Arostocles at birth, but is known to history as Plato.

Plato, whose philosophical writings remain one of Greece's best-known exports, came of age amid the aftermath of the Sicilian expedition. The city of Syracuse had transformed the philosopher's life before he ever set foot there, and Professor Ingrid Rowland has argued that the physical geography of Syracuse served as the inspiration for his world-famous allegory of *The Cave*.

Near to the Greek theatre is the 'Ear of Dionysius', named so by Caravaggio, because legend claims it was the cave in which Dionysius I held his prisoners. It has a curved ceiling that puts me in mind of a human spine, but the space itself put Caravaggio in mind of the human ear canal. The other reason for its name is that the unique acoustics of the space meant that guards posted at the entrance of the cave could hear what prisoners were plotting within. It is certain that every pin drop echoes in that ancient place, and amid the coos of various birds, you can almost hear the murmuring of mutinous Athenians, echoing down the ages to this day. In the heat of the Syracusan summer, I am grateful for the coolness inside the cave, but I wonder how cold it must have been for the Athenians at night, and how unbearable the conditions would have been with thousands of ill and unwashed bodies crowded into that space. The soldiers left there must have been in hell. Perhaps it was this cave, and the story of the unhappy Athenians, that put into Plato's mind an image of prisoners kept in a cave, looking hungrily at the shadows on the walls beyond.

On the arm of his excited student Dion, Plato came to Syracuse and to the court of Dionysius I. He was drawn not by Syracuse itself, a city about which the Athenian must have had mixed feelings, but by the potential and earnestness of Dion who Plato wrote was 'eager to learn everything' and 'listened with such keen attention as I have never experienced with any other young person, and resolved to live his life differently than most Italians and Sicilians. Loving virtue, rather than luxury.'

Whatever Plato's reasons for going to Syracuse, it was perhaps the defining journey of his life. He writes in his seventh letter: 'How, then, can I declare that my arrival in Sicily was the beginning of everything? In keeping company with Dion, only a youth at the time, I dare say that in disclosing to him in words what I thought was best for humankind, and counselling him to put these things into action, I failed to realise that I was unwittingly contriving a future means of overthrowing tyranny.'

Dion was advisor to his brother-in-law, Dionysius I, and Plato hoped through his efforts with both Dion and the tyrant to make out of Dionysius a 'philosopher king'. Plato stayed at the court for a long while, but eventually his teaching began to irritate the rulers, and he fell foul of the tyrannical regime. Dion told his teacher to return to Athens, but Dionysius went a step further and had the philosopher captured and sold into slavery. This was not quite as bad as it sounded, and was intended to prove a point: Plato had argued that man could be happy in any social role, provided his education was complete and his mind was free. Dionysius meant for Plato to put his money where his mouth was and live as a slave, but in any case Plato did not languish in captivity long, and was quickly ransomed and freed by his friends.

Plato was not the only intellectual who incited the petty wrath of Dionysius. The poet Philoxenus, a former slave educated by his master, was a celebrated writer who came to live in Syracuse. He was incarcerated in the same quarries used to imprison the unfortunate Athenian prisoners of war. The reason why is disputed, with some sources claiming he had attempted to seduce Dionysius's wife Galateia, but others insisting it was because he criticised the tyrant's own attempt at poetry. In the second version of events, when Dionysius had been persuaded to release Philoxenus and asked to try another poem on him, Philoxenus requested to be returned to the quarry.

Once he was freed, Plato did not dawdle in Syracuse and made for Athens. However, his relationship with the city was not over. Remarkably, when Dion summoned him some years later, to help improve the mind and rule of Dionysius's wayward son and successor Dionysius II, Plato accepted. He was ready once again to try and use his teachings to create a virtuous ruler. He believed fervently in justice, and the necessity of training rulers just as doctors and generals must be trained. Whatever his feelings regarding Syracuse and the heir of Dionysius I, he saw the chance to educate the ruler of the greatest Greek city in the world in the philosophy of just rule as an irresistible opportunity to put his life's work to a practical use.

The second Dionysius was to prove even more fickle than his father.

Plato writes with horror of the decadence of the Syracusan lifestyle under Dionysius II. The excessive banqueting and flagrant promiscuity was at odds with the path of 'virtue' that he was trying to extol:

[That] so-called blissful life of Syracusan banquets pleased me not-at-all – living by stuffing oneself twice a day and never spending a night alone ... no city can remain stable under the rule of law when its citizens are convinced that everything should be pursued to excess, and that they should exert themselves in nothing but feasting, drinking and Aphrodite. Cities like these are condemned of necessity to pass from tyranny to oligarchy to democracy in an endless cycle.

Plato's predictions proved correct, in the Greek period at least. Dionysius II would tire of both his uncle Dion and Plato's advice. He would banish his uncle, and place Plato under a kind of house arrest, so that he alone could have access to the philosopher's teachings. Plato's legacy has continued in Syracuse, especially among politicians: the current mayor – Francesco Italia – laughs and tells me that he constantly thinks of Plato. Whenever he is deciding to do something against the political grain, or make a controversial decision, he always casts his mind back to Plato and his teachings.

For all his clear admiration for Plato, Dionysius II made little effort to put his teachings into effect. While dabbling in cerebral thought, just as his father had dabbled in the arts, Dionysius II's style of rule was quickly to come to reflect the brutality of his father's, only to a less successful extent. He eventually released Plato back to Athens, where he would once again be joined by Dion, his most favoured pupil.

Over the following decade, Dion and Dionysius II would war against each other, forging various alliances with Corinthian Greeks and Carthaginians. During Dion's banishment, Dionysius II forced his wife Arete to marry another man. When Dion returned to Syracuse at the head of an army, successfully forcing his nephew out of the city, he took her back. The struggle was far from over, and while Dion was indeed a more moderate ruler than either Dionysius I or Dionysius II, he was still not accepted by the citizens of Syracuse, who had borne the yoke of oppression far too long, and he was murdered in mysterious circumstances in 354 BC. Following this, Dionysius II would return to Syracuse to reassert control. His second period of rule proved still more short-lived than his last.

The Syracusans, weary of the chaos and economic ruin into which they had been plunged since the death of Dionysius I, sent an urgent envoy to Corinth, their historic mother city, to beg for aid. The more well-known leaders of Corinth were unwilling to dirty their tunics with the vicious and unstable politics of Syracuse. The man chosen for the job was a distinctly able but relatively unknown general, Timoleon, who led a mercenary force to Syracuse. He captured the city, exiled Dionysius II and placed himself in control, presiding over a new democratic regime.

Timoleon was the saviour of Greek Syracuse. He did as much for the glory of the city as Gelon. He restored it to democracy and prosperity, and raised it to still loftier heights than it had seen before. He is remembered primarily as the antithesis of the two Dionysii. Plutarch lavishes such soaring praise on Timoleon that it is hard to glean anything about who the man actually was – he was, simply, perfect.

TIMOLEON, AGATHOCLES AND SYRACUSAN RECOVERY

The struggles between Dion, Dionysius II and their various allies along the way had equated to a fifteen-year civil war that had robbed Syracuse of the majority of the wealth and power that the city had garnered under the rule of Dionysius I. The city that Timoleon liberated was a shadow of its former self, and characterised by destruction, weariness and neglect.

Timoleon was pragmatic. One of his first acts was to pull down the tyrannical fortress in Ortygia that Dionysius I and II and Dion had ruled from, as a visual signifier of his break with their style of rule and oppression. He cleared the mess of neglect from the city, and called for new settlers from Corinth to repopulate the city. On top of this, he auctioned off the public statues – impressive marble sculptures decorating the city – to the highest bidder, both to generate income for public works and to visually destroy the hegemony of tyrants in the city. One statue alone he preserved – that of Gelon, the first tyrant of Syracuse, whose popularity had endured in the hearts of the citizens.

Carthage still represented a major concern to security, but Timoleon roundly defeated the armies of Hamilcar and Hasdrubal in battle near Segesta. The result was not the ousting of the Carthaginians from Sicily, but an agreement that they would remain in the west of the island, and not ally themselves with other tyrants on the island.

The greatest mark of Timoleon's prowess as a leader, and a differentiating factor from his predecessors, was his willingness to give up power when he believed his task of restoring order to Syracuse was completed. After seven years of tireless rule, he retired, leaving Syracuse a democracy, and spent his remaining years living quietly near the city and dispensing wisdom to those who came in search of it.

For all this, his legacy was complicated. While he had established a moderate form of democracy, it was fragile, and it did not take long for political intrigue and infighting to lead once again to the establishment of oligarchic rule in Syracuse. Around 330 BC an oligarchic pack of 600 wealthy citizens seized power, under the leadership of two men named Sosistratus and Heracleides. These men did not establish a peaceful state, and they were constantly entangled in conflicts with the proponents of democracy and others who opposed oligarchic rule. It took twenty years for a decisive new ruler to emerge to take control, and when that leader did come he proved to be a mixed blessing. His name was Agathoclesto; a man from humble origins and born on the northern coast of Sicily, he was famed for his ruthlessness but also for his military skill. He was certainly relentless in his wars against the Carthaginians: what Timoleon had started, Agathocles would continue with gusto and still more success than Timoleon himself. We have encountered Agathocles already in this book, as he took the battles with Carthage from Sicilian soil to African soil, and beyond this he was still masterminding attacks against them when he was in his seventies. When Hamilcar threatened Syracuse, Agathocles would leave the defence to his brother and launch a counter-attack with fifty ships on Carthage herself. Although he was eventually beaten back to Sicily, the resulting peace treaty left him master of nearly the whole island. It was images of his battles that would come to adorn the temple of Athena, until the age of Cicero and Verres.

Agathocles' excessively aggressive policy towards Hamilcar would result in tit for tat, with Hamilcar besieging Syracuse and nearly succeeding in taking it, before being rebuffed and killed himself. His campaigns against the Carthaginians were marked by peaks and troughs, but Agathocles must be remembered as a successful leader of Syracuse, carving out vast territories and dominating nearly all of Sicily, with Syracuse standing as his glorious capital. He acted as tyrant of Syracuse for thirteen years from 317 BC to 304 BC, a position he took on the point of his sword and with the deaths of the 600 defeated oligarchs, and a sizeable number of citizens of Syracuse as well, and then styled himself 'King of Syracuse' – a position he held until his death in 289 BC.

Niccolò Machiavelli used Agathocles as an example of the pinnacle of the self-made prince. Agathocles engineered his own fate, rising from a mere potter, and not even a native of Syracuse, to the successful ruler who drove the Carthaginians out of Sicily. However Machiavelli's tone is one of grim admiration:

> Therefore, he who considers the actions and the genius of this man will see nothing, or little, which can be attributed to fortune, inasmuch as he attained pre-eminence ... not by the favour of anyone, but step by step

in the military profession, which steps were gained with a thousand troubles and perils, and were afterwards boldly held by him with many hazardous dangers. Yet it cannot be called talent to slay fellow-citizens, to deceive friends, to be without faith, without mercy, without religion; such methods may gain empire, but not glory.

Agathocles' memory has been doubtless tainted by the extreme negativity of Timaeus and Diodorus, who focused on his cruelties and failings, but has been somewhat mitigated by Polybius's quest for balance. In a similar vein to Machiavelli's analysis, Polybius focused on the achievements of Agathocles, highlighting that he must have possessed some excellent qualities to rise the way he did, and that once he had subdued his dominions and driven off his enemies, he was far more mild.

Agathocles of Syracuse was a direct contemporary of Alexander the Great, born just six years before the great general. He would of course outlive him. Alexander made his conquests, and forged the world's mightiest empire, but he died at the age of thirty-two, leaving his empire to fragmentation, and the Seleucid and Ptolemaic empires were forged out of its remains. Alexander's general Ptolemy had made himself master of Egypt, and it was to his son-in-law Pyrrhus – King of Epirus – that Agathocles would marry his daughter Lanassa, who brought with her the island of Corfu as a dowry. This marriage was not to last, however: Lanassa gave her husband two sons but would leave Pyrrhus, allegedly as a result of his polygamy. Despite this, even without Lanassa on his arm, Pyrrhus would attempt to claim Syracuse in the political turmoil that followed his father-in-law's death.

In his later years Agathocles would rebuild and strengthen his capital's defences, and never cease to plot war against the Carthaginians. At the age of seventy-two, he would fall ill, potentially as a result of poisoning by one of his would-be successors. On his deathbed he attempted to prevent any single man – particularly his sons or grandsons – succeeding him as tyrant and said he wished to reinstate the democracy of Syracuse and end the tyranny. When Agathocles was placed on his funeral pyre, it marked the end of his twenty-eight-year rule of Syracuse. One source presents this as the end of a reign of terror, and claims that his bitter attendants threw him onto the flames while he was still alive.

Turmoil followed the death of Agathocles, as it so often follows the death of a strong leader who has ruled by force for many years. There was a power vacuum left, in which many men jostled for position, and the stability that Agathocles' later years had brought to Syracuse was undone. Before long the Carthaginians had re-established themselves in Sicily, going so far as to sail their fleet into the Great Harbour of Syracuse. In despair at the progress made by the Carthaginians and the damage inflicted upon the island, the interim rulers of Syracuse sent envoys to Pyrrhus, Agathocles' erstwhile son-in-law, offering him control of Syracuse in exchange for driving out their enemies; an offer Pyrrhus gladly accepted. In 278 he crossed to Sicily, and in 276 he defeated the Carthaginians. But, it was not long before he left Syracuse and returned to Italy. Much of the territory that had been regained under his leadership swiftly fell again, but Syracuse remained secure, and one of Pyrrhus's officers was elected to be the new leader.

HIERON AND ARCHIMEDES

During the reign of Hieron II, Syracuse entered a period of cultural flourishing that it had not seen since Plato's time, and took its place as perhaps the most famous city of the ancient world. New buildings and works of art proliferated. The theatre was significantly enlarged and rebuilt, and a great altar was built and dedicated to Zeus. This is not an altar in the Christian sense of the word, essentially an elegant table large enough for a couple of chalices. This was a monumental altar, larger than most theatre stages, on which hecatombs – hundreds of oxen – could be slaughtered for the glory of Zeus. The temple of Athena was decorated with paintings representing the military triumphs of Agathocles.

Hieron sponsored both the arts and the sciences in his city, and by far the most significant beneficiary of his encouragement of the sciences was Archimedes. He was a native of Syracuse, who as a young man completed his studies at the University of Alexandria, where a well-established community of Syracusan expats had been established for some time. During his time there, he would create the first of his marvellous inventions that has been handed down to modern historians: a hydraulic screw that could draw water up a tube, which was a great leap forward for the mechanics of irrigation and agriculture.

On his return to Syracuse, his patron Hieron encouraged the young prodigy to focus his skills on inventions that would protect and enrich the glory of his mother city. Perhaps the most famous story regarding Archimedes – committed to history by the writer Vitruvius – is that of how he solved a puzzle given to him by Hieron, and celebrated by leaping naked out of his bath and running a lap of the city shrieking 'EUREKA!' Hieron asked Archimedes to fathom whether or not he had been cheated by a craftsman, and reveal whether the golden crown was truly made of pure gold, rather than an alloy. When mulling the problem in his bath, Archimedes realised that by sinking the same quantity of gold into water, and submerging the crown as well, he could measure how much water each displaced and thereby reveal if they were made of the same material. This revelation came to him when he sat in an overfull bath and saw his body displace the water. The glee this discovery ignited in him is what inspired that naked sprint.

Following the solution of this problem, Hieron took a still more active interest in sponsoring Archimedes' inventions, and directing him towards practical rather than theoretical pursuits.

The first result of this was the *Syrakosia*. This was the *Titanic* of the ancient world. An unsinkable ship on a scale unthinkable to contemporary minds. Syracuse had always relied on trade, its position at the centre of the Mediterranean making it a crucial juncture on the ancient trading networks. Archimedes' new ship was designed to carry cargo – with twenty banks of oars and state-of-the-art defences including catapults and siege towers.

The Greek writer Athenaeus recorded that for the construction of the *Syrakosia* materials were sought from across the known world, including timbers from Etna and Italy and hemp and pitch for ropes from Iberia and the River Rhone. It was a miracle of nautical engineering and grandeur unrivalled in the ancient world. The ship had three masts, was decorated with luxurious apartments adorned with statues and art, a marble bathroom and a gym. On an upper deck was a temple to Aphrodite made of cypress wood, with an agate floor and adorned with still more marble statuary. The ship had stalls for horses, and room for a crew of over six hundred men. The bilges were emptied with Archimedes' spiral screws, which effortlessly would draw water upwards to be poured over the sides.

The one problem with the ship was that its immense size of 104 metres meant that only two significant trading cities in the entire Mediterranean had a harbour that could accommodate it. One was Alexandria, and the other was Syracuse. *Syrakosia*'s maiden voyage was a journey from Syracuse to Alexandria therefore, laden with wheat. When Ptolemy, the ruler of Egypt, received the ship in his harbour, he not only unloaded the grain but hauled the ship out of the water, renamed it the *Alexandris* and turned it into a museum.

This ship, then, while marvellous, did not spend much time practically serving Syracuse. More pressing threats loomed. Carthage and Rome found themselves in a vicious deadlock better known as the Second Punic War, in which the house of Barca and its most famous son Hannibal pitched themselves against Rome for blood, territory and glory. These extensive campaigns locked Syracuse's near neighbours in a deadly struggle that lasted seventeen years from 218 to 201 BC. Syracuse, situated so perfectly between Carthage on the North African coast, and Rome in southern Italy, became strategically vital to both belligerents, and it was only a matter of time before one or other of them attacked. Archimedes set his brilliant mind to the craft of war.

Hieron II would die in 215 BC, and his underwhelming grandson would immediately take the reins of government, and swiftly switch the city's allegiance from Rome to Carthage – for reasons unknown. This youth would soon be assassinated, and the government that replaced him would choose to ally itself with Carthage rather than Rome. This made Roman attack inevitable, and when the armies of Rome did come knocking in 214 BC, Archimedes would prove to be the Sicilian capital's secret weapon. When Archimedes designed his machines, he doubtless envisaged them harrying Carthaginian ships; little did he know they would soon be used to blast Roman galleys from the harbour waters.

THE ROMAN SIEGE

The leader of the Roman army was named Marcellus, a man who had earned the epithet the 'Sword of Rome' and was the sort of adversary to make generals flinch. Some of the troops disembarked and set up a camp near the Olympieion; meanwhile Marcellus commanded the fleet in the Great Harbour. They attacked together, but while they might have hoped to steam through the Syracusan lines, outmanoeuvre their ships and breach their walls, they were repelled again and again. In fact, the siege would last nearly two years, and give ample opportunity for the by now elderly Archimedes to put many of his mathematical theories into practice.

Plutarch testifies to this in his *Life of Marcellus* in his description of the siege, describing the pinpoint accuracy of the defending catapults of Syracuse which were honed so as to 'throw [the enemy] into much difficulty and distress; as soon as these engines shot too high he continued using smaller and smaller [missiles] as the range became shorter, and, finally, so thoroughly shook their courage that he put a complete stop to their advance'. Plutarch goes on to describe one of Archimedes' most famous inventions, the great iron claw which would rip ships out of the sea by the bow, putting one in mind of the game to win fluffy toys with a descending claw in modern arcades. When one visualises it, it seems an improbable and ungainly invention, but Plutarch's description describes exactly that. He wrote:

some of them [...] were seized at the bows by iron claws or by beaks like those of cranes, hauled into the air by means of counterweights until they stood upright on their sterns, and then allowed to plunge to the bottom, or else spun round by means of windlasses situated inside the city and dashed against the steep cliffs and rocks.

It's hard to look at the serene and often perfectly still surface of the sea in Syracuse in quite the same way after reading these descriptions. Archimedes' other famous defence device wheeled out at this time is the legendary 'death ray' or 'heat ray'. Many historians and scientists have allowed the possibility of the claw and precision catapults existing, but most are sceptical of this heat ray, which reportedly used sunlight, mirrors and magnifying lenses to direct beams of intense light onto the ships in the harbour, causing them to catch fire and burn in the sea. Some have suggested that this was a cannon rather than a heat ray. Whatever this mystery machine was, Livy recorded Marcellus's despair in the face of Archimedes' defensive genius: 'Shall we not make an end of fighting with this geometrical Briareus who uses our ships like cups to ladle water from the sea, drives our sambuca [siege engines] off ignominiously with cudgel-blows, and, by the multitude of missiles that he hurls at us all at once, outdoes the hundred-handed giants of mythology?'

For all this, Rome would be victorious, conquering the districts around Syracuse one piece at a time. From their camp at the Olympieion, they pressed through to capture Tyche and Neapolis and also succeeded in taking Euryalus castle. Plutarch wrote that when Marcellus looked down on Syracuse from the heights of Euryalus, he wept at the magnificence of the city he was about to sack. This is unconvincing and perhaps more in line with poetic convention than reality: a man who has dedicated two years of his life to wearing down a city that taunts him and rips apart his ships is unlikely to weep for its demise. That said, when the opportunity presented itself, Marcellus – against the grain of conquest – decided not to raze Syracuse, murder its people and bathe its beautiful monuments in blood. Syracuse would be spared.

In the meantime, Marcellus's army could advance no further. The two armies reached an impasse, with the pro-Carthaginian Syracusans holding Achradina, the Epipolae and Ortygia itself, and the Romans holding Tyche, Neapolis and Euryalus. And Ortygia still had Archimedes. To make matters worse for the Romans, the Carthaginian fleet arrived in the harbour to support the Syracusans – but before their presence could have any real impact they were routed by disease.

In the way of well-defended cities – and seemingly never was there a better-defended city – Syracuse did not fall through strategic fault, but rather through intrigue and betrayal. The Romans, for all their famed military prowess, did not outwit or outmanoeuvre Archimedes, but rather were granted entry by traitors from within – a Spanish mercenary, clearly sympathising with the pro-Roman and anti-Carthaginian faction of the city – opened the gate above the fountain of Arethusa for the invaders. As has been seen, Marcellus decided not to sack the city, wishing instead to preserve its beauty and wealth for the glory of Rome. Cicero would later praise the conqueror's leniency, writing:

> Having with the help of his army attacked and captured this magnificent city, he took the view that it would not tend to the credit of Rome that he should blot out and destroy all this beauty, the more so as it threatened us with no danger. He therefore spared all its buildings, public and private, sacred and secular, as completely as if he had come with his army to defend it, instead of to assault it. In dealing with the city's treasures he did not forget either that he was a conqueror or that he was a humane man. As a conqueror, he thought it proper to remove to Rome many objects that might fitly adorn our city: as a humane man, not to strip the place completely bare, especially as he had resolved to prevent its destruction. The result of his division of its treasures was that his humanity preserved at least as much for Syracuse as his conquest secured for Rome.

Marcellus allowed his men to plunder freely however – it would be impossible to deny them this after years of hardship and service away from home – and this brought grief to the citizens who found their property seized. Marcellus gave specific instructions that the freeborn citizens were not to be harmed, in particular the mastermind Archimedes. His mind was too valuable to waste on petty revenge. That said, soldiers rampaging through a city in the aftermath of hard-won victory are not the most discerning of men, and against Marcellus's command Archimedes was killed by a Roman soldier, apparently in a case of mistaken identity and insolence.

Several accounts of this story are given across the sources – most notably by Plutarch and Livy. Livy asserts that in the chaos that reigned after the capture of the city, a marauding Roman soldier stumbled upon a stubborn old man drawing circles in the dust, and when the man ignored his commands, struck him dead, never realising that it was Archimedes. Plutarch gives a similar account, but one which does not assert that the soldier did not recognise the man. He writes:

> the philosopher was by himself, engrossed in working out some cal-
> culation by means of a diagram, and his eyes and his thoughts were
> so intent upon the problem that he was completely unaware that the
> Romans had broken through the defences, or that the city had been
> captured. Suddenly a soldier came upon him and ordered him to
> accompany him to Marcellus. Archimedes refused to move until he
> had worked out his problem ... whereupon the soldier flew into a rage,
> drew his sword, and killed him.

Most famous is the claim that Archimedes cried out '*Nōlī turbāre circulōs meōs!*' ('Do not disturb my circles!') in defiance of the soldier who wished to drag him away from an incomplete diagram. This myth seems to have been inspired by Valerius Maximus's quotation of the mathematician's last words as '*Noli, obsecro, istum disturbare*' ('Do not, I entreat you, disturb that'). The sources all align in one respect – that Archimedes was absorbed in his calculations until his final moments, and used his last breath to defend his work. Today, little is left of Archimedes' legacy in Syracuse, beyond the Piazza Archimede, and a statue of him, holding an orb, beside the second harbour. More than this, the Syracusans love him to this day.

For all that Marcellus attempted to preserve the glory of Syracuse following his conquest, and indeed that it was retained as the capital city of the newly formed province of Roman Sicily, it seems that with the death of Archimedes, the city's most famous son, the star of Syracuse – glittering at the heart of the Mediterranean – began to wane. Following Roman domination Sicily would experience a series of economic crises, and with the addition of the repression of Greek culture in the island, Syracuse's time as a major power centre and cultural capital was up. The city would remain politically important as the home of the Roman gover-nor or *praetor* – but never again would it rise to dominate Mediterranean politics, culture or trade.

In the immediate aftermath the capture of the city was a disaster for its citizens and those of other surrounding Sicilian cities. It marked the end of Syracuse's independence as a city state which had lasted for over five centuries. Families found themselves dispossessed of their lands and properties, which were given to Romans. Food was scarce, and even the fish of Arethusa's fountain were devoured by starving citizens. Others surrendered themselves as slaves to be sure of food and shelter, not that slaves were treated well by the Roman governors of Sicily.

Marcellus became the ruler of the city, but was accused by the Syracusans of violating the terms of their surrender. Following an investigation and trial, he was found not guilty – and in an apology the citizens heaped honours upon him. A cult sprang up around him, and a vow was made that whenever he or his family members landed in Sicily, the Syracusans would adorn themselves with garlands and make sacrifices. He was further honoured with games and festivals in much the same way the Greeks had formed cults and celebrations around Greek kings. Indeed it is in Syracuse that we find the first evidence of Hellenistic ruler cult honours being centred on a Roman. Perhaps this was a way of packaging a new regime in familiar trappings to make it more palatable to local people.

Marcellus's career did not end with his capture of Syracuse. He would go on to fight for Rome in Carthage, and would die in battle against Hannibal. Out of respect for his generalship, that legendary leader would have Marcellus's body burned with honour, and the ashes sent with due respect to his son.

The cult around Marcellan rulership would long outlive his memory, and his descendants, who would maintain close ties to Sicily and Syracuse, would continue to be honoured by the citizens.

The next great general to come to Syracuse was none other than Scipio Africanus, who used the subdued Sicilian capital as the base for his preparations for his wars in North Africa. Before going to do battle with Carthage, the sources attest that he enjoyed a luxurious and indolent lifestyle in Syracuse, dressing in Greek style and fully absorbing the lingering Greek culture of the city. Despite this, when the time came to attack Carthage, as has been seen, Scipio was ready.

ROMAN SYRACUSE

The Roman governorship of Sicily from Syracuse was marked by poor management of the agricultural system and abuse of the enslaved population. This would result in the revolts and wars known collectively as the First and Second Servile Wars, from 135–32 BC and 104–100 BC respectively. These were no mere blips, but major uprisings involving tens of thousands of enslaved men and women rebelling against their masters and attempting to form independent new countries and territories, in defiance of Rome.

Roman slaves came from a variety of sources: many were purchased, but many more were the enslaved local populations following conquest. Sicily – known for years as the bread basket of Rome for its abundant wheat production – was home to a great many low-status, labouring slaves. They were mistreated by their Roman masters, and this led to the First and Second Servile Wars. In both cases the slaves were initially successful, with slaves crowned King of Sicily, before always eventually succumbing to Roman counter-strikes. Syracuse itself was never captured by slaves, but was instead the nerve centre of the Roman counter-attacks.

The Third Servile War would take place in 73 BC, and for the first time it would not originate in Sicily. This is perhaps the most famous of the Servile Wars – and was led by a man named Spartacus, who thanks to Kirk Douglas needs little introduction. His rebellion began in a gladiatorial school in southern Italy, and would progress to challenge Rome itself. Knowing that Sicily had form as a fertile ground for slave rebellions, when Spartacus found he could no longer resist Rome in Italy he planned to sail his army to Sicily and establish a slave kingdom there; however he was swindled and let down by the pirates he paid to transport him. The slaves were cornered, routed and crucified. For all that Spartacus never set foot in Sicily, it did not stop the then governor using the fear and trepidation caused by the events in Italy to scaremonger and extract money from his population.

Gaius Verres had been installed as governor of Sicily in Syracuse in 74 BC. His tenure was short, but infamous. There was no limit to his greed, and he used his time as governor to extort and abuse his citizens. During the Third Servile War, he would accuse slaves most indispensable to their masters of being in league with Spartacus, and ransom them back to their households for exorbitant fees to avoid trial or punishment. Beyond this however, he stripped Syracuse of her wealth and artworks. Most notably, he pillaged the temple of Athena, stripping down the painted panels showing the wars of Agathocles against the Carthaginians. He was also negligent as a defender, with pirates succeeding in docking in the Great Harbour and raiding the city during his command. Verres is the ultimate example of the corrupt Roman official, and this became apparent even during his lifetime. He was prosecuted for his crimes against Syracuse and the empire by a rising orator known as Marcus Tullius Cicero, and it is thanks to Cicero's prosecution, and his writing down of his speeches against Verres, that we not only have a clear account of Verres' crimes, but also of life in Roman Syracuse.

Early in his political career Cicero had gone to Sicily to serve as *quaestor*, an administrative office similar to a low-level magistrate – often involved with official investigations and the like. He clearly liked Syracuse, and Syracuse liked him. The citizens requested him personally to prosecute the recalcitrant and immoral Verres. When he did so, he gave full rein to his rhetorical skill and bitterness against Verres and wrote a detailed account of the beauty of the city that Verres had profaned. In Cicero's words:

> You will often have been told that Syracuse is the largest of Greek cities and the loveliest of all cities. Gentlemen, what you have been told is true. Its position is not only a strong one, but beautiful to behold in whatever direction it is approached, by land or sea. Its harbours are almost enfolded in the embrace of the city buildings, their entrances far apart, but their heads approaching till they meet each other. At their meeting place, that part of the town which is called the Island, being cut off from the rest by a narrow strip of sea, is re-united with it by a connecting bridge. So large is the city that it is described as being four great cities joined together.
>
> One of these is the Island already mentioned, girdled by two harbours, and extending to their mouths or entrances. In this quarter there is the house, once King Hieron's, which our governors regularly occupy. Here also are a number of temples, two much finer than the rest; namely that of Diana [now known as the temple of Apollo] and the other one that of Minerva [Athena, now the duomo], a place rich in treasures in the days before Verres arrived there. At one extremity of this island is the spring of fresh water called Arethusa; an incredibly large spring, teeming with fish, and so placed that it would be swamped by the sea waves but for the protection of a massive stone wall.
>
> Then there is the second town in the city, called Achradina: this contains a broad market-place, some fine colonnades, a richly adorned

town hall, a spacious senate house, and the noble temple of Olympian Jupiter, besides the rest of the town, which is filled with private houses, and divided by one broad continuous street crossed by a number of others.

There is a third town, called Tycha from the ancient temple of Fortune that once stood there; this contains a spacious athletic ground and several temples, and is also a crowded and thickly inhabited part of the city.

And there is a fourth town, which being the most recently built is called Neapolis: on the highest point of this stands the great theatre; besides which there are two splendid temples, one of Ceres and the other of Libera (Persephone) and a large and beautiful statue of Apollo Temenites.

Master of rhetoric as he was, Cicero emphasised the beauty of Syracuse before laying into how Verres abused it. The polemic against Verres was so ferocious – detailing his despoiling of temples, blackmailing of citizens, failures as a defender and commander – that his defence counsel declined to make any defence at all, and advised that Verres go into exile, immediately. Among his various crimes and corruptions, Verres was accused not only of plundering the temples for his personal art collection, including stripping the ivory doors from the temple of Athena, but also of compromising the security of the city in order to steal one of his commander's wives, crucifying citizens without trial, and generally breaking the morale and faith of the population through rampant corruption and extortionate and illegal taxation. He went to live in Marsalia (Marseilles) and was eventually killed under the same order from Mark Antony that would also see Cicero condemned. It was Cicero's searing rhetoric that earned him his death sentence, with Mark Antony's wife Fulvia reportedly cutting the tongue out of his severed head and stabbing it with a hairpin, in cold revenge against his criticisms of her family. Verres in contrast was eventually killed in a dispute over a statue, which in typical fashion he refused to surrender.

Verres, then, had stripped Syracuse of all the art, wealth and ornamentation that had survived Marcellus's initial plundering, hastening the city's decline. While Verres slunk away in disgrace, and Cicero basked in the admiration of all Rome, the empire became the battleground for a tortuous civil war, beginning with the struggle between Caesar and Pompey, culminating in the assassination of Caesar by Brutus and Cassius. This led to the famous triumvirate formed by Octavian, Mark Antony and Lepidus who went to war against the assassins.

Sicily would be strategically significant during this war, in no small part because Roman soldiers lived off Sicilian wheat. It would become a pawn in the war, and despite being granted more Roman rights during this period, the island suffered hugely. One of Pompey's sons would seize control and '[abuse] not only other cities but Syracuse in particular'. As Octavian would struggle to regain control, the population would suffer still more hardship and turmoil.

Octavian would eventually triumph alone, styling himself Caesar Augustus, and ushering in some years of peace. Syracuse, like the rest of the empire, had endured hardship during the political turmoil of the preceding decades, and Augustus did his best to mitigate this with an ambitious building programme. He gave Syracuse, along with the four other most prominent cities of Sicily, the status of *colonia* – and built the Roman amphitheatre, the remains of which remain impressive in the archaeological park of modern Syracuse. The city evidently made an impression on Augustus, for it was the nickname he gave to what is best described as his 'man cave' – the little workshop he retired to in his palace whenever he wanted to do secret or private things.

The fact that the name of Syracuse resounded so clearly with Augustus stands as testament to the status of the city in the popular Roman imagination* and cultural consciousness. Historians, classicists, archaeologists and amateur enthusiasts have speculated for decades, if not centuries, if not millennia, as to why Augustus named his inner sanctum after the humbled Sicilian capital. It has even been a question in entrance interviews for Eton College. Some have suggested that the room was like an island, or hard to penetrate – thus likening it to the city. Others have said it is because of the connection with Archimedes, or because it was so quiet it reminded him of the state he found the ruined Syracuse in when he visited in 21 BC. Any or all of these theories could be true, and it could also be the case that it was not Augustus himself that named the room. It is all conjecture, and we will never know.

However, what is clear is that Syracuse and the history that was not so mythic and distant in the time of Augustus loomed large in his mind and in his view of the world. Greek identity – and particularly Greek brilliance – was a major force in the Roman world view, and was certainly aspirational.

Moreover, Augustus had a personal reason to be invested in the memory of Sicily and Syracuse. His sister Octavia had married firstly Gaius Claudius Marcellus, a descendant of the conqueror of Syracuse

* Emily Gowers, *Augustus and 'Syracuse'*.

himself. This link would only be made stronger by his adoption of his nephew – Marcellus – as his heir. The Marcelli, as members of the family were known, would dine out on Marcellus's conquest of Syracuse and subsequent fame for generations, and certainly played up the connection with their famous ancestor who had died so heroically on the point of a Carthaginian spear. By the time Augustus was doing DIY in his Syracuse chamber, the Greek city had become symbolic of Hellenistic culture at its best, but also of Roman contrition. Marcellus allegedly wept for the fall of such a gorgeous city, and Verres was lambasted and exiled for its plundering. Roman politics had tortured Sicily and Syracuse together, and ushered in the age of the city's decline. There was a trend for restoring Syracuse; not only did Augustus attempt to regenerate the city with a building programme, but Caligula followed suit, rebuilding both the damaged walls of the city and the religious temples. Hadrian also wished to jump on the bandwagon of benign benefactors of the Sicilians, depicting himself on a coin raising a kneeling Sicily.

Rome regarded Syracuse in a special light. They had conquered the city, reformed it and moulded it to their ways, but there was a Greek glamour around it – a legitimacy and brilliance that inspired respect and admiration. A Roman expat community sprang up, as many well-to-do Romans went to spend their holidays in the well situated and historic city, just as they do today. They created a Latin-speaking ruling class, and Syracuse would enter a period of rare peace. Peace that would be disrupted by two features of the third century – the spread of Christianity, and Viking raids. When the Norsemen sacked the city, tradition has it that the citizens sheltered in the many networks of Christian catacombs mazing under the city's streets.

Roman Syracuse would take on a new identity with the advent of Christianity in the Roman Empire and Mediterranean. St Paul, when being conveyed to Rome via Malta as a prisoner, spent three days in Roman Syracuse.

A CHRISTIAN CITY

St Paul is one of the most revered figures in the history of early Christianity. Despite never meeting Jesus, he was one of the most zealous apostles, preaching Christianity to Gentiles across the Mediterranean and Asia Minor from his base in Antioch. Originally named Saul and a Jewish persecutor of Christians, he converted during his famous journey to Damascus, where he beheld a vision of Christ that changed his life, his identity and his name. So successful was he in his preaching of Christianity that he ruffled Roman feathers, and soon found himself imprisoned and being conveyed to Rome to stand trial. It was on this journey, following a shipwreck in Malta, that Paul would come to Syracuse, and bring the seeds of Christianity with him.

It seems that – despite technically being under arrest – Paul enjoyed much freedom during the journey to Rome, perhaps because he was accused only of non-violent crimes and had not yet been found guilty or sentenced in a Roman law court. Thus he used his time both in Malta and Syracuse to preach. During the three days he spent there, he spoke to audiences underground, in the crypt of what would become the Church of San Giovanni. He was fortunate – a native Greek speaker, he was easily understood in Syracuse, as for all that the ruling class were Latin speakers, much of the populace continued to speak Greek as their native language. All across Ortygia and on the mainland, networks of tunnels survive, linking parts of the city. Some are the catacombs beneath early Christian churches, but others date from the Greek period, an elaborate system of water cisterns and escape passages. Today visitors can enter the Greek tunnels in the Piazza Duomo, pass through the labyrinthine network, and exit into the bright sunlight of the harbour – just as ancient Greeks might once have done, blinking and stepping into the light. The most spectacular examples of these catacombs today are those associated with the Church of Santa Lucia, and San Giovanni. These tunnels have survived well-preserved to the modern day and visitors can wander in the darkness, clutching torches to light their way. With the help of a guide, it is possible to find graffiti of war images, sketched by frightened children who sheltered there during the Second World War, just as their ancestors had sheltered there when the Normans came. Beneath the Church of San Filippo, one Syracusan child drew pictures of parachuters, and captioned them in Sicilian dialect 'The British are coming to save us.' When the tunnels were converted to air raid shelters, the bones of the long dead were removed to make way for the living, but the grim atmosphere must have remained, along with the frescoes of dancing skeletons that adorn the walls.

When Paul arrived in Syracuse, he would have already found the beginning of what would become a thriving and established Jewish community. The Roman response to the Jewish revolts in the Holy Land had been brutal, with the result that much of the Jewish population fled as refugees across the Mediterranean.

However, Christianity would not truly take hold and spread in Sicily until the third century AD. In response to this spread and strengthening of Christianity throughout the empire, the advisors of Diocletian would urge him to take drastic action. Christians, who had for a hundred years enjoyed reasonable safety in most territories throughout the empire, now found themselves in the midst of the worst persecution to beset the followers of Christ since the apostolic age. In 303, the emperor issued the first 'Edict against the Christians', and the Diocletian Persecutions had begun.

SANTA LUCIA

In all the pages written on the history of Syracuse, few books give much credit to the less developed but no less ancient section of the city lying just across the bridge from Ortygia, adjacent to the ancient shipbuilding harbour. In the Borgata of Santa Lucia the history of Christianity in Syracuse is written in blood.

It is impossible to write about the history or identity of Syracuse without touching on the story of Santa Lucia. Many cities do not celebrate their patron saint, but in Syracuse the entire city flocks to the procession celebrating her feast day, in which an exquisitely worked silver reliquary, in the likeness of the young girl, is held aloft above the adoring devotees. This silver sculpture is carried through the streets for hours on the shoulders of devoted citizens. Babies are raised up from the crowd and pressed to the silver lips. Santa Lucia has a place in the hearts of the citizens, whether they are Christian or not. The neighbourhood surrounding Lucia's church is less expensive and prestigious than the area surrounding the duomo in the centre of Ortygia. Many of Syracuse's immigrant communities – primarily Bangladeshis and North Africans – live in this area, and children play cricket and kick footballs in the piazza outside the church in the evenings. On the weekends, it hosts a flea market.

I first explore the area with a friend, a Syracusan serendipitously named Lucia – for the saint of course. In fact, Lucia's mother had desperately wanted to name her new baby Patrizia. It was her third daughter; she had named the first for her mother, the second for her mother-in-law, and now it was her turn to choose. But the baby girl was born with wide, clear blue eyes and on the evening of 13 December, Santa Lucia's feast day, just as the fireworks exploded in the sky. The nurses confronted her: 'You cannot name this child anything but Lucia.'

The basilica of Santa Lucia is vast and dominates the piazza, beside an octagonal sepulchre of marble. As we arrive, the priest emerges from the vestry, wearing a wine-red T-shirt decorated with the crosses of Jerusalem. He is a Franciscan, and they are the guardians of Santa Lucia in Syracuse. He is busy preparing for the six o'clock mass, and hastily throws a white robe and collar over his T-shirt. He agrees to quickly show us the basilica and the sepulchre. Fixing his collar he reminds us, 'The robes make not the monk.'

The first thing he tells us is that the basilica stands where Santa Lucia was murdered and thus became a Christian martyr. A pillar of porphyry marble stands beside the altar. 'This is where they cut her throat,' he tells us. 'They tied her to a column. We don't know if that's the *real* column that she was bound to, where she was martyred – it probably isn't, but that *is* the spot where it happened.'

Lucia was a young woman of noble family, and Christian during the reign of the Roman Emperor Diocletian. She was born around AD 283, an inauspicious time to be a young woman and a Christian; it was the time of the Diocletian Persecutions – a period of intolerance and aggression towards Christian citizens of the Roman Empire, following a period of relative tolerance during which the religion flourished and spread. Diocletian himself was not a zealot, but was persuaded by his advisors and an oracle that the Christians needed to be rooted out of the empire. Presumably his advisors were acting out of self-interest, and a desire to preserve the status quo: Christianity was seen as a dangerous and extreme sect, which extolled equality and poverty and threatened to upset the established social and political order of the Roman Empire.

It was during this period that the stories of Christians being thrown to lions in amphitheatres became common currency in conversation and literature. The emperors before Diocletian had not been tolerant of Christians, but they had been reluctant to pass empire-wide laws attacking them. Diocletian did not hesitate. He wished to stamp out the resistance, and Christians across the empire found their heads being struck off, including bishops in Egypt and Antioch.

According to Christian tradition, in Syracuse, the young Lucia decided she wished to preserve her virginity for Christ, but her mother arranged a marriage for her with a man of good social standing, out of concern for her daughter's future. Her father was dead, and doubtless her mother felt she needed the protection of a man. However, Lucia was adamant, and convinced her mother to let her break the betrothal, thus rejecting a passionate pagan suitor. Moved by her belief that St Agatha healed her mother's illness, Lucia went a step further and distributed

The coastline of Tyre with Byzantine columns visible under the sea.

The sarcophagus of Antipater, the *murex* fisherman, in the Al-Mina archaeological site.

Left The fishing harbour of Tyre presided over by the statue of Mary.

Middle The Roman road in the Al-Mina archaeological site of Tyre.

Below The remains of the hippodrome of Tyre.

Top Dido Building Carthage,
by J. M. W. Turner.

Left The Tophet of Carthage.

Above Bust of Hannibal, depicted on
a Tunisian banknote.

Ortygia viewed from above.

Duomo of Syracuse with baroque façade.

Silver reliquary of Santa Lucia, housed in the Duomo of Syracuse.

The entrance to the 'Ear of Dionysius'.

The Greek theatre of Syracuse.

Portrait of Galla Placidia.

Mosaic portrait of Emperor Justinian
from the Basilica of San Vitale.

Intricately decorated mosaic ceiling in the Mausoleum of Galla Placidia.

View of the modern city of Antakya, prior to the February 2023 earthquakes.

bove The synagogue of Antakya, prior to
ıe February 2023 earthquakes.

Right The Iron Gate of Antioch.

Left Destruction in the streets of Antakya, February 2023.

Middle The ruins of the Greek Orthodox Church in Antakya, February 2023.

Below The ruins of Cindi Hammam in Antakya, February 2023.

the dowry that her suitor had hoped to claim among the poor and needy. In his bitterness, her would-be bridegroom denounced her to the Roman authorities in the city. He revealed to them that she was a secret Christian.

The governor, Paschasius, initially proved lenient by Roman standards, certainly at the height of the persecutions. He ordered Lucia to make a pagan sacrifice to the emperor to reconfirm her submission and loyalty to him and the pagan faith, and renounce her Christianity. Lucia, much in the way of martyrs, refused. Incensed, Paschasius ordered her to be thrown into a brothel to be gang-raped by whoever happened to be there. This is essentially the storyline presented in Handel's opera *Theodora*, and seems a common theme of female saints. The world of early Christianity was a gritty and visceral place; it is easy to forget in the tranquillity of modern churches, but the early Christians were perceived as the raving members of a cannibalistic cult, and they fought for their beliefs against one of the most brutal and martial-focused forces of history. Mercy was not often dispensed by the Roman Empire.

The story goes that when the governor's men came to drag her away to carry out her sentence, they found the defiant Lucia rooted to the spot. For all their efforts, even going so far as to tie a team of oxen to her, they could not move her. God helped her and she would not budge an inch towards the gateway of the brothel. Unwilling to embarrass themselves through further failure, the Romans decided to burn the proof of this resistance and heaped bundles of wood around Lucia and thrust burning faggots into them, but though the wood blazed around her, Lucia stood serene and resolute and did not burn. Late sources say that they then proceeded to gouge out the young girl's eyes. This detail is missing from earlier accounts and is likely a fabrication; nevertheless it has not prevented Lucia from becoming specifically associated with protecting the eyes in the subsequent centuries of veneration (from the fifteenth century onwards). Finally the soldiers slit her throat, and she bled to death on the spot from which she could not be moved, where the pink marble pillar stands today. Her blood bathed the ground. The priests tells us emphatically that the Borgata of Santa Lucia, the poorer area of modern Syracuse in which the church stands, has been given a special energy and is blessed by God, for it is here that the blood of the martyr was spilled, and every day they walk on the land made rich by Santa Lucia's blood.

Back in Ortygia, in a church on the Piazza Duomo, a Caravaggio painting depicting Santa Lucia's burial is housed. It shows the darkness, tragedy and squalor of the story. In dark browns, the fragile body of the dead girl lies on the floor in humble clothes while a mostly male assembly of mourners gathers around her. In the painting, the eye is drawn not to the saint, but to her powerfully built gravedigger. Caravaggio painted this altarpiece during his stay in Syracuse after fleeing Malta.

Santa Lucia's body was buried first in a simple tomb in the catacombs of the area to which she would give her name. George Maniakes, a famed Byzantine general whose life intersects with that of Antioch as well as Syracuse, would move her remains to the then imperial capital of Constantinople. When Constantinople was sacked by the Venetians during the Fourth Crusade, her relics were seized by the invaders and moved to a church in Venice, where they remain to this day. The feast of Santa Lucia in December 2004 was a momentous occasion. For the first time in over a thousand years, the relics of Santa Lucia were brought from Venice to Syracuse, to mark the 1,700th anniversary of her death. It was an emotive day for the city, with the residents flocking to the marina to watch the ship entering the historic harbour. Joyous tears fell thick and fast that day.

The miracle of Santa Lucia is not Syracuse's only miracle. The priest tells us of another that occurred on this land, many years later, the miracle of the *Madonna delle lacrime*, the crying Madonna. A young woman, newly married, thought that she was dying, and the icon of the Madonna on her wall wept real tears for four days. The priest in the Church of Santa Lucia also asserts that the white marble statue of Mary in the crypt of the sepulchre – while she has not shed tears – has sweated.

The facade of the Duomo of Syracuse is home to many statues. Together, they tell the story of Christianity in the city. This narrative is, of course, debated. The apostles St Peter and St Paul stand outside the cathedral, St Peter with his eyes raised heavenwards, Paul admonishing citizens. These statues reference the connection between Peter and Paul in Antioch – legend has it they came and preached together and founded the church – but this is not substantiated in any historic documents, nor the Bible for that matter. The next level above them houses statues of the famous martyrs, Santa Lucia and St Marcian, although somehow the builders responsible mixed them up – Santa Lucia stands on the left of the Duomo, clutching her eyes on a plate, above a label naming her St Marcian, and St Marcian stands on the right, his iron crook in hand, labelled Santa Lucia.

St Marcian was claimed to have been the first bishop of Syracuse, sent by St Peter and martyred by the Jews of the city – however the historical record places his time in Syracuse two centuries after the death of St Peter. For Santa Lucia, historical record and legend match up well. She was venerated immediately following her death by a cult that formed around her martyrdom and legacy. In the catacombs of San Giovanni, a stone tablet was discovered by the archaeologist Paolo Orsi testifying to the celebration of Santa Lucia's feast day less than a century after her death – suggesting that she truly did capture the hearts and minds of the city's residents who witnessed the atrocity first hand.

Above the statues depicting the saints and martyrs presides Virgin Mary, carved in white marble by the Palerman sculptor Marabitti, standing serenely in a niche. Beneath Mary is a rigid eagle, the royal emblem of Charles III of Spain, who reigned as King of Sicily in the eighteenth century when the facade was created. Above them all are winged cherubs. Everything is supported and framed by gorgeous marble swirls and Corinthian columns, with their ornate acanthus leaf capitals. The overall effect, framed dramatically by the invariably bright blue sky of Ortygia, is one of coherent busyness, in stark contrast to the simplicity of the Doric columns that stand in the walls.

Diocletian would eventually repeal his edicts for the persecution of the Christians in his empire, seeing that the effect was not what he had hoped for. The Christians were not stamped out; if anything the martyrdom of many of their leaders only strengthened their resolve and drove them underground which made them harder to control. Eventually they would resurface, stronger than ever before. As the early Christian writer Tertullian put it, 'The blood of the martyrs was the seed of the Church.' By 324, just two decades after Santa Lucia's death, Rome was ruled by a Christian emperor, Constantine the Great – the same man who founded Constantinople and ordered the building of the Church of the Holy Sepulchre in Jerusalem.

THE BYZANTINE CAPITAL?

Despite Constantine ruling as sole emperor and his many successes, following his death in the fourth century the western Roman Empire would begin to unravel in the wake of barbarian invasions. This would have serious consequences for Syracuse. The Germanic tribes – Vandals, Goths and Lombards – would make incursions into territory in the western Roman Empire, sacking and occupying as they went. The peak of these invasions would come with the 410 sack of Rome by the Visigoth King Alaric. This siege and its aftermath – and indeed the

disintegration of the western Roman Empire – are discussed in depth
in the section of this book on Ravenna, which would soon find itself at
the heart of these conflicts.

As for Syracuse, it was peripheral to the great battles taking place in
Roman Italy, but far from immune. Syracuse would be sacked by the
Vandals and come under the control of the Goths, until the general
Belisarius retook the city for Byzantium under the rule of the Emperor
Justinian and restored Roman rule and Greek language and culture to
its streets.

Belisarius's troops took Syracuse not long after his triumph at
Carthage, which had seen the historian Procopius himself stop in the
city as part of a reconnaissance mission. In fact, it is disappointing
that Procopius was not so moved by the beauty of the city that he
chose to write a description – perhaps this can be seen as 'evidence
of omission' that Syracuse had indeed dwindled and suffered under
the period of Germanic harassment. Belisarius was welcomed as a
hero by the Sicilians, whose cheers rang out for him as he made his
triumphal entry into the city, scattering gold coins among the jubilant
population. Belisarius could have been seen as offering a period of
relief, prosperity and security – but really what he brought more than
anything else was organised, Byzantine taxation. Sicily would stand
as the capital of the Byzantine province of Sicily for 300 years, and
become an important Christian centre and strategic foothold for the
remainder of the Roman Empire once again. It was in the Byzantine
period that the already extensive catacombs were enlarged and decorated
with frescoes depicting scenes from Christian history, and also that the
pagan temples would be consecrated as churches, including the ancient
temple of Athena.

In 663 Syracuse would take on new significance. The then emperor,
Constans II, decided to make it his capital. Historians differ in opinion
as to whether Constans moving his court to Syracuse amounted to the
city taking on the status of capital – and that brings with it a discussion
of what exactly a capital is. However it seems that for much of history,
the capital has indeed been the primary residence of the ruler, and the
place from which he conducts business and gives orders – from this
perspective, Syracuse *was* the capital. During his time in Italy and Sicily
(Constans travelled to Rome before making his way south) he is reported
to have stripped the cities of their wealth – even from the holy places –
and carted it off to Constantinople. Beyond this Constans levied a severe
tax regime against the Syracusans and citizens of surrounding lands.
The emperor's time in Syracuse did not serve to benefit or beautify the

city as might have been expected. This adds weight to the argument that Constans never in fact intended to make Syracuse a long-term imperial capital.

Part of what engendered this move by Constans was a growing threat from a group that would become known as the Arabs. The Prophet Muhammad had united the Arab peoples into a distinct polity, that would in turn become the caliphates. These groups had an expansionist policy and were beginning to threaten Byzantine-held Italy and Sicily. As has been seen, they were soon to wage war against them. By physically moving his capital to Sicily, Constans may have hoped to deter invasion and strengthen the defences and his control over the region, but perhaps he was simply seduced by its beauty.

Whatever his motivations, his time in Syracuse was ill-fated and short-lived. After just five years in the Sicilian capital he was murdered by an attendant named Andrew while he was bathing. Readers should not imagine a knife and a tub, but something rather less romantic. He was killed in the Roman baths – similar to a Turkish hammam – and was not elegantly stabbed but bludgeoned to death with a soap dish. Archaeologists have recently uncovered the remains of a bath complex beneath an apartment building – formerly a car park – which may be where Constans II met his end. One of the noblemen who had accompanied him to Syracuse, an exceedingly handsome Armenian man by the name of Mizizios, usurped the throne in the wake of Constans's assassination. This revolt was short-lived and Constans's eldest son regained control of Syracuse and the wider empire before the year was out. Mizizios was executed, but not before he had succeeded in proclaiming himself King of Sicily, and had coins bearing his image and name minted in Syracuse.

Constans II had been a divisive figure, and while history does not relate the names of those who had plotted his death, or put Andrew up to the murder, there was no shortage of candidates. He had made enemies in Rome through his stripping of the riches of the city, in Constantinople for quitting the city, and for the murder of his monk brother who was perceived to be a threat to his authority, and in Syracuse he had rankled the population with his harsh tax regime. Additionally, the Church regarded him with some fury as he had refused to weigh in on the Arian controversy, and indeed tried to ban its discussion, which infuriated Church leaders on both sides of the debate. Beyond this he had gone so far as to limit the powers of the Pope, informing him that he had no authority over the archbishop of Ravenna. Bad as this may have been, his treatment of the previous pope was worse: when Pope

Martin condemned the ruling Constans offered on the Arian controversy (namely, no ruling at all) he had the Pope arrested, dragged to
Constantinople to stand trial, and exiled for contradicting the emperor.

THE ARAB CONQUEST

The next great scandal to erupt in Syracuse would not come for several
centuries after Constans's demise. This time it would not centre around
the Byzantine Emperor, but a would-be Sicilian king – a Greek usurper
by the name of Euphemius – in the year 826.

Euphemius had been appointed commander of the Sicilian navy
under the governorship of another Byzantine named Constantine
Sounas. Euphemius was dispatched to lead an expedition raiding along
the North African coast. In his absence the emperor sent a decree for
his dismissal from his position and his arrest. Catching wind of this
impending disgrace, Euphemius resorted to open rebellion.

Sources disagree as to the exact cause of Euphemius's fall from
favour, but the argument put forward by the nearest contemporary
chronicler was that he had abducted and forced marriage upon a Sicilian
nun named Homoniza. According to a chronicler, Homoniza's brothers
complained to the emperor about Euphemius's vile conduct and abuse
of his position. The emperor's verdict was that, if the charges were true,
Euphemius should be subjected to rhinotomy – the Byzantine practice of
the punitive cutting off or slitting of the nose. Doubtless it was wishing
to avoid this fate that forced Euphemius's hand. Not only did he rebel,
but he forged an ill-advised alliance with the Aghlabids of North Africa.

Euphemius was not the first Byzantine to rebel or defect in this
way; in the previous century two generals had plotted similar manoeu-
vres, and their swift defeats and deaths should perhaps have warned
Euphemius of the futility of such acts. But it seems Euphemius was not
a student of history. With the support of his fleet he landed in Sicily,
marched on Syracuse, which he captured easily, and sacked Enna as
well. Constantine Sounas was captured and executed and Euphemius
proclaimed himself *basileus* of Sicily. He went a step further and called
himself Emperor of the Romans in some official documents. This
clearly indicates the intrigue in Sicily was now about much more than
a love affair with / abduction of a nun: Euphemius was playing for the
imperial crown.*

---

* Vivien Prigent, 'Pour en finir avec Euphèmios, basileus des Romains'.

However, his initial glory was short-lived. Euphemius had entrusted the subjugation of the western parts of the island to a confederate known only as Balata and named only in Arabic sources. This man betrayed Euphemius and pledged allegiance to Constantinople before marching on Syracuse and ousting Euphemius. This was far from the end of the matter. It was then that Euphemius appealed to his Muslim neighbour, Emir Ziyadat Allah of Ifriqiya, for aid. They hatched a plan in which Ziyadat Allah would provide Euphemius with the troops and resources he needed to capture Sicily in exchange for regular tribute. When Euphemius summoned up this storm, he had no idea of the destruction it would cause. When he landed on the west coast of Sicily at Mazara with a hundred ships, laden with ten thousand infantry and seven hundred mounted knights, he started a war that would thunder for half a century. The Arab conquest of Sicily had begun.

Euphemius would swiftly change sides again, but small good would it do him. His co-conspirator died first of disease and then Euphemius himself was stabbed by men he thought were coming to negotiate with him outside the fortified hillside town of Enna.

The Arab conquest of Sicily was not a smooth, premeditated operation. Rather it was haphazard and opportunistic. Nevertheless, it was effective, and for 260 years from 831 to 1091 the Byzantine Theme of Sicily become the Emirate of Sicily, ruled first by the Aghlabids and then by the Fatimids. Palermo fell to the Arab invaders in 831, and in time would replace Syracuse as the capital of Sicily. In 843 Messina would fall. In 859 it was Enna. Their siege of Syracuse was initially unsuccessful, due in no small part to the disease that spread through the marshlands that had crippled many other invading forces before them. The attacks were relentless however, and some reports even claimed the Aghlabids had something akin to Greek Fire in their arsenal – the legendary burning chemical with effects similar to napalm used in ancient warfare. In 878, after fifteen hundred years as the capital of Sicily, Syracuse was not only captured but sacked by the conquerors.

A Christian monk named Theodosius living within the city testified to its ruin in vivid terms. He was sincerely traumatised by his experiences in the city, and the letter he wrote to Leo the Deacon describing them is more like a confession – a catharsis – than a report. He asserts that the fall of Syracuse and the sufferings of the Syracusans were at least as bad as the sacking of Jerusalem. Theodosius wrote to Leo the Deacon:

Such was the slaughter that on the same day every weapon with which defence had been made was broken to pieces, bows, quivers, arms, swords, and all weapons; the strong were made weak [. . .] We were vanquished after many attacks made upon us by night, and many a hostile ambush [. . .] we were taken captive after we had suffered hunger long, feeding upon herbs, after having thrust into our mouths in our extreme need even filthy things, after men had even devoured their children – a frightful deed, that should be passed in silence, although we had before abhorred human flesh – oh! hideous spectacle [. . .] we did not abstain from eating leather and the skins of oxen [. . .] Now this thing came to pass, by far the most terrible thing; a most grievous pestilence, alas, followed upon famine.

For what else can I do than condense and crowd such great things into few words, being shut up in prison where I have not one hour of peace and quiet? The thick darkness of my prison, which hangs over my eyes, weakens and dulls my sight [. . .]

First they slew to the last man those who were drawn up in line against them at the porch of the Church of the Saviour, and with a great rush they opened the doors and entered the temple with drawn swords [. . .] Then indeed people all ages fell in a moment by the edge of the sword, princes and judges of the earth, as we sing in the psalms, young men and maidens, old men and children, both monks and those joined in matrimony, the priests and the people, the slave and the free man, and even sick persons who had lain a long time in bed. Merciful God, the butchers could not even spare these; for the soul that thirsts for human blood is not easily satisfied by the death of those who first face it in anger.

Theodosius and his bishop were spared and imprisoned, after revealing where the cathedral's treasure was kept. They had hidden it behind the altar in the temple of Athena turned cathedral in the heart of Ortygia. They were spoken for by a less bloodthirsty invader named Semnoës, who clearly respected the lives of churchmen and asked for them to be spared. They were then imprisoned in rat-infested darkness in the basilica of San Giovanni for a month while the Aghlabids summarily destroyed as much of the city as they could in that period, massacring those of the population who resisted – or simply who it pleased them to massacre – and enslaving the rest. The sack of Syracuse did not spell complete dominion over the island however. Famously Taormina would hold out until 902, and a handful of small forces near Messina resisted longer – but soon the entire island was subjugated.

Theodosius and his brothers were then packed onto the back of mules and sent on the long march across the island to Palermo.

Palermo was chosen as the capital of the Emirate of Sicily because it had fallen more easily and quickly to the invaders, and thus had been in their possession longer and was in better shape than Syracuse. Following this conquest, Syracuse would never again be a capital of the Mediterranean, nor even of the island of Sicily. Palermo would eclipse it in size, wealth, political importance and as a cultural centre. Much was destroyed in Syracuse, and moneylenders set up shop in the corner of the Christian cathedral, Athena's former temple. The Italian American writer Francis Crawford wrote of the Arab conquest:

> Syracuse lived again, and lives today, a military stronghold, a naval station, a commercial town; but its life as a source of power and as a fountain of individuality was arrested forever on the fatal day ... the five cities upon which Marcellus looked down with tearful eyes have sunk out of sight, never to rise again, and a small Italian town, crowded together and irregularly cut by quiet little streets, covers the island, and extends over a few hundred yards of the opposite peninsula. That is all there is left of her that rivalled Athens and Alexandria, and that once far outdid Rome in extent, in wealth, and in beauty.

The result of the Aghlabids and their Fatimid successors choosing Palermo as the capital of the emirate over Syracuse is that in Palermo one can *feel* the three centuries of Arab rule. In Syracuse, this period of Sicilian history escapes the senses – visually at least. There are scarcely any examples of Arab art and architecture remaining in Ortygia. A handful of inscriptions and mosaic decorations have been found, but no buildings. It is possible some were built, but if they were they were levelled without trace by subsequent earthquakes and rulers and never restored. Roaming the crooked streets of Ortygia, crossing the Piazza Duomo, dipping underground to visit the Jewish mikvah, one does not cross paths with Muslim Syracuse. The language also did not leave much of an imprint, as it did in Malta – Sicilian dialect carries only light traces of Arabic.

However, in the food of Syracuse, one can taste the Arab conquest. Perhaps the chief and lasting impact on Sicily of the Arab conquest is in the senses of taste and smell. The Arabs brought with them sugar cane, aubergine, date palms, pistachio and more. *Pasta alla Norma*, the Sicilian classic – would be nothing without its North African aubergines. The traditional Sicilian sweet – cannoli – was created under Arab rule.

Following the conquest of various major cities many Arabs emigrated from North Africa to Sicily, attracted by the fertility of the island and the prospects of a new life and greater opportunities. These immigrants formed a new ruling class, altering the social hierarchy of Sicily and pushing the native Sicilians, Greeks and Jews into an underclass of tradesmen and farming peasants. The Sicily that the Arabs conquered was a multi-ethnic and multiconfessional society, and the arrival of immigrants from Ifriqiya brought a still greater mix to the island including Arabs, Berbers and Andalusians.

The Aghlabid administration did not last long. Ifiqiya, the North African territory spreading across modern Tunisia and Algeria, was conquered by the Fatimids in AD 909. Thus Sicily transitioned to Fatimid rule, and with it so did Syracuse. This also brought with it a religious change as the Fatimids were a Shīa dynasty who traced their provenance to the Prophet's daughter Fatima, whereas the Aghlabids were Sunni. However, despite the difference in religion of the new ruling classes, tolerance existed in Syracuse. Religious conversions were not forced upon the inhabitants – perhaps in no small part because the Christians and Jews of the island were required to pay higher taxes.

Sicily would prosper under Arab rule, with Palermo becoming what Syracuse once had been – a city renowned for beauty, luxury and culture. The Sicilian Arabs took on a distinct cultural identity from the Arabs of the east, with Ibn Hawal, a celebrated Shīa Fatimid geographer from Baghdad, deriding their loose adherence to standard Islamic devotions and the nonchalance with which they married Christians, and criticising their pronunciation of Arabic.

However, for all the prosperity of the Emirate of Sicily, it began to disintegrate due to internal conflicts in the eleventh century. From one unified emirate it fragmented into separate territories ruled by rival local leaders. Perhaps the beginning of the end was spelled out one night in around 1060, when Ibn al-Thumna, Lord of Syracuse and Catania, decided to beat and abuse his wife to within an inch of her life. Her son witnessed the altercation, and summoned a doctor, which probably saved his mother's life. As she recovered, her husband was penitent and conciliatory, and the battered woman used this as an opportunity to obtain leave to travel without him to visit her brother, a lord in the centre of the island. Eager to make amends, her husband agreed.

On seeing the sorry state of his sister, Ibn al-Hawwas was incensed and refused to allow his wife to return to her husband, and cut off all communication with him. This resulted in Ibn al-Thumna marching on the siblings at Castrogiovanni, but he was soundly defeated by his brother-in-law's troops. In desperation, the furious and embarrassed emir took drastic action. In the year 1061, he appealed for help from a band of marauding Normans, recently arrived in Sicily. This would lead to the conquest of Enna, and little by little, the Normans gaining more and more traction on the island. By 1062 Ibn al-Thumna had paid for his treachery, assassinated by his own people.

THE ARRIVAL OF THE NORMANS

The southernmost tip of Ortygia is dominated by the magnificent Castello Maniace. This limestone fortress, with its high walls that drop down to the sea, was named for the Byzantine general George Maniakes, who took a ship for the Emirate of Sicily in 1038.

Maniakes was, according to the Byzantine historian Michael Psellus, a giant of a man:

> I myself saw the man, and marvelled at him; for nature had combined in his person all the qualities necessary for a military commander. He stood to the height of ten feet, so that to look at him men would tilt back their heads as if towards the top of a hill or high mountain. His countenance was neither gentle nor pleasing, but put one in mind of a tempest; his voice was like thunder and his hands seemed made for tearing down walls or for smashing doors of bronze.

With him came an invasion force comprised of Italian Lombards, French Normans, Varangians and Scandinavian Vikings – including none other than Harald Hardrada – future King of Norway, who would later jostle with William the Conqueror for the English throne. Maniakes and his motley crew of highly able soldiers swiftly managed to capture the less thoroughly Islamised areas of the island. This included Syracuse in 1040. The siege of this city was – as it had always been – dramatic, and one of the mercenary Normans, William of Hauteville, earned himself the nickname of William Iron Arm by killing the Emir of Syracuse in single combat; so forceful was his blow before the walls of Syracuse that the emir was nearly sliced in half. Following the capture of Syracuse, Maniakes exhumed the remains of the patron saint Santa Lucia and shipped them to Constantinople as a trophy of conquest.

For all the speed of its success and heroic posturing, this conquest of eastern Sicily was short-lived and the territories were lost within a few years. Maniakes was a skilled general who, left to his own devices, might have succeeded in keeping the coastal territories and making inroads into the island; however intrigue in Byzantium resulted in him being summoned back from Sicily and imprisoned in Constantinople. The Arabs quickly regained the cities conquered by Maniakes and the Varangian and Norman mercenaries.

However they would not remain in their possession long. Disunity continued among the Arab rulers of Sicily, which was by this stage less a unified emirate and more a collection of rival city states. In 1061, one of the leaders – casting around for allies to help him dominate the island – lighted upon a pair of brothers, Norman mercenaries who were garnering a reputation for ruthless efficiency and conquest. He approached these two – Robert and Roger – for aid, and they were only too happy to oblige. These men were the half-brothers of William Iron Arm – two of the twelve sons of Tancred of Hauteville – the founder of a dynasty of Norman conquerors who would snap up Italian lands throughout the eleventh century. Robert – later known as Robert Guiscard – would himself be the father of Bohemond who would capture and rule Antioch during the First Crusade.

But who were these Hautevilles, these Normans, suddenly dominating Sicily and southern Italy? They were the descendants of Vikings. When the Vikings tired of raiding and chose instead to settle on lands in northern France, convert to Christianity, and intermarry with the local Gallic population, their early name – Norsemen – eroded to become Normans and they gave their name to the area known ever since as Normandy. Their centuries of travelling and warring remained strong in their blood and that of their descendants, and so the Normans were never quite content to sit and till their fields – they had a taste for conquest. Before they proved this in England, they would prove it in Italy, attracted by the richness of the countryside. Once established in southern Italy, these Normans turned their minds to Sicily.

Even without an invitation from an Arab emir, Tancred of Hauteville's sons were already hatching Sicilian ambitions. The Pope in fact approved of their plans, and went so far as to name Robert Guiscard 'future Duke of Sicily' in 1058.

He and his youngest brother Roger had carved out territories in Apulia and Calabria. In their conquest of southern Italy, they had the support of the Pope who was in conflict with the Byzantine Empire, and the Normans agreed that in exchange for the legitimacy that papal approval offered them they would refuse to recognise the Church or Emperor of Constantinople.

It took them thirty years, but by 1091 the Normans had brought Sicily to heel. Roger had taken Syracuse in 1085, sailing his fleet into the Great Harbour and successfully besieging it. With the blessing of his brother

Robert Guiscard, Roger would become Roger I, the Count of Sicily, and following the inclination of his Arab predecessors he would hold court in Palermo. He entrusted the rule of Syracuse to his son Jordan who had fought beside him during the siege. Roger made Syracuse a Latin bishopric along with the other provinces of Sicily, forever throwing off the influence of the Byzantine Church and unifying Sicily more closely with mainland Italy and Rome.

Unsurprisingly, just as the Arab conquest had sparked an influx of Muslim immigrants from North Africa, the Norman conquest sparked an exodus. While the Normans – like their Arab predecessors – implemented a system of tolerance in their multi-ethnic and multiconfessional new lands, many Muslims chose to leave. Among them was the celebrated Arab Sicilian poet, Ibn Hamdis, who was born in Syracuse. He was in his late twenties when the Normans took his native city, whereupon he packed his bags, his wife and his children and moved to North Africa. From there he would travel to Seville, but he would always carry Sicily in his heart, which would bleed through in his poetry.

In the Norman period, despite its many harrowing sieges, Syracuse would rise to flourish again. It would never again rival Palermo, and never again be a power of the Mediterranean, but it had risen from its ashes, as it had time and time again. Merchants still flocked to the town, the harbours were functioning once again, and the gardens were abundant with fruit.

HIGH MEDIEVAL PERIOD

Sicily would pass through successive kings, and importantly queens as well, not least Constance I who would rule as queen regnant from 1194 to 1198. Her son, Fredrick I of Sicily, was also Fredrick II – Holy Roman Emperor – through his father the Swabian Emperor Henry VI of the Hohenstaufen dynasty. It was under Fredrick's rule that Sicily nominally came into Swabian hands, but Fredrick was a Sicilian through and through: born in northern Italy, following the death of his father he was rushed to his mother in Palermo where, at the age of three, he was crowned King of Sicily. After the death of his mother the kingdom and indeed the whole island was subject to political turmoil as different agents vied for power. When the young king was twelve years old, a Genoese naval officer – more frankly, a pirate named Alamanno da Costa – took control of Syracuse and proclaimed himself count of the city, ruling it as a Genoese trading outpost and clashing with Pisans who also wanted control of Syracuse.

By 1220, Fredrick – now twenty-six – had begun to assert his rights in Sicily and wanted to bring Syracuse under his control as well. He succeeded in expelling 'Count' Alamanno in 1221. Fredrick would establish himself as one of the greatest rulers of the age, and was hailed by chroniclers as *stupor mundi* – the wonder of the world. In Syracuse he built the Castello Maniace, the spectacular fort that guards the harbour, in 1239. He left a horde of children, both legitimate and illegitimate, and in time three of his sons would succeed to the throne of Sicily. Ten of his children would die either in prison or by violent means in the struggles for power that consumed the island in the aftermath of his death. He had been the lynchpin of his empire. The last of these unfortunate children was his illegitimate son Manfred, and on his death the throne of Sicily was seized by Charles of Anjou, who had been awarded the right to Sicily by the Pope. As ever, different Sicilian cities had differing opinions on the regime change, and Syracuse and Messina came out in support of Charles.

This may have suited the Pope's political agenda but it meant nothing good for Sicily, and not long after the Angevin takeover, Sicily would revolt against the exploitative and abusive system of government that had been imposed. This bloody uprising would become known to history as the Sicilian Vespers, immortalised in countless books and Verdi's epic opera *Les vêpres siciliennes*.

The rival who presented himself against Charles for Sicily was King Pedro of Aragon who had married Manfred's daughter Constance, thus giving him a claim to the Sicilian throne.

On Easter Monday, 1282, a conflict broke out between the Sicilian locals and Angevin French soldiers before the walls of Palermo. A French officer searching people for weapons was suspected of either insulting or groping a woman, and in the outraged chaos that ensued he was murdered. This precipitated a vicious riot against anyone with a French accent, and many thousands of French officers were slaughtered by the assembled crowds. The pent-up fury towards the French regime came rushing out, and the violence spared neither the elderly, nor children, nor even local Sicilian women pregnant by French soldiers – all fell victim to the anarchic butchery. The revolution spread, and before long Sicily was cleared of Frenchmen. In the aftermath, Peter of Aragon sailed to Sicily and promised the people that he would grant them the ancient rights they had enjoyed under the Norman kings; they accepted him, and he was proclaimed king on 4 September. The house of Aragon would rule in Sicily until the eighteenth century.

Under the Hohenstaufen rulers Syracuse had ceased to be a city of tolerance. Fredrick had forced the Jewish community to wear identifying clothing, attempted to forbid marriage with foreigners, and had cast prostitutes out of the city (they could still work, but not live within the city limits or use the same baths as 'respectable' ladies). Under the Spanish, tolerance would reduce still further. During the rule of Frederick II of Sicily, an Aragonese king, Jews were further segregated and persecuted. In 1402, following an urgent appeal by the Jews of Marsala, the king repealed some of the laws against them, and the Jews enjoyed some religious freedoms and prospered as traders. In some cities, including Syracuse, they made up as much as one tenth of the urban population. Jews in Sicily were particularly respected for their practice of medicine, and one of the first recorded female doctors was a Sicilian Jewish woman named Virdimura, who came from the province of Syracuse and married a resident of Catania in the fourteenth century. However for all this relative prosperity, disaster would soon strike under the Spanish government. I am writing of course of the Spanish Inquisition.

The Jewish community of Syracuse had been established for longer than any Christian community, certainly longer than any Latin Christian sect, any Islamic group and any Hohenstaufen, Angevin or Aragonese rulers. Through all the many conquests, sieges and destructions of Syracuse, the Jews had remained, conducting their rites and passing down their traditions. Nevertheless they were about to find themselves violently ejected. In 1492, a decree was signed by the reigning monarchs of Spain – Ferdinand of Aragon and Isabella of Castile – expelling the Jews from Spain and Spanish territories, including Sicily. The residents of Palermo protested against the decree, arguing that the Jews were not causing problems and trade would be disrupted by their removal, but the Spanish crown did not budge and Sicily could do nothing. In 1493 thirty thousand Sicilian Jews became religious refugees.

It must have been a sorry day in 1493 in the streets of Ortygia, when the Jewish population packed up what possessions they could carry, and left the city. They had inhabited the narrow, jagged streets of the Giudecca, now ironically one of the trendier places to stay in Syracuse, with boutique hotels, wine bars and shops selling local handicrafts. Vestiges of their presence remain in the mikvah on Via Alagona, the oldest preserved Hebrew baths in Europe, dating from the sixth-century Byzantine period. Before they left, the evicted Jews of Syracuse filled in this sacred space with rock and earth, to preserve it for when they would one day return. Their synagogues could not be concealed, and were either destroyed or converted to other uses, but the baths remained a secret and as such survived. These subterranean pools have damp, gritty floors and punishingly low archways, and echo with the trickle of the freshwater spring. Eighteen metres underground, the baths lay undisturbed for centuries, waiting for their makers' return, until a hotel owner began renovations and stumbled upon the carved stone chamber, with five ritual baths, a natural flowing water source and direct light channel.

While most of the city's Jewish inhabitants were expelled, many chose to convert to Christianity instead. The result is that many in the population of modern Syracuse are of distant Jewish heritage, even if they have left their faith behind.

During my second visit to Ortygia I meet a man named Gabriele. He is one of the handful of Jews still practising in Syracuse. He tells me the story of how he discovered his faith. In 2008 a rabbi came from Israel to Syracuse, keen to re-establish a Jewish community. He wanted to reach the *anousim* of Syracuse – people of Jewish heritage but who had either been forced to convert or whose faith had worn away. He wanted to persuade them to return to their ancestral religion. Perhaps surprisingly, some answered his call. Seven Jewish families now exist in Syracuse, practising their religion and using the historic mikvah. The rabbi has since left, but the faithful remain. In 2022, a small Jewish bookshop opened in the Giudecca, selling sacred texts and keeping the memory of Syracuse's Jewish past alive.

Following the departure of the Jews, a group of Christian refugees would arrive in Syracuse in need of a place to rest and regroup. These were the Knights of St John, the military order of the hospitallers who after being kicked out of the Holy Land had set up shop on the island of Rhodes. In 1529 twelve ships arrived in the harbour of Syracuse carrying what was left of the military order following their expulsion by the Ottomans following the siege of Rhodes. Syracuse hosted the fragmented order for a year, before the king settled them on Malta. However, while the presence of the military order in Syracuse was short-lived, and famously they would thrive on Malta, their arrival served as a wake-up call to the King of Sicily of the threat posed by the growing Ottoman Empire to Mediterranean islands. Rhodes had fallen; Sicily might be next. This spurred a hasty overhaul of Syracusan defences. During the epic siege of Malta that would take place in 1565, Syracuse would send a somewhat tardy relief fleet to help raise the siege.

It was during the Spanish period that the streets of Ortygia would become more recognisable as what they are today. In the wake of devastating earthquakes, which miraculously did not destroy the internal temple of Athena but which did fell much of the external Christian casing and razed much of the city, almost the entirety of late medieval Syracuse was rebuilt in the style that has become known as Sicilian baroque. The scowling faces supporting wrought iron balconies, now such a feature of the city, emerged in this time.

The earthquake of 1693 was a disaster of an unprecedented scale, similar in scale to those that had razed Antioch in the sixth century, and indeed in the twenty-first. It had an estimated magnitude of 7.4, and is the single largest earthquake recorded in Italian history. Ninety thousand deaths were recorded and cities across the south of Sicily were left in ruins. Syracuse was rare in that it was rebuilt on its same site to the same city plan as before, whereas Noto was moved to a different site entirely.

This was the city in which a fugitive painter would arrive. Caravaggio, fleeing prison in Malta, would take refuge with a former assistant of his who was an established painter in Syracuse. Through his connections the painter would gain the commission for the now iconic altarpiece depicting the burial of Santa Lucia.

Following his departure, two more tragedies would devastate Syracuse: another grievous earthquake in the seventeenth century, and plague in the eighteenth. These disasters gave rise to the Ortygia we see today, but it was modernism and fascism that formed the Syracuse we see on the mainland, with its modernist blocks and broad, sweeping corsos.

Admiral Horatio Nelson would anchor his fleet at Syracuse before the Battle of the Nile, taking on water for his ships from the fountain of Arethusa.

An outbreak of cholera would ravage the city in 1837, and the poverty and suffering which it precipitated and the meagre intervention of the government led to a revolt by the Syracusans against the Bourbon government. In retaliation, Syracuse was deprived of its status of provincial capital, which was transferred to Noto. For the first time in its millennia-long history, Syracuse was no longer even a regional capital; the magnificent city was humbled. For all this, the Syracusans still participated in the Sicilian revolution of 1848. Seventeen years later, the status of capital was restored following the unification of Italy. In the twentieth century, Syracuse would be captured by the Allies as part of Operation Husky and the Allied invasion of Sicily.

With unification came a striving for modernity, which took the form of an exodus of many citizens from the island of Ortygia to newly built and more functional homes on the mainland. The urban centre of the city moved. Ortygia itself became dilapidated, and a red-light district. The *lungomare* that encircles the island became a place for prostitutes to solicit clients, and the romantically crooked alleys became the sites of drug deals and extortion. The current mayor, Francesco Italia, remembers these days from his own boyhood – when he wasn't allowed to play in the streets of Ortygia after dark. With increased tourism has come a revival of the historic heart of Ortygia. Fifty years ago, the gorgeous Piazza Duomo was dark with pollution and hosted four lanes of traffic and a car park. In the eighties, a slow revival began, transforming Ortygia into the beautiful centre it is today. For all that Ortygia might once have been a setting of crime and Mafia wars, today it is known as *la province barbar* – which in Sicilian means the 'stupid' or 'naive' province. Crime rates are lower here, and the Mafia is less active than in other parts of the city. The mayor is trying to push this further, applying the law as cleverly as he can to eliminate monopolies on public services.

When fascism came to Italy, Sicily and the architecture of Syracuse was not spared. Fascist architecture dominates much of the city on the mainland. Industry came to Syracuse, and sulphur mines and oil refineries began to spring up in the environs of the city. A Syracusan named Carlo, a married man with a young family, asserts that with the coming of the chemical industry the old identity of Syracuse was lost irrevocably. The oil industry brought wealth, but also brought complications. Many gained employment, and the city's main industry shifted from fishing and agriculture. It separated the people from the land, and also brought manifold health risks and decimated the beauty of the landscape. Those who approach Syracuse by train rather than sea will see the towers of the chemical plants before they see the spires of the churches.

Syracuse is no longer a great power of the Mediterranean; it hasn't been since the Arab conquests. However it is still the cultural heart of the Mediterranean. Its history is touchable, breathable. The memories of ancient people whisper to visitors in the Ear of Dionysius, Greek tragedies are played out in the ancient theatre. The food is rich in Arabian influence, and the sound of French is never far away. It is a city where the centuries of conquest, invasion, settlement and art seamlessly coalesce. It is a perfectly preserved pocket of Mediterranean richness, diversity and splendour.

Looking at the sea from a balcony in Ortygia one cannot help but be put in a mood of calm, and in mind of eternity. The rolling of the waves on a calm morning – cerulean, shot with threads of light and shallows. The sun breaking round the corner of the headland carelessly strews diamonds across the surface of the water, and the brilliant blue turns to frothing white on rocks where young and old bodies bask together.

Bathers, swimming from these rocks, have perfected the art of hanging in the water in a state of meditation, lying cruciform like martyrs on the surface. When one does this, ears under the surface, saltwater lapping over the face, the sounds of the shore dissipate to be replaced by an eerie crackling, like popping candy or breaking crystals – the sound of the living coral reef. The soul of Syracuse is in its history. Wherever you are – a roof terrace, a back alley, a sea cave – you are rubbing shoulders with the shadows of those who went before, with the multitude of civilisations that have made this island their home. Syracuse is a city of memories. You live and breathe half-forgotten stories as you stroll around its streets. You can still hear the Ancient Greek sandals on the stone.

RAVENNA

Dante's tomb, Ravenna, 1832

In 1877, a young Irishman with floppy hair and a penchant for brocade waistcoats arrived on horseback outside an ancient walled city in the north-east of Italy, a stone's throw from the Adriatic coast. He had galloped through the thick pine forests and marshlands that surrounded the antique stones, before finally drawing reins before the imposing walls, beholding the 'crown of towers'. A queen among cities, Ravenna captured his imagination, perhaps more so than any place he'd been before. The poem he composed about his experiences there, when submitted for consideration at New College, Oxford, won him the Newdigate Prize, and cemented his status as 'one to watch' in literary circles. His name was Oscar Wilde.

Wilde was struck by the silence of the city, and its poetic heritage as Dante's final resting place, and where Byron 'loved to dwell'. The silence moved him because it was here that some of the most beautiful lines of poetry were composed, and where the might of Rome once assembled to cross the Rubicon. Ravenna was a city of action and of song, but when Wilde visited, as now, it had declined to something quieter and more modest. Only the glowing interiors, with ceilings like liquid gold, roused the mind to the splendours of its past.

Wilde did however lay his lament on a little thick, he wrote:

> O lone Ravenna! many a tale is told
> Of thy great glories in the days of old:
> Two thousand years have passed since thou didst see
> Cæsar ride forth to royal victory.
> Mighty thy name when Rome's lean eagles flew
> From Britain's isles to far Euphrates blue;
> And of the peoples thou wast noble queen,
> Till in thy streets the Goth and Hun were seen.
> Discrowned by man, deserted by the sea,
> Thou sleepest, rocked in lonely misery!
>
> . . . .
> O fair! O sad! O Queen uncomforted!

Even when Wilde visited, provincial as it may have seemed compared to Venice or Rome, Ravenna was far from desolate. As Wilde himself acknowledged, it was the place where Byron chose to spend his time, engrossed in his last true love affair with the beautiful and married Countess Teresa Guiccioli. Today, their letters are preserved in the Biblioteca Classense in Ravenna's ancient centre, including a glorious love note idly penned in the back of a velvet-bound novel.

Today, the city is a quiet one, with neat, red-brick streets lined with expensive boutiques selling French swimsuits, frescoed wine bars, and broken up with leafy squares and splendid churches. The surroundings are beautiful: Ravenna is in the heart of the Po delta, close to the Adriatic coast, at the northern reaches of the Mediterranean. Undoubtedly a Mediterranean city, and key to Mediterranean history, it no longer stands on the shores of that sea. Once a thriving port, Ravenna no longer boasts a harbour. The waters of the Adriatic have long since receded. The nearest beach, Lido Dante, is now eleven kilometres from the city centre. But the nexus of the Po delta still surrounds the city, and wild horses still graze in the pastureland and pine forests that Oscar Wilde once galloped through.

For all that its canals are gone, Ravenna – like Venice – is slowly sinking. This can be starkly seen in the crypt of the Church of San Francesco, near Dante's tomb – in fact where his funeral mass was held. The ancient, mosaic-floored crypt has flooded, and repeated attempts to clear the water have been unsuccessful. Defeated, the conservators have shrugged and now charge admission. Visitors can descend halfway down a flight of submerged steps, squint into the eerie darkness and pay a coin to turn on the light. If they do, they will behold a damp chamber, flooded to perhaps knee height, and through the water they can glimpse dark mosaic patterns, and the slippery orange bodies of goldfish.

In ancient, medieval and Renaissance times, the city was built along canals which bustled with barges and gondolas. Indeed, when the Greek geographer Strabo described Ravenna, he portrayed a city:

> built entirely on wooden piles and coursed by rivers, it is provided by thoroughfares by means of bridges and ferries [...] hence human settlement becomes possible in a space usually populated by insects, frogs and snakes, and a flourishing economy develops, mainly based on controlling trade and inland waterways. The place is considered so healthy that it is chosen for feeding and training gladiators.

Today the canals and river-streets that made Ravenna a second Venice (although it was founded long before) have long since silted up and been paved over. Perhaps the only remaining trace of the city's watery heritage is the fact that some of the paved streets are labelled 'canal' rather than 'via', and of course the occasional flooded basement.

The citizens of Ravenna are varied. Ambitious young people often leave in search of the opportunities afforded by big cities, drawn away to neighbouring Bologna, or to Milan and Rome. That said, for a small city in the north of Italy, slightly off the well-beaten tourist track, it has a diverse population. Romanians, Senegalese, French – the town is full of people with different stories. In the evenings, people play ball games in the shadow of the Venetian fortress, or drink full-bodied red wine in the *ca' de vin* – a former grocery still decorated with medieval accents and dark mahogany furnishings. The city is tidy, functional and atmospheric. The quality of life is high. The council puts on magic shows and concerts for children in its many parks, and culture flourishes. Art galleries and artists abound. The Teatro Dante mounts regular productions, and *aperitivi* last hours in twilit Italian squares, while Ravennate enjoy Aperol spritzes under the watchful eye of the twin pillars in Piazza del Popolo that mimic those of San Marco. The bellinis are cheaper than in Venice, and the wine as rich as in Tuscany.

At sunset, what feels like the entire city spills onto the neat terracotta streets for an evening promenade, adults holding dog leashes, children clutching *gelati*. Strolling through the gently crooked, modest streets, one would be hard pressed to realise that for three centuries the city stood as the capital of the western Roman Empire, Theoderic the Great's Ostrogothic kingdom, and the nerve centre of the Byzantine exarchate of Ravenna. It was in Ravenna that the western Roman Empire drew its last, faltering breaths.

But Ravenna is a red-brick city with a golden soul. Beneath the unassuming facade, the city's hidden heritage glitters. For all that its history is more august than that of Venice, its story is not half as well known. Older and formerly far grander than its more famous cousin, this city's glories have faded out of popular memory. But beneath the surface, the memories remain. Those who linger long enough to look, are dazzled. The city is home to no fewer than eight UNESCO World Heritage Sites. While the western Roman Empire was in its death throes, the fortified city of Ravenna, nestling amid marshland, became a haven for the vestiges of Byzantine culture and power in Italy. The marshes, rivers and canals both kept invaders at bay and supplied the city with necessities. Within Ravenna, encircled by protective walls and water, artistic culture thrived.

The churches, Catholic and Arian, built by Romans, Byzantines and barbarians alike, gleam with the splendour of Ravenna's imperial past. The best preserved, most lavish examples of Byzantine art are not to be found in Constantinople, but in Ravenna. Craftsmen in the pay of the emperor and leading churchmen painstakingly sealed gold filaments between fine squares of glass. These they pressed into wet mortar to create the glowing domes and wall panels that Ravenna is famous for today. Every colour imaginable was used to create psychedelic scenes of saints, of animals, of Christ, all set in a golden sea, symbolising eternity, and heaven. The swirling stars and imposing figures have inspired poets, artists and kings for centuries. Dante and Charlemagne both looked on these scenes in wonder. It was while he stayed in Ravenna that Dante described skies 'the sweet colour of oriental sapphire'.

But more than a city of gold, Ravenna is a city of love stories. It is here that Dante wrote *Paradiso*, thinking always of Beatrice Portinari. It was where the English Romantic poet Lord Byron pursued and lived with Teresa Guiccioli. Dante's love for Beatrice is famous through the city, immortalised not only in the cantos of *Paradiso*, but also in the work of the controversial street artist Dicky Cock, who across from Dante's demure sepulchre added a ceramic mosaic depicting a red-caped, laurel-wreathed Dante with a nude Beatrice, with emphasised breasts, lips and genitals. They are pressed together with arms outreached, as if in euphoric flight. The Ravennate have mixed feelings about this art, many deeming it lewd. Byron's love for Teresa is widely known as well. This passion is revealed in his poetry, while the pages and pages of letters the lovers wrote to one another are preserved in the Biblioteca Classense. Teresa's house, where Byron spent many nights, is conserved as a museum.

Rarely has a city so un-renowned been so adored by poets. Oscar Wilde hailed it as a 'city of poets' in his poem *Ravenna*, and certainly it is a city for the soulful, where the body may rest and the mind can climb. Dante finished *Paradiso* while in residence in Ravenna. In the final stanza '*Puro e disposto a salire a le stelle*' translates roughly as 'Pure and willing to rise to the stars'. This line is now written in light above the streets of Ravenna. When I visit, the city is commemorating the legacy of the poet in their city on the 700th anniversary of his death. Residents of Ravenna grow up with Dante; they study him in school, and they walk past his famous yet modest tomb each day. He is like a relative, they say, a great-uncle whom they visit sometimes. Always there, certainly respected, but taken for granted, really.

The mosaics of Ravenna are like this too. 'They are like the sky, they're always there,' one resident tells me. 'Of course we value them, but they aren't always looked at, or wondered at.'

Ravenna's origins are perhaps the most mysterious of all. Antioch was founded by Alexander's general, Syracuse by Corinthian Greeks,

Tyre and Carthage by Phoenicians, but Ravenna's foundation myth is conspicuously absent. Ancient historians, it seems, were too lazy or divergent when it came to conjuring grand origins for the city. Traces of early settlement go back to the ninth century BC, but it took until AD 89 for it to be acknowledged as a Roman town. It is hard to say when exactly it began to take shape as the city of Ravenna.

Water has always been the city's lifeblood. Not only the lapping waves of the Mediterranean Sea, but the canals and rivers that diffused throughout its landscape, spreading like a network of arteries and veins, giving fuel for commerce and barriers for defence. Throughout the centuries Ravenna has been described as the little sister of Venice, with early maps likewise presenting the city as a group of islands split up by canals and linked by bridges. But Ravenna is not the little sister of Venice. When Venice was merely marshland inhabited by obscure fishermen known only to history as 'the lagoon dwellers', and established as a city with the foundation of its first church, Ravenna was already the capital of the Roman Empire. The city rose from a ragtag group of dwellings within a marshy lagoon, and prospered under Roman rule to become the rallying point of Julius Caesar's armies and eventually, following the fall of Rome, the new capital.

Today Ravenna is nestled in obscurity, but with flashing gold tesserae telling its secret history.

Ancient historians variously believed Ravenna to have been founded by Pelasgians, Thessalians or Tyrrhenians, and then later refounded by Sabines or Umbrians. Modern experts believe the data conclusively points to an Etruscan identity, created by persecuted Etruscans fleeing the spread of Gallic peoples in inland Europe, who settled on the Adriatic coast and lived a life of trade and piracy.

Since ancient times it has been possible to hear a medley of languages spoken throughout the city and to witness traditions and rites of different peoples and ethnic groups. The history of humanity in Ravenna and the surrounding territory of Romagna goes back millennia, and from the ninth to the third centuries BC Greeks, Etruscans, Umbrians and even Celtic peoples vied for control of this marshy region.

In the third century BC, the Romans conquered Ravenna. The archaeological record testifies that at this time the city was square shaped and fortified, facing the sea to the east across a lagoon. The forum occupied the space now occupied by Piazza Kennedy, and traces of villas with intricate mosaicked floors have also been found, indicating the strength and sophistication of the Roman presence. The earliest walls of Ravenna were built in the third century BC, around the time that it was conquered by the Roman Republic, and set on the road to greatness. It was then it began to assume the identity that would lead it to become a Mediterranean capital.

The rise of Ravenna was to begin in earnest in the last century BC, when two events of great significance occurred within the city. The first was that a semi-disgraced general made a decision, while headquartered in the city, to cross a rather small river. This might seem insignificant, except for the fact that the general was Julius Caesar, and the river was the Rubicon.

Caesar's decision to ford the stream at the head of a legion, one of the legions which had conquered Gaul for him no less, marked the beginning of the end for the Roman Republic and the birth of the Roman Empire. With this in mind, Caesar's crossing constitutes a pivotal moment in Mediterranean history. For some time Ravenna had served as Caesar's headquarters in the region, where he planned his strategies and received his guests.

The relatively shallow river, running through the Italian countryside just south of Ravenna, marked the border between Cisalpine Gaul and Italy. Today, it is heavily polluted, and not much more than a sludgy stream. Roman law prohibited Caesar from entering Italy with his legion, and in flagrantly breaking this law, Caesar made a declaration of war on the ruling figures of the Roman Republic. This decision, taken in Ravenna, is seen by many historians as the point of no return, where Caesar purportedly announced 'alea iacta est' – 'the die is cast'. The crossing launched a violent and protracted civil war, which would eventually see the republic toppled and Caesar ruling as dictator of Rome.

The crossing is unlikely to have been the glorious affair that Oscar Wilde fantasised about when he wrote his prize poem. In reality, it would have been very cold and logistically challenging, and filled with tension and wet boots that soldiers had little time to dry out or replace. The journey took place at night in January, and teeth must have chattered with cold and trepidation as the soldiers moved their kit across. Wilde's poem puts us in mind of glorious sunshine glinting on the wings of Roman eagles, but the reality was less glorious, though it is of course possible that moonlight breaking through the January clouds glinted on the bronze eagles.

On the evening of the crossing, Caesar did not act as a man about to make history, and take the greatest gamble of his career. Instead, he dined well and inspected the city of Ravenna, listening to plans for the new gladiatorial school. Meanwhile he issued instructions for the legion to furtively decamp to the banks of the river and await instructions.

Caesar's choice was doubtless a tricky one. He had risen through the Roman political system, which at the time of his adolescence and early career was fraught with conflicts about the best way to govern Rome, and tensions between the aristocratic class and populists. Eventually he withdrew, having been given command of a legion. Caesar played this well: with a legion, he could achieve military victories which would enhance his power and influence, and if he could win the loyalty of the men, then he was to all intents and purposes the king of a small army. Caesar did win victories, subduing all of Gaul. At this point, Roman law dictated that a general should relinquish his command, but Caesar did not. In Rome his former ally, Pompey, had become his rival. Gold was changing hands, and bribery and skulduggery were the currency of the day. In marching his legion across the Rubicon, Caesar was declaring war on Pompey. The poet Lucan attributed to Caesar the declaration: 'Here I abandon peace and desecrated law. Fortune, it is you I follow. Farewell to treaties. From now on, war is our judge.'

From Ravenna, Caesar exchanged many letters with senators in Rome, variously angry or conciliatory. At the beginning of January, fuming and mulling over his options in Ravenna, he sent the senate a final letter, purportedly with the aim of bringing matters to a peaceful conclusion. What Caesar wanted was consulship, which Rome had agreed to give him on his giving up of his armies. But he had been betrayed many times, and he believed that the minute he gave up his armies he would be in danger of disgrace, exile, death, or all three. His great enemy now was Pompey, and he said he would resign his command of his legions simultaneously with Pompey, but certainly not before, fearing an attack from this senator if he let his soldiers go. This and other suggested compromises were rejected, under the influence of Pompey, Mark Antony and Cato the Younger. Caesar gave his commands, and around 13 January, the legion crossed the Rubicon and marched for Rome. The senate fled before them.

The second event of great significance followed not long after. Caesar's great-nephew, known formerly as Octavian and latterly as Augustus, became the first Roman Emperor of the new-forged empire, following the assassination of Caesar by Brutus et al. Augustus visited Ravenna, and perhaps remembering its strategic importance to his great-uncle, decided to establish a Roman naval base. From here, the imperial fleet was to roam the eastern Mediterranean. This established Ravenna, then a medium-sized town, as a city of importance, and it was adorned with new monuments to chart this progression. Augustus built a much-needed aqueduct to bring a plentiful supply of fresh drinking water, and in AD 42 built the Porta Aurea, a monumental gateway which served as a monument testifying to the city's importance. Although the gateway itself is now lost, decorative relief carvings of lions and trees have survived.

In the quality of marble monuments being created in Ravenna we can read the beginnings of greatness. Along with this visible richness, a cultural diversity also developed. Between 6,000 and 10,000 sailors settled in Ravenna with their families at this time, bringing with them languages and customs from across the Roman Empire and from all corners of the Mediterranean.

Between the fifth and eighth centuries, Ravenna reached an apogee of greatness.

In 402, the Christian Emperor Honorius transferred the imperial capital from Milan to Ravenna following a disastrous siege. He was the son of Theodosius – the last emperor to rule both halves of the Roman Empire. His brother Arcadius was given control of Constantinople, and arguably become the first Byzantine Emperor. Honorius made Ravenna his new capital on account of its harbour and geographic situation, facing east towards Constantinople. In recognition of this, the city expanded at an unprecedented rate. A palace was built for Honorius, as were magnificent churches. The city was transformed from a military outpost to a cosmopolitan centre that would serve as the seat of the sprawling, yet crumbling, western Roman Empire. The empire was coming apart at the seams under the pressure of encroaching barbarian tribes. Power had begun to be divided into eastern and western realms, and true power was now in Constantinople rather than Italy.

It was also during this time that Galla Placidia, one of the most important women in the history of Ravenna and its politics, would be frogmarched onto the scene. Galla Placidia was Honorius's half-sister; Honorius was the product of Theodosius's first marriage, and Placidia his second. She had two other half-siblings: Arcadius, and Theodosius's adopted niece, Serena.

When Theodosius died the siblings converged on the then capital Milan to attend their father's deathbed and reap their inheritance. For Honorius and Arcadius that meant half an empire each. For Placidia it meant being absorbed into the household of her adoptive older sister Serena and her husband Stilicho. As Honorius and Arcadius were both underage, Stilicho stepped into the power vacuum and effectively ruled the western empire on Honorius's behalf.

Eventually, while still very much a child, Galla Placidia was betrothed to Serena and Stilicho's son Eucherius, to further cement this ruling couple's power. If this was not enough, Stilicho married two of his daughters successively to Honorius. Placidia's marriage to Eucherius however, although much anticipated by the bridegroom's parents, never came to pass.

While Stilicho was attempting to solidify his grip on power, Alaric, King of the Visigoths – a barbarian tribe presenting one of the greatest threats to Rome's security – harried the fringes of the empire. Alaric spread his soldiers across Greece, and threatened to break through into northern Italy. It was in the wake of this threat that Honorius moved the western capital to Ravenna, at Stilicho's urging. This was a practical move, as Alaric was capturing city after city and besieged Milan as well.

Nevertheless, three years after Ravenna became the imperial residence and capital, the western empire was still beset by external threats and internal turbulence. A rogue Roman general named Constantine set himself up as an alternative emperor, going so far as to mint his own coins in Arles, and various barbarian armies continued to harry Gaul. Under these various pressures, Honorius took the decision to bring Alaric – busy attacking Italian towns – into the imperial fold, and gave him a military command and an official position and authority in exchange for help against the usurping general Constantine.

The process was not smooth, and scandal after scandal unfolded at the Roman court. Eventually enmity brewed between Honorius and Stilicho: when the latter was unable to effectively quash the usurpation of Constantine, rumours began to swirl that he himself had imperial ambitions and planned to install his own son – Galla Placidia's betrothed – on the imperial throne in Constantinople. While the veracity of this cannot be proven, Stilicho's actions certainly looked ambitious. In the shadow of these doubts, Honorius ordered Stilicho and Eucherius to be executed. Despite the pair taking refuge in a church in Ravenna, the emperor's orders were carried out. This left Placidia – now in her late teens – free to be betrothed once more.

The fallout following these deaths was vast. A witch-hunt was mounted for allies and enablers of Stilicho, and their wives and daughters were targeted too. Even Serena herself was executed in Rome, some even said with the consent of her young ward, Placidia.

In the wake of all this upheaval, Alaric, Honorius's erstwhile ally against the usurping Constantine, took the opportunity to march on Rome. He mounted a comprehensive siege of the city, taking control of grain supplies, and harrying the population. He continually demanded to be given total control of the military of the western empire, and envoys travelled tirelessly between the besiegers at Rome and Honorius's court at Ravenna in an attempt to broker terms, seeing as the Visigoth could not be defeated outright and occupied a position of great strength.

It is possible Placidia tried to escape the city and make her way to Ravenna. No one is exactly sure of her movements, but what is known is that the Visigoths encamped before the walls of the city managed to take her hostage. Beyond this, Alaric forced the captive senate in Rome to elect a new emperor over Honorius; they acquiesced to his demand to be appointed supreme military commander, and commissioned him to lead an attack on Ravenna to dislodge the 'other' emperor. Honorius had the loyalty of the eastern empire and Africa, who sent a 4,000 strong relief force, which clashed with Alaric and drove him back. Incensed, Alaric returned to Rome, took it, and in his fury sacked it. This was the great sack of Rome of AD 410, lamented by Roman writers across the empire, and epitomising the decline of the western Roman Empire.

According to Procopius, the court historian of the later Emperor Justinian, Honorius was fond of his pet chickens. When the news was conveyed to him that 'Rome has perished' his first thought was grief for a favourite cockerel named Rome, but when he realised that it was the ancient capital and not the bird, he breathed a sigh of relief.

Thus began a different kind of life for the captive princess, Galla Placidia. She was hustled from pillar to post by her Gothic captors. Alaric, the brilliant general, died, and 'guardianship' of Placidia passed to his brother-in-law Athaulf as he fought his way out of southern Italy, over the Alps and into the province of Gaul in 412. During this period, despite Placidia being held as a hostage, relations improved between her captor and her half-brother, securely holed up in Ravenna. They allied together against various common enemies, and friendly feeling between the two leaders reached its zenith on 1 January 414 when Placidia was spectacularly wed to her erstwhile jailor Athaulf in the cathedral of Narbonne. She was around twenty-one years old. On this day, Galla Placidia, Roman princess, became Queen of the Goths. They married in traditional Roman costume, and the Gothic king gave his bride dishes of treasure that he had stolen from Rome as a wedding gift.

This marriage might have heralded the birth of a new line of Gothic-Roman emperors, but such a dream never came to fruition. While Placidia and Athaulf were blessed with a son, he died in infancy, and that put paid to that idea. Shortly after the death of his son, Athaulf died too, assassinated by members of his retinue. Following the murder of her husband, Placidia was forced by his enemies to undergo the public ritual humiliation of walking twenty kilometres out of the city and back in front of a chariot ridden by her husband's murderer. The queen was a hostage once again.

The trials of Galla Placidia may not at first glance have much to do with the fate of Ravenna, where her brother held court while she suffered in Gaul and Hispania, but in reality they have everything to do with it. Within ten years of losing her Visigothic captor-husband, Placidia would have manoeuvred herself into power, and would be ruling the western Roman Empire from a glittering throne in Ravenna.

Following the death of Athaulf, Placidia was ransomed back to Honorius in Ravenna as part of a peace treaty. She brought with her a bodyguard of fiercely loyal Visigoths who would continue to serve her during her time as a Roman *Augusta*. Honorius received his half-sister with due honours, but promptly forced her into marriage with a member of his retinue – his military commander Constantius, who may well have met the princess on her journey back from Gaul to Ravenna. They were married on Placidia and Athaulf's second wedding anniversary on New Year's Day 416. Within three years Placidia had given birth to both a daughter named Honoria, and a son named Valentinian. With Honorius childless, these two children were in line for the imperial throne.

On 8 February 421, Constantius – in recognition of his military achievements – was pronounced co-emperor with Honorius, with Placidia now being recognised as *Augusta*. Constantius was not destined to enjoy his exalted rank for long: he was dead within seven months of receiving this honour. Relations in the imperial palace then took a strange turn. Honorius's enthusiasm for his widowed sister's company would become so intense that soon tongues were wagging that their relationship was more than it should be between siblings. Reports of them spending all their time together, and frequently kissing each other's lips, abounded. In the way of Roman politics, sparks began to fly, and soon there were also whispers that Placidia's servants were plotting to kill Honorius, and her Gothic guard was openly clashing with the imperial guard in the street. To quell all kinds of gossip, and perhaps genuinely fearful for his life, Honorius banished Placidia and her followers from Ravenna, and they took refuge at the court of Constantinople.

Honorius would rule alone following the death of Constantius and the exile of his sister, before dying in 423, leaving a political vacuum into which Galla Placidia, leading her young son by the hand, would stride. Following her half-brother's death she and her son returned to Ravenna.

In 424, following the typical political scuffles, five-year-old Valentinian was named Emperor Valentinian III, and Placidia took on the role of regent – essentially assuming the role of empress of the western empire. Meanwhile her niece Pulcheria was pulling the strings of government in Constantinople, and so for twenty-five years both eastern and western empires were essentially ruled by women. However, this was a time of military turbulence in both the eastern and western parts of the empire, while would-be invaders gnawed at the borders and raided their lands. The eastern empire bought off the attackers with rich gifts from the seemingly bottomless coffers of the imperial treasury in Constantinople, but in the west gold reserves were low, and the armies were the main defence. This diluted the power of the empress and young emperor, transferring it instead into the hands of the generals keeping the marauders at bay. Nevertheless, Placidia had become one of the most important women in the world, and following various inauguration ceremonies in Rome, she and Valentinian returned to Ravenna to rule from there. In a time before the printing press, coins, ceremonies and building projects were the main tools of political communication and propaganda – and Placidia exploited them all.

Around the empire, ordinary citizens quickly found themselves paying for goods with coins that bore the image of the empress. Placidia was resilient, surviving the sack of Rome, kidnap, multiple political marriages and childbirths, dangerous journeys, the political machinations of the Roman court, and more. Now she had achieved supremacy and was depicted on gold, silver and bronze coinage seated on a throne; across the empire people could be in little doubt that they were ruled by a woman. She was also active in her son's investiture ceremonies, and would commission the building of some of the earliest Christian architecture still standing today. All of this emphasised her power and prestige in the city, and has left subsequent generations visual reminders of her presence.

One building commissioned by Placidia surpasses all others: the so-called Mausoleum of Galla Placidia. Many tourists who visit the little brick shrine, which feels like an afterthought in the grounds of the much grander Basilica of San Vitale, do not pause to read the information board, small and tucked away as it is. If they did, they would learn that this is in fact no mausoleum of Galla Placidia. Perhaps it was designed as such, but her remains are not there.

The building, like most of Ravenna, is made of neat red bricks. It is small, modest, just one storey high and without particularly soaring ceilings, and is laid out in a cross formation with a tiled terracotta roof. There are four tiny windows, but to preserve the solemnity of the interior they are made not of glass, but thin slices of alabaster, letting only muted, pearly light filter through.

The dazzling jewel-box interior does indeed contain stately marble sarcophagi – three, to be precise. They rest in suitable magnificence under a fiery, star-encrusted night sky. But none contain the bones of the Gothic queen and Roman *Augusta*. Placidia is not buried in Ravenna, but in Rome. No one knows for sure whose remains the sarcophagi once contained.

Placidia commissioned this building and its decorations during her years as regent for the young Valentinian, and it stands as a visual emblem of her power, wealth and status. She is remembered as a devout empress, who took a close personal interest in the management and building of the churches in her capital, and is described as praying for hours on end, with tears streaming down her cheeks, in the monumental houses of worship that she raised from the ground and decorated so lavishly.

She built a second church, the Church of St John the Evangelist, a saint to whom she was always grateful, supposedly for saving her and her family from shipwreck during a storm-tossed voyage to Constantinople. In this church, she would assert her imperial status and authority still more clearly, in soaring portraits of her dynasty with her own inscription above.

This trend set by Placidia was followed in subsequent centuries, and Ravenna today is home to numerous astounding buildings boasting unrivalled examples of early Christian art. Some might shrug that the mosaics of Palermo, Cefalu, Monreale and Aachen are more splendid, more impressive, more creative, but it must be remembered that those mosaics were made centuries later, and were uniformly inspired by the art of Ravenna. The mosaics of Ravenna are the best, and best preserved, of early Christianity.

It was also under Placidia that the city of Ravenna expanded most and truly established itself as a commercial, theological, political and religious centre.

With Placidia's attention focused on adorning and embellishing her capital, her two children were running amok. While Valentinian's political education seems to have left much to be desired, it was the exploits of his sister Honoria that would really bring chaos to Ravenna's gates.

Unusually for an imperial princess, Honoria did not make a political marriage in her early teens. It is unclear why neither her mother nor her brother arranged this for her. Instead she lived with servants in

Ravenna, and it seems grew up without the meticulous supervision normally imposed on valuable young princesses from wayward families. There is evidence of an affair and a pregnancy in her twenties, and stronger evidence yet that the still unmarried Honoria at the age of thirty tried to break away from court life and elope with a steward named Eugenius. Clearly she lacked proper supervision, and probably also craved affection, and with her immediate family neglecting her and no marriage arranged for her, it is only natural that she turned for comfort to the arms of the highest-status and best-educated servants in her household. Her brother's fury focused on covering up the scandal by arranging a marriage between his sister and a tame senator to smooth things over and curtail her freedom at last. He did not reckon on the form his sister's resistance would take.

Instead of climbing down from her tower on knotted sheets, drinking poison or doing a deal with the devil, or whatever conventional methods princesses use to evade unwanted marriages, Honoria acted by making another proposal herself. Taking matters into her own hands, she sent an emissary to none other than Attila the Hun, who was currently ravaging Rome's borders. She begged him, a powerful rival to Rome, to rescue her from this unwanted match, and enclosed a ring with her letter. The message may have been lost in translation, or Attila's cultural advisors may have enthusiastically assured the Hun leader that in Roman culture, a ring was a symbol of marriage. In any case, Attila believed that Honoria's letter constituted a formal proposal and betrothal, and he would thereafter use the motive of 'claiming his bride' as an excuse for daring incursions into Roman territories. Honoria was as valuable a bride as they came – the sister of the western emperor – and her dowry would be unparalleled.

Valentinian's eyebrows must have hit the ceiling and his jaw the floor when he heard of his sister's antics. Consulting with Theodosius II – his co-emperor in the east – they were in disagreement about how to proceed. Theodosius took the view that the rash princess had committed treason and made her bed, which she should now be forced to lie in. He proposed sending her straight away to Attila, to become part of his harem. Valentinian was not convinced. Incensed as he must have been with his sister's blatant treason, he did not want to send her off to the camp of his enemy, who had a ferocious reputation, was pagan and practised polygamy. Instead he executed the servants who had helped her, and forced through the planned marriage to the senator, whom he promoted to consul to sweeten the deal – he was no longer receiving a prize princess, but a disgraced and mutinous one. Meanwhile, Attila marched through Roman lands, running rings around the Roman military and sacking multiple cities. He went as far as to threaten Rome, before negotiating a peace, and promptly dying. He never rattled the gates of Ravenna, or managed to 'rescue' Honoria, who from that point onwards is lost to the historical record, living out what was left of her life in quiet disgrace.

How Placidia reacted to her daughter's rebellion is not known. Maybe she saw something of herself in the daring of the action, but Placidia never made such a miscalculation. Maybe she blamed herself for not paying closer attention to Honoria. In any case, during these years Placidia gradually ceded power to Valentinian, although it is clear she retained a good deal of authority, with various visitors to Ravenna asserting that she still presided as grand dame over the ceremonies and running of the city.

In addition to her role as regent and raiser of cities, Placidia was also deeply engaged with the theological debates of her day, which raged around her empire and within the walls of her capital. Only two documents penned by Placidia survive, letters written to influence a debate over the nature of Christ. One letter was addressed to Theodosius II, urging him to protect and back the bishop of Constantinople, and to preserve the 'true faith'. The second was written to her niece, urging her to use her influence to see to it that decisions made at the Council of Ephesus did not hold, and that the matter of the status of the bishop of Constantinople be referred to councils at Rome.

Placidia was without doubt the most influential woman of her era, and greatly increased the status of Ravenna, her capital. She died in Rome in the year 450 and was entombed there alongside other members of her dynasty, but her legacy in her capital was nevertheless profound. Her marriages inextricably linked the Roman and Gothic cultures, and ushered in a new era for the western empire.

Just one month after his mother's death, Valentinian decided to move his capital from Ravenna to Rome. While the notion of ruling from the ancient seat of power and rejecting his mother's world may have appealed to Valentinian, the move was to be his undoing. It was also around this time that Constantinople was beginning to indisputably outstrip Rome and Ravenna as the primary, even sole, true capital of the crumbling empire. Valentinian dismissed his stalwart general Aetius in a bid to consolidate his waning power in the west – another error, as he misjudged the popularity of and loyalty commanded by Aetius; shortly after ordering the assassination of this man, Valentinian himself was also assassinated, by men loyal to the fallen general, in the year 455, just five years after the death of his mother. The murderer was Petronius Maximus.

Valentinian left a widow – the Empress Eudoxia. Eudoxia soon found herself prey to the advances of men who wished to seize imperial authority through marriage to her. Some time before, Eudoxia's namesake daughter had been betrothed to a Vandal prince, as a way of cementing an alliance between the Vandals and Rome. Just as her aunt Honoria had appealed to Attila for help against such palace intrigue, now Eudoxia appealed to the father of her future son-in-law for aid. A Roman senator was attempting to force himself upon her, and Eudoxia in desperation sent a message to the Vandal king in Carthage, Geiseric, the very man who had captured Carthage from the Romans. Eudoxia implored him to save her. Geiseric did not need telling twice, and marshalled his ships to sail for Italy. His approach was doubtless hastened by the plot by Valentinian's murderer – Petronius Maximus – to marry the princess Eudoxia himself, thus depriving Geiseric's son of his betrothed.

Of course, just as Agamemnon did not sail to Troy to claim Helen, Geiseric did not sail for Rome to rescue Eudoxia. She was saved from the unwanted match, but the city burned. Carthage finally sent her revenge on the Roman destroyers. The fleet sailed from the ancient Carthaginian harbour, 600 years after the Roman sack of Carthage by Scipio's forces. The Vandals of Carthage earned their reputation in the thorough sacking of this city, which made the Gothic conquest look like little more than holiday guests overstaying their welcome. For two weeks the Vandal hordes ransacked, pillaged and burned the Eternal City. Eudoxia and her daughter were conveyed safely to North Africa, and the daughter was swiftly married to Geiseric's son Huneric. This sack spelled twilight for Rome. In contrast, Ravenna's star was on the rise. The city would go from strength to strength.

While Rome's monuments were laid low, Ravenna was building hers. Imperial attention had been drawn elsewhere, but wealthy citizens were continuing to buy their spots in heaven and publicly demonstrate their status through the construction of glorious churches and public buildings. One such was the renovation of the baptistry originally built by Bishop Ursus, which now has the name of the Baptistry of Neon, named after its decorator, rather than the original builder. As with the mausoleum of Galla Placidia, the simple exterior belies the glory inside – the slightly psychedelic mosaic decorations around the octagonal building and large central dome. Built for baptism, the font is large enough for the immersion of adults. The centre of the dome depicts a fully grown

Christ receiving baptism in the River Jordan, flanked by concentric rings of saints.

Meanwhile, chaos reigned in the western empire, and its security wavered on a knife edge. Emperors came and went, with ten emperors and usurpers claiming the title of western emperor within one twenty-year period from 455 to 475. The last of these was Romulus Augustus, a child emperor, who was deposed by a Germanic barbarian soldier who had risen through the ranks in the Roman army and become a commander of considerable influence. His name was Odoacer, and he certainly saw himself as more fit to rule Italy than a child amid a den of wolves fighting for control. He took matters in hand and claimed the throne for himself. Odoacer's ethnicity is debated, with some early historians naming him a Goth. The likelihood is he was of mixed and at least partly Germanic descent. In any case, he was not considered a 'Roman' by contemporaries. This did not hold him back from becoming the King of Italy.

The soldiers in the army were unhappy with the policies of those governing, specifically unhappy to not receive regular payments or any grants of lands. With this in mind, they rose up and Odoacer took charge. He did not take an imperial title for himself, but rather announced that there was no need for a western emperor at all. While he did not receive official approval from the eastern emperor, he succeeded in styling himself King of Italy, and ruling in practice from that day forward. This moment, Odoacer's rise, is often seen as the final sunset of the western Roman Empire, bookending decades of decline, beginning with Alaric's sack of Rome and the abduction of Galla Placidia in 410.

While Odoacer's rule might have heralded the end of the western Roman Empire, it also marked a new era of importance for Ravenna. Unsacked, the city was splendid, and not since Galla Placidia's days had a ruler made it so unequivocally his capital. The intervening emperors had flitted between Rome and other cities, but Odoacer made Ravenna his clearly designated royal capital and set up residence in the palace there.

Crucially, Odoacer was an Arian Christian, which set him against the Catholic bishops who had great influence in the city, and much of the general population. He was not however an intolerant ruler. A man who had fought his way up, his mind was not preoccupied with the oppression and division of the population, but rather with functionality. Arians and non-Arians would coexist in relative harmony. Odoacer outreigned his ten predecessors, ruling unopposed for thirteen years until 489, when at last a mighty challenge came in the form of the Ostrogothic general Theoderic.

This commander was sent by the eastern Roman Emperor, by this point a man named Zeno, who saw Odoacer's stable rule in Italy as a direct threat to his empire. Zeno, doubtless somewhat disingenuously, promised Theoderic Italy if he could dislodge Odoacer. Why exactly he would have preferred Theoderic to Odoacer ruling as an independent Italian king from Ravenna is unclear, therefore it is unlikely that he intended to fully honour this promise. It should also be noted that Theoderic exacted this promise at sword point, having encamped before the walls of Constantinople, cut off the fresh water supply and refused to leave until Zeno conceded him some legitimate Roman power: the promise of Italy if he could capture it was the result. Theoderic advanced across the Alps and into Italy, and before long – despite some internal turbulence in his own army – Ravenna was under siege for the first time in decades. This is where Ravenna's strange geography played to its advantage: the marshlands and waterways served as well as high walls to make the city impregnable.

Unable to starve the defenders out, given the many hidden entry points to the city, the siege lasted for three years, during which time both the besiegers and the besieged suffered. Eventually Odoacer and Theoderic agreed terms, agreeing in essence to share the Kingdom of Italy. Shortly after this, Theoderic entered Ravenna, ostensibly to co-operate with the Germanic king who had resisted his entry for so long. However, once inside the city, Theoderic claimed to hear rumours that Odoacer was planning to double-cross him. This was exactly the opportunity he needed to double-cross Odoacer, and he quickly instructed his men to assassinate him. They demurred, too afraid to attack the old king, and Theoderic was forced to slaughter Odoacer with his own hands. Ravenna was no longer capital of the decaying western Roman Empire, but capital of the new Ostrogothic Kingdom of Italy. Its status had risen.

Theoderic ruled like a king. Barbarian he may have been by pedigree, but not by upbringing: he was trilingual, speaking not only the Gothic vernacular, which he used to communicate with his troops, but also Greek and Latin. He summoned luminaries to his court, most notably the up-and-coming philosopher and writer Boethius. He had acted as something like a patron to Boethius, favouring him politically and granting both him and his sons important offices within his kingdom. Under Theoderic, Boethius became a senator and then a consul by 510, around his thirtieth birthday. For twenty years he rose at Theoderic's court, eventually becoming the Master of Offices in Ravenna. However the friendship between the two men was not destined to last. An invented scandal in 523 caused Theoderic to imprison the greatest mind at his court, and eventually execute him. This spell of unjust incarceration, with only death awaiting him, triggered Boethius to pen one of the great philosophical works of the era: *The Consolations of Philosophy*. In this prison text, Boethius laments and is comforted by a female embodiment of Philosophy as he ponders the problem of evil in a world ruled by God, and concepts of predestination, virtue and free will.

Like his predecessor Odoacer, Theoderic was an Arian Christian but allowed the non-Arians to continue their worship and way of life relatively unchecked. Theoderic's move to Ravenna had not simply been a military campaign, but a migration. His troops had marched with him with the promise of new, fertile lands to settle, not to be sent back across the mountains when a city or two had been taken for their lord. Thus one of the first tasks of Theoderic's new regime in Ravenna was to settle his hordes. For his family, this was easy enough – he and the royal women swiftly took over the apartments in the imperial palace – but it was a little more complicated for the thousands of Ostrogoths who had crossed the Alps with him. Perhaps 100,000 Ostrogoths had migrated to Italy, and they needed land and livings. They also needed churches. Although Odoacer had also been Arian, he had not built new houses of worship in the city, and once Theoderic had organised lands for his people in northern Italy (presumably by taking them off the defeated supporters of Odoacer), he began to build. He started with a cathedral, the fabulous baptistry of which still stands, adorned with the original decorations that Theoderic commissioned for it. It is strikingly similar to the Baptistry of Neon, except for one key difference: Christ as depicted during his baptism is not ageless, but an adolescent, emphasising one of the key differences in Arian and Catholic doctrine – that Christ was not an extension of God, only *like* him.

Theoderic's most spectacular architectural achievement was the Basilica of Sant'Apollinare Nuovo. In Theoderic's day however, this building was his palace chapel, and dedicated instead to Christ the Redeemer. Today, it is Catholic in dedication, but of course under Theoderic it was a proud bastion of the Arian religion. A confection of white arches, with a slightly incongruous and perfectly cylindrical bell tower, like all of Ravenna's early Christian buildings the exterior – while here a little quirky – does nothing to prepare one for the splendours of the interior.

Inside are the best mosaics in Ravenna. The scale and state of preservation, and the movement depicted, is phenomenal. And there used to be more. Today, only the mosaics processing along the nave survive, but when Theodoric finally looked on his finished church, the gleaming tesserae would have covered even more of the interior, spreading over the apse like molten gold. The walls of the long nave are lined with rows of an almost overwhelming number of intricately robed figures, all processing down the aisle of the great church towards the altar. They are going to make offerings – saints and virgins, angels and ships – all moving towards the altar against the gold sea of eternity, in patterned robes, bearing crowns and gifts for Christ. Almost at the front of the procession, near the altar itself, can be spied the three Magi, almost tripping over themselves in deference to Christ, clutching those precious silver salvers presumably holding gold, frankincense and myrrh, and dressed in elaborate Persian costume. They have jaguar-print trousers, spotted cloaks, slightly misconstrued turbans, curl-toed slippers, and everything – of course – is trimmed in lustrous gold.

Perhaps the best details to be found in this elaborate glass tapestry are not figurative at all, but rather the absence of figures. Near the entrance, far from the altar, is a contemporary depiction of Theoderic's palace. White marble Corinthian columns are depicted in mosaic tiles, under terracotta roofs, and white and gold curtains are drawn between the arches to reveal precisely nothing. Something is conspicuously absent from the palace. The drawn curtains reveal only backgrounds of gold and black tiles. On a couple of the columns beside these curtains can be glimpsed disembodied hands. One wrist, raised in exclamation or gesticulation (we will never know) wears lavish gold bangles. Who did these hands belong to, and what has happened to the rest of them?

The answer is simple: they belonged to members of Theoderic's court.

Theoderic may have presided over a golden age in Ravenna, but it was certainly not viewed that way by the eastern emperor – who despite initiating Theoderic's conquest of Ravenna did not like his independent way of doing things, the Arian religion, or the dynasty and legacy he left behind when he eventually passed away. Furthermore, following years of weaker hands at the helm, the rule of the remaining pieces of the Roman Empire passed in 527 into the hands of Emperor Justinian, and his more-than-feisty wife Theodora. This was just one year after the death of Theoderic, and Justinian had expansionist ideals and a very capable general – Belisarius – at his command. Theoderic's heirs were less successful than himself, and while rule passed briefly to his daughter Amalasuintha and grandson, the boy died and the mother was assassinated. Justinian used Amalasuintha's death as a pretext for launching a full-scale invasion of the Ostrogothic kingdom, under the command of Belisarius.

This is the same Belisarius who had landed at Syracuse and conquered all of Sicily with a force of only 7,500 soldiers, before going on to capture Carthage from the Vandals, along with many other North African territories, and parade the Vandal King Gelimer in chains through the streets of Constantinople. For all Belisarius's undeniable skill as a commander, Italy would be a more complicated project. Fierce resistance was raised to the advancing Byzantine armies. Belisarius took Milan, but lost it again, and found himself having to divide his army and leave garrisons to hold the towns and cities he took in order to stop the Goths regaining them. Under the command of their recently elected King Witigis, the Goths counter-attacked and besieged Rome, which Belisarius had already retaken and installed his wife in. Eventually however, the Goths were forced to raise the siege in order to rush north and defend their capital, Ravenna, from Belisarius's advancing war host, which arrived in early 540.

Witigis made various attempts at negotiating peace, even offering Belisarius his job, and suggesting he take the title of Western Roman Emperor, so desperate was he to keep his territories from Justinian. Belisarius feigned interest in this offer, but ultimately did not betray his master. He entered the city without fighting a decisive battle following extensive surrender negotiations with Witigis, and it is to this day unclear why Witigis surrendered – perhaps he was tricked by Belisarius. Justinian – perhaps hearing rumours of potential skulduggery from Belisarius – summoned his general home, and although the general obediently returned at his master's call, laden with plunder and captive barbarian royalty, he was not received in glory as he might have expected to be. His welcome was decidedly less warm than following his conquest of Carthage, and despite his victory he was denied an imperial triumph through the streets of Constantinople.

Despite the lack of immediate imperial recognition of the magnitude of his victory, Belisarius's conquest of Ravenna would have lasting ramifications. The Gothic royal family was deposed and brought as captives to Constantinople, and an imperial administration was set up in Ravenna. The city became the centre of business for the Byzantine emperors in Italy, and would remain so for two hundred years. Although the Goths in Italy elected new leaders and sought to oust the Byzantine forces from their lands, they failed to retake Ravenna. Under the new rulers, it underwent a series of sudden and dramatic changes.

Arianism in the city was reversed. This is the explanation for the floating hands on the walls of Sant'Apollinare Nuovo. Theoderic the Great had glorified himself and his wife and his court in the wall mosaics. The conquerors had different ideas for the decoration. Originally, those almost never-ending processions of virgins and saints approaching Christ had been led by the figures of Theoderic and his wife, but these portraits were transformed by the new masters. Theoderic was turned into St Martin of Tours, a saint who had earned his status by opposing Arianism, and Audofleda, Theoderic's formerly pagan Frankish wife, was replaced by St Euphemia at the head of the female procession. Other portraits of Gothic courtiers and leaders were replaced either with pure gold, or with curtains hanging in the windows – it is unclear why they were not replaced with new imperial portraits, or why the hands were left. Perhaps it was simply because a greater and more important building project was taking place a stone's throw away, and the resources and time of the master craftsmen were being poured into that instead.

Following the imperial conquest of Ravenna, a serious construction project was brought to completion under the watchful eyes of the new Roman Catholic bishop, Maximian. This was the Basilica of San Vitale. Design and construction had begun in the last years of Theoderic's reign, but it was finished and decorated under the rule of Emperor Justinian. It is his face that glowers down from the mosaic decoration on the left of the apse.

His eyebrows are dark and arched as if to suggest unimpressed incredulity. His irises are made from the same glinting golden pieces as the sea of eternity that surrounds him, and the steely gaze exudes power. He wears an imperial crown, encrusted with pearls, rubies and a greeny-blue stone, and pendant pearls swing from his ears. Dark tendrils of hair wreath his low forehead and his lips are fixed in a stern and impassive almost-pout. A fiery halo encircles the portrait. Across his shoulders is draped a cloak that might once have gleamed imperial purple, but has faded away to a brown. The brooch that fixes it in place, almost as large as the emperor's face, has not lost its colours, an egg-sized ruby encircled with white pearls.

In the hands of the emperor rests a golden liturgical dish, and he stands front and centre amid an entourage of soldiers, noblemen and priests. One historian has argued that the man directly behind him is Boethius, the philosopher imprisoned by Theoderic, although this claim is tenuous. Others believe the man to be Belisarius. Beside him stands Maximian, the man who oversaw the building of the church. Maximian, while initially unpopular, would carve out an immensely influential role for himself in the government of Ravenna under Justinian, as bishop – truly blurring the lines between Church and state in the city. In recognition of his power and achievements, Justinian commissioned an intricately carved ivory throne to be made for him in Constantinople, and shipped to Ravenna. Today the delicately panelled armchair, which Maximian once sat in dispensing policy and issuing orders, resides in a glass case in the Archiepiscopal Museum of Ravenna, beside the other gilt treasures of the Roman Church. Some argue that the throne was too grand to be intended for daily use, and instead stood symbolically empty, as a reminder of the overarching authority of Justinian in Ravenna. However, if the throne were made for this purpose, why does John the Baptist hold a medallion with Maximian's name above it, not Justinian's? The carvings on this throne entice the eye, drawing one into the biblical narrative of Joseph, perhaps the most finely executed, and maybe drawing parallels between the boy of humble birth who rose to become the right hand of the pharaoh.

Justinian is an interesting figure to now preside over Ravenna, albeit through his deputy Maximian, immortalised by his side on the walls of San Vitale. Emperor from 527 to 565, his reign was a remarkable one, which marked a period of great challenge and change for the imperial office. From humble beginnings, born in a small Latin-speaking Balkan village, Justinian rose to prominence through the favour of his opportunistic uncle, eventually the Emperor Justin, and after years at his side influencing, building and plotting, Justinian finally ascended to the office of emperor himself. The major events of his reign – his wars, his law codex, his controversial choice of wife – have remained some of the most prominent areas of study in Byzantine history; the most striking visual legacy of his reign is undoubtedly his buildings. Many of these still stand as tangible proof of the force of character of Justinian I, and the ingenuity of his architects. Justinian's great architectural triumph, the church of Hagia Sophia, completed in 537, dominates the skyline of modern Istanbul; below, the Basilica Cistern attracts visitors to its subterranean depths. Over the course of his reign, Justinian undertook one of the most prolific building projects of any emperor, recorded in unparalleled detail by Procopius in his panegyric *De Aedificiis*. Justinian's buildings can be seen as the physical embodiment of the values he espoused as emperor and the agenda he pursued.

Directly opposite Justinian and his imperial posse in San Vitale stands an image of Empress Theodora and her girl squad. This is the controversial wife who engendered so much gossip, both late antique and modern. Theodora is decked out in still more finery than her husband. Her robe is as dark as his, edged in gold, and accessorised with a necklace-cum-breastplate dripping with gems that makes her husband's gigantic brooch look modest. Her crown also dwarfs his for decadence, as high and as rich, with a profusion of pearls dripping from it in ribbons to her chest. Her eyes however are not quite as golden as her husband's.

Theodora, it is known, had a taste for finery. Some years before the imperial couple commanded Belisarius to retake Italy, they were almost thrust from their thrones in the midst of riots in Constantinople that could have ended in their deaths. As the mob raged through the city, Justinian lost his nerve and declared that he and his retinue should flee to safer territory. Theodora steadfastly refused. She purportedly declared that she would rather die in her imperial regalia, shrouded in purple, than go somewhere where she would not be hailed as empress. She would rather die in her pearls than live without them.

This imperial regalia, her imperial status, were Theodora's trophies. The signs that she had hoisted herself out of poverty. Knowing where Theodora had been before, perhaps it is understandable that she was unwilling to risk her position. Like her husband, Theodora was self-made, and had climbed the ladder with a mixture of luck, sex appeal and hard graft. She was born somewhere in the eastern Mediterranean, maybe Syria, maybe Cyprus. Her father trained bears, her mother was a dancer, and from a young age Theodora and her sisters were prostituted in various brothels. In her teens, she starred in a show performing sex acts on stage, not unlike those popular in seedy destinations around the world today. She attached herself to different men, who variously travelled with her and abandoned her. She trailed around North Africa for a time, before finding herself in glittering Antioch. One lover introduced her to another, and eventually she found herself entangled with Justinian, before he became emperor. He was twenty years older than her, and became completely infatuated with his mistress.

At this time, his uncle was an emperor, and passed a special law to allow his nephew to marry a woman of such low rank. Two years after the wedding, Theodora became the empress of the eastern Roman Empire. Her portrait in San Vitale shows her on equal footing to her husband. On the same physical level, and at the front of her own entourage, not simply a part of his. The women who stand with Theodora are almost as richly attired as her, in intricately embroidered robes and gilded headgear.

The irony is that despite these dazzling portraits of the imperial couple staring imperiously down on tourists in perpetuity from the walls of Ravenna – the only remaining, perfectly preserved images of this brilliant couple – neither Justinian nor Theodora ever set foot in Italy, let alone Ravenna. The conquest of Ravenna was Belisarius's victory, not theirs, and the emperor and empress celebrated in Constantinople; there was no reason for them to visit their new territories. It is possible that the artists worked from other images or studies of Justinian and Theodora, or it is possible that they did not. These mosaics might be likenesses of them, or they might just be an artist's imagining of how they looked. We will never know. What we do know is that these portraits reflect how the new rulers of Ravenna wanted to be seen by their subjects.

San Vitale stood as a visual statement of imperial authority in the new-won city of Ravenna. It signified the triumph of imperial Catholic Christianity over the Arianism of the Goths, and the final return of the empire to Italy.

To this day, the building is imposing – the diamond in Ravenna's crown. Lacking the intimate splendour of Galla Placidia's mausoleum, or the bright openness of Sant'Apollinaire, it instead is loaded with weighty majesty. The building is octagonal, and is one of the few buildings in Ravenna where the red-brick exterior is as complex and impressive as its interior. Sprawling, almost like an octagonal pyramid, cylinders, squares, triangles and arching buttresses all lean in, coming together under the tiled roof that covers the central dome, with an iron cross surmounting it all. Under this complicated exterior is a still more complicated interior: a many-apsed nave, decorated with luminescent mosaics in every colour, heavenly frescoes, imported marble and soaring domes.

The art of making mosaics is one that has been carefully preserved in modern Ravenna. The local institute for mosaic art is one of the foremost in the world, and the city is filled with artisan shops creating mosaic decorations, and also with the work of fine artists, who use mosaics as a medium. Some of the sculpture is elegant and abstract, other pieces are quirky. Others are political, engaging with the modern history of the Mediterranean and using this ancient art form to pass comment.

If a visitor crosses the street from Sant'Apollinare Nuovo, they will find themselves staring into the window of a gallery with a very different type of mosaic in the window. It is the gallery of Luca Barberini, a local artist who has made assembling the carefully clipped pieces of glass his life's work.

Luca remembers the first time he saw the mosaics in San Vitale and Sant'Apollinare, and even as a child was in awe of them, but not because of their majesty, but because they reminded him of manga. He understood straight away, as a child who had not yet learned to read, the power these images had to communicate key concepts to an illiterate population. While they stun now as art, at the time of their creation they were a vital means of communication.

The French artist Invader has installed mosaic images of Space Invaders around the city, and on other city walls in Europe; he has added pixelated mosaics of Theodora and Justinian, in comic homage to his mosaic antecedents. The Museum of Ravenna holds marble sculptures and mosaic ones too. Marc Chagall designed mosaics that were made by modern masters of the craft in Ravenna.

A lot of Barberini's work has been inspired by the modern issues facing the Mediterranean region – specifically the refugee crisis. At one exhibition, he divided the room in two with barbed wire, with the buffet on the opposite side to the viewers. Guests who wanted to access the wine and food and see the mosaics up close had to clamber through the barbed wire. It sent a provocative message. Like Gea Casolaro, Barberini's work has explored the drowning of immigrants and the refugee crisis.

Ravenna has always been a city of mosaics, but primarily of restoration. Then in the sixties things changed: mosaic art began to emerge as a modern art form and a new way of communicating ideas.

Art is important to the soul of Ravenna. It seems it always has been. Walking around the streets of the modern city, images are everywhere. The city has revitalised itself, capitalising on its artistic and poetic heritage. Street art has proliferated, with a campaign whereby residents volunteered to host a mural on the side of their building, but the finished product would be a surprise – they had no say in the content or design of the mural for which their buildings would act as a canvas. Many were unhappy with the designs chosen by the various street artists, and it is true, massive insects and monstrous babies can be seen adorning otherwise meek apartment blocks around the city. Every now and then, a pixelated mosaic Space Invader can be glimpsed. Irreverent and unsettling as much of this art is, it is still a homage to the Byzantine heritage of the city, which, although long faded, is still important to the city's memory.

The Byzantine period was brief, and hectic. As has been seen, under Justinian plague ravaged the empire, and the emperor had his hands full with warfare and earthquakes in other territories. For all this, at the time of his death he held almost the entire Mediterranean coast.

THE COMING OF CHARLEMAGNE

Control over these realms was precarious at best, and Justinian's holdings in Italy would fall. Not on his watch, but in the years of his successors. Three years after Justinian's death, the Lombards – or 'long beards' – would march into Italy from the north in 568, commencing the Byzantine–Lombard wars. These were a Germanic people from northern Europe, and exploited the weakness of Byzantine rule in Italy – Belisarius was absent at this time. They took numerous towns, and within a year had taken Milan. Ravenna however was safe for the moment. It stood in the eye of the hurricane that was engulfing Roman Italy, protected by its marshy surroundings and high towers. Ravenna would exist as a Byzantine exarchate for another 167 years, until the final exarch was murdered by encroaching Lombards. During this period, it may have weathered the storm but continued to lose territory, and no longer expanded or undertook monumental building projects of the scale of San Vitale or Sant'Apollinare.

The fate of the once mighty cities of Ravenna and Carthage mimicked each other during this time. Both became the capital cities of exarchates: Carthage the centre of the Byzantine Exarchate of North Africa, and Ravenna the centre of the eponymous exarchate in northern Italy.

Despite the turmoil erupting in Italy in the wake of the Lombard invasions, Ravenna remained a centre of learning for much of its time as an exarchate, an unexpected haven where culture and scholarship could flourish. It was during this time that another powerful faction would begin to emerge that would further destabilise the crumbling Byzantine Empire. The Franks were forming the empire that would one day be expanded and united under the first Holy Roman Emperor Charlemagne, and become known as the Carolingian Empire. At first, the Byzantines attempted to harness Frankish power through an alliance against the Lombards, but this came to nothing.

In 712 Liutprand, King of the Lombards, invaded and occupied Ravenna itself, but was unable to hold it, and after a few short weeks passed the towered city back to Byzantine control. In 751 King Aistulf finally succeeded in doing what his predecessor could not, and conclusively wrested Ravenna from Byzantine control, thus ending the era of the Byzantine Exarchate of Ravenna.

Through wars with the Franks and the turn of the wheel of fortune, Ravenna gradually came under the control of the Papal States, who put themselves on friendly terms with the Franks – in particular, with Charlemagne. Charlemagne and his dynasty always felt a keen legitimacy deficit, coming as they did from 'the ranks'. Charlemagne's grandfather Charles Martel and his family had been household stewards – 'mayors of the palace' – to the Merovingian kings, but had eventually seized power from these 'legitimate' monarchs. As such, they felt they had something to prove. Charlemagne certainly proved it. He was a formidable leader and succeeded in defeating many of the disparate groups in Europe, and uniting their territories, including that of the Lombards. He subdued much of central Europe, and eventually in the year 800 the Pope agreed to finally seal his legitimacy, and crown him emperor – making him the first western emperor since the child-Emperor Romulus Augustus was deposed by Odoacer.

The Carolingians – as they came to be known in the wake of Charlemagne's achievements – did not see themselves as masters *only* of the western empire. At the time of Charlemagne's coronation in Rome on Christmas Day 800, the Byzantine court was in a state of complete disarray. A woman – the Empress Irene – was now running things, having blinded her own son in order to seize power, and he had subsequently died of his injuries. The Pope refused to recognise an empress, and a murderous one at that, as sole ruler of the empire, and thus he argued that the imperial throne was vacant and granted it to Charlemagne. This was in name only, of course, as Charlemagne never made it to Constantinople, and the Byzantine court never recognised him. Irene would reign from Constantinople for two more years before being deposed and replaced by her finance minister. Despite the ruckus in Byzantium, the Pope and the remains of the western empire in Europe submitted to Charlemagne. As confirmation of Charlemagne's imperial status, Pope Leo gave the newly anointed and crowned emperor leave to strip whatever treasures he liked from the former capitals Rome and Ravenna, to take them with him to decorate his own new capital, Aachen, in southern Germany.

The first Byzantine-era mosaics I ever laid eyes on were not in Ravenna, or Constantinople, or Sicily, or any area ever occupied by the Byzantines. They were in Charlemagne's palace chapel, in Aachen. I was overwhelmed as I looked up past the marble columns, to the liquid-gold ceiling, adorned with saints and stars. It was a taste of all that I would discover in Italy and Turkey later in life, copies of the style that had marked Ravenna and Constantinople out as capitals in the afterlife of the Roman Empire. Charlemagne wanted to build a new Ravenna at Aachen, taking all the splendour of late Roman Christian art, and fusing it with his own Germanic tastes. He did not want Aachen to look princely, nor even kingly, but imperial, and to this end he minutely copied imperial style in the designs of his monuments.

Charlemagne carried off many objects from Ravenna, but more importantly, he took inspiration. He was entertained magnificently by the archbishop of Ravenna when he visited in 787, and it was in this city, rather than Rome, that he found the image of the emperor he wanted to be. It was in Ravenna that he learned what a capital should look like, and saw what it meant to be an emperor. Charlemagne stood in San Vitale and raised his eyes to meet Justinian's flinty stare, and in that moment he knew what he wanted his palace chapel to look like, and he knew how he wanted to be remembered. He plundered treasures, and commanded his architects to build an octagonal chapel, raised on marble columns, with a glittering apse. He recreated the wonders of Byzantine Ravenna in central Germany, and called it Carolingian. From Ravenna, as from Rome, he carried back not only imperial ambitions, but porphyry marble columns and monumental capitals that he would use to adorn the palace at Aachen.

One of the key art pieces that Charlemagne removed from Ravenna to Aachen was the great equestrian statue of Theodoric the Great, which exuded as much imperial authority, if not more, than Justinian's mosaic, and was easier to carry; the statue was made of bronze, but plated with gold, so that to the casual observer it might seem to be struck from pure gold. It depicted the barbarian king astride a destrier with a shield on one arm and a lance couched in the other. Charlemagne might have related to this king even more than Justinian, as he represented a Germanic-Roman hybrid ruler, who had successfully tamed Italy. The statue embodied this in more ways than one: having originally been built to honour a Roman Emperor, it was relabelled and slightly remodelled by Theodoric. Appropriation of Roman frippery was a favourite hobby of the barbarian invaders.

The force of Charlemagne's iron will and personality played a major role in keeping his European empire together, and following his death in 814, the empire began to disintegrate. Ravenna would slip into obscurity, futilely struggling for independence from the Papal States. Subsequent regimes looted from and endowed Ravenna, and the city was ruled largely by her bishops.

The office of Holy Roman Emperor persisted following the collapse of Charlemagne's empire, but subsequent incumbents of the office took a very different attitude to the papacy. For Charlemagne, co-operation with the pontiff had bestowed upon him a much-craved claim to legitimacy, but later German emperors resented the power of the Pope. In the various conflicts that would arise, Ravenna would take the side of emperor against pope. The city by this time had a history of resisting papal dominance.

Theoretically under the rule of the papacy, the bishops of Ravenna retained rule of the city and region in all but name, and the story of Ravenna slipped into the story of northern Italy. Powerful Renaissance families began to rule cities, as seen more famously in Florence on the part of the Medici. In Ravenna the ruling family was the Da Polenta family – a clan not without its own woes.

It was during the supremacy of this ruling family that the legendary poet Dante Alighieri, author of the *Divine Comedy*, was chased out of Florence in a political dispute, and retired to Ravenna to finish his magnum opus and breathe his last. Dante, while in Ravenna and a guest of the Da Polenta family, was moved to include a piece of their family history in *Inferno*. He spent days alone there, walking in the ancient pine forests and marshlands surrounding the city, lamenting the strife in Florence, and composing *Paradiso*.

Walking in Ravenna in 2021, the 700th anniversary of the poet's untimely death from malaria, it was impossible not to be aware of Dante's contribution to the city and its poetic identity. Each evening, at sunset, verses from the *Divine Comedy* were read out to faithful crowds gathered around his simple sepulchre. Illuminated calligraphy spiralled over the streets, spelling out snatches of his poetry, and one night, overnight, fifty Ravennate came together and rolled out a giant mural of Dante in the central square, assembling it from wallpaper-like sheets, almost like a modern mosaic. Citizens were then invited to tear a piece and take it home, and so it was dismantled as quickly as it came. The legacy of this red-robed, laurel-crowned poet looms large in this small Italian city.

The tomb is simple though, tucked away in a corner of the city centre, in a side street near the Church of St Francesco, with the flooded crypt and where Dante's funeral mass was heard. The simple white stone stands in contrast to the red-brick wall it nestles beside. A simple dome surmounts the structure, edged with carved sheep skulls, grim mementos mori for the dead poet. Inside, a sarcophagus contains his bones, beneath a relief carving in porphyry marble. An inscription above expresses Dante's bitterness towards Florence, the city he loved, calling it a 'loveless mother'. Some centuries after his death Florence decided they loved their most famous son once again, and started making fervent requests for the bones of the great poet to be returned to his mother city. For centuries, Ravenna has refused. Even when in 1519 Pope Leo X issued a decree, monks in Ravenna packed up an empty box and sent it to Florence. To this day, the far more ornate tomb in Florence remains empty. Dante's bones stay in Ravenna, and the citizens love their poet.

The city Dante lived in was different to that inhabited by Galla Placidia and Theoderic, but just as Dante casts a long shadow in the city today, so too did these figures in his time. The walls that stood in Dante's day were those built by Honorius. Moreover, still more mosaics and churches survived in Dante's time that have since been lost. Justinian, who glowers down from the wall of San Vitale, is found in Dante's heaven, occupying the sphere of Mercury. Justinian is cast as the 'historian' of the Roman Empire, whose justness as a law giver is demonstrated in the victories of Belisarius. Can we imagine that Dante was not inspired to write this verse while staring up in wonder at the mosaic portraits that Charlemagne also marvelled at, and visitors can still gaze up at today? Art historians have also been quick to draw parallels between the stars of Galla Placidia's starry sky and verses in *Paradiso*, and the procession of saints in Sant'Apollinare.

Of more influence perhaps even than the mosaics and the eyes of Justinian was the story of a young woman of Ravenna, a daughter of the Da Polenta family which hosted Dante during his time in the city.

The Lady Francesca Da Polenta was born in 1255, just ten years before Dante, and only a handful of miles away. She was Ravennate by birth and, as a woman of this noble house, was expected to make a strategic marriage. At the age of twenty a match was made with Gianciotto Malatesta of the house of Rimini, a still more prestigious family. There was no love between the couple, with Gianciotto at least a decade older than Francesca and physically deformed. Instead she found love in the arms of his younger brother – the more aesthetically blessed Paolo 'il Bello'. The pair embarked on an impassioned, illicit affair. As shall be seen, affairs were tolerated among the noble families of Ravenna in later centuries, but at this time, they were not. The two were discovered *in flagrante delicto* by Gianciotto, and murdered together in bed with one stroke of his sword.

Francesca and her sorry story were propelled to immortal fame by Dante. He wrote that he encountered the doomed lover in the second circle of hell, and fainted out of pity for the girl. While he described her with great sympathy and sorrow, she is still portrayed as damned for her lust, and her lack of agency. It's not a crime to fall in love, but to relinquish self-control. When she tells her story, Francesca acknowledges no responsibility for her actions or those of Paolo, but instead she depicts them as powerless in the face of love. Francesca and Paolo were condemned to be trapped forever, clinging to one another in a vicious and fiery whirlwind in the circles of hell reserved for the lustful. The eternally doomed Francesca recalls her homeland on the beautiful Po delta and laments that the greatest punishment of all is to 'remember days / of joy when misery is at hand'.

Dante never really met Francesca. She was killed at the age of thirty, following her ten-year impassioned affair, years before Dante arrived in Ravenna. But he would have been well acquainted with her story. They were born just ten years apart, and had Francesca lived, she would certainly have known Dante, as it was her own nephew, Guido da Polenta II, who hosted Dante during his years in Ravenna.

Dante began the relationship between the city and poetry, a relationship that would flourish down the centuries, and like the glinting mosaics of San Vitale, would stand the test of time.

Many years after Dante wandered the streets of Ravenna thinking of Beatrice, the English Romantic poet Lord Byron would come lovelorn to the city and write poetry. In the intervening years Ravenna would pass through the hands of the Venetians, the papacy and the French.

The Venetians did not take the city by force, but rather accepted control when it was offered to them by a group of high-ranking Ravennate, evidently fed up with the internal politics and strife that took hold of the city following the decline of the Da Polenta family. Nevertheless, they made the city their own and left the most imposing visual marks on Ravenna, building the fortress on the north-east side of the city, a stone's throw from Theoderic's mausoleum. In the central square, Piazza del Popolo, they erected the two granite columns that still stand today. Originally, Venetian-instructed craftsmen put a winged lion atop one of the columns, alongside the statue of the patron saint, Apollinare. When the city managed to finally chase the Venetians out, the triumphant winged lion was replaced with San Vitale.

The Papal States would once again take control for some centuries, until they became involved in a decades-long struggle, with the French among others. These struggles became known as the War of the League of Cambrai, in which the Papal States, France and Venice found themselves embroiled with new participants arriving all the time and alliances changing just as regularly. At the Battle of Ravenna in 1512, the Kingdom of Spain and the Papal States allied against France and the Duchy of Ferrara. Ravenna was very much caught in the middle. It was during this Battle of Ravenna, which brought thousands of soldiers into the environs of the city, that the renowned French leader, Gaston of Foix, was killed. This was not an ancient or early-medieval battle, but an early-modern one; cavalry was still a key part of combat, but now artillery was on the scene as well, and cannon fire played a role too. Some weeks before this bloody conflict, a perceived omen heralded the papal defeat in Ravenna, in the form of the birth of a grossly deformed child. This infant, which purportedly had horns and an eye in its knee, became known to history as the Monster of Ravenna.

A diary entry by the Florentine apothecary Luca Landucci in 1512 describes the unfortunate infant thus:

> A monster had been born at Ravenna, of which a drawing was sent here; it had a horn on its head, straight up like a sword, and instead of arms it had two wings like a bat's, and at the height of the breasts it had a [y-shaped mark] on one side and a cross on the other, and lower down at the waist, two serpents, and it was a hermaphrodite, and on the right knee it had an eye, and its left foot was like an eagle's.

At this time, superstition led people to interpret such events metaphorically. The underdeveloped arms could be a sign of inaction or lack of initiative on the part of the Ravennate. The deformed genitals could be a sign of sexual misconduct. The claw could be greed, the eye avarice, and so on. All in all, it was seen as great misfortune for the city of Ravenna, and when the French army descended upon the city and beat back the forces of the Papal States, it seemed the misfortune foretold had indeed come to pass. Despite the death of Gaston of Foix, the French army was victorious, and under its new commander they besieged the city of Ravenna itself. Quick to victory, the soldiers entered Ravenna full of bloodlust and spent three days sacking the city, robbing and raping the citizens. At that point, even their commander could not stomach looking on their actions any longer, and bid them march away.

French control of the city was short-lived. The Papal States regained control shortly after the siege, and Ravenna stayed in papal hands almost uninterrupted until the unification of Italy. However it was before unification was achieved in 1871 that another poet, this one bent on adventure, careened into Ravenna's streets, many decades before Oscar Wilde followed suit. Lord Byron arrived in Ravenna, drawn there by love or lust for a married teenager he had met recently in Venice.

One of the brief interludes in which Ravenna was not subject to papal authority in the intervening years was when Napoleon's armies took the city at the tail end of Napoleonic supremacy in Europe. While Napoleon held much of Italy, a nobleman named Count Alessandro Guiccioli made himself useful to the French forces, co-operating with them and being rewarded with power in return. As Napoleon's empire crumbled, he conveniently switched sides to support the Papal States, and as such navigated the period of transition with limited personal loss. It was following Napoleon's defeat, in the newly stabilised Italy, that Guiccioli – at the age of fifty-seven – married a nobly born and comparatively well-educated eighteen-year-old named Teresa Gamba, and made her Countess Guiccioli. They lived together in Ravenna, Teresa being the daughter of another count of the region. Shortly after the wedding, Countess Teresa met Lord Byron at a party in a Venetian palazzo, and although she did not know it at the time, the trajectory of her life was permanently altered.

The life of Teresa, a noblewoman of Ravenna coming of age amid the Napoleonic wars and growing up to see the unification of Italy, gives a good glimpse of life in Ravenna during this in-between phase. The truth is that life in the city followed the pattern of other Italian towns, although this was certainly a twilight phase for Ravenna. Tourism and the riches it brought with it had not yet taken hold in the city, and it was comparatively poor, with its monuments unloved by modern standards.

When Byron arrived in Ravenna, he was unimpressed with what he found. Nevertheless, he stayed. He went to the theatre looking for Teresa, who had said it was there that they should meet. But due to illness she stood him up. He wrote her a letter:

I have tried to distract myself with the farce of visiting antiquities – it seems quite intolerably tedious – but at the moment everything else is equally displeasing. The little that interests me, Dante's tomb and a few things in the library – I have already seen with an indifference made pardonable by the state of my heart... I am a foreigner in Italy – and still more a foreigner in Ravenna – and naturally little versed in the customs of the country – I am afraid of compromising you. For myself these is little more to fear – my fate is already decided. It is impossible for me to live long in this state of torment – I am writing to you in tears – and I am not a man who cries easily. When I cry my tears come from the heart, and are of blood.

Byron was enraptured with Teresa, and the feeling was mutual, for all that the reception he received in Ravenna was a little faltering. The pair began a passionate love affair, seemingly with the knowledge and at least tacit acceptance of Teresa's much older husband, the Count Guiccioli. No matter how much Byron complained, he was clearly inspired by his surroundings, penning *The Prophesy of Dante* while in Ravenna, and dedicating it to Teresa. When he went to fight and die in Greece, he went with a lock of Teresa's hair in a locket by his heart, which his daughter dutifully sent back to the countess after his death, and which she treasured for all of her life.

We know from other sources that Byron enjoyed his time in the city. His fellow poet Percy Bysshe Shelley visited him in 1821 while he stayed in the Palazzo Guiccioli – owned by Teresa's absent husband. Shelley was equally bemused and amused by Byron's lifestyle there, which he described in a letter home:

> Lord Byron gets up at two. I get up, quite contrary to my usual custom... at 12. After breakfast we sit talking till six. From six to eight we gallop through the pine forests which divide Ravenna from the sea; we then come home and dine, and sit up gossiping till six in the morning. I don't suppose this will kill me in a week or fortnight, but I shall not try it longer. Lord B's establishment consists, besides servants, of ten horses, eight enormous dogs, three monkeys, five cats, an eagle, a crow, and a falcon; and all these, except the horses, walk about the house, which every now and then resounds with their unarbitrated quarrels, as if they were the masters of it...
>
> P.S. I find that my enumeration of the animals in this Circean Palace was defective... I have just met on the grand staircase five peacocks, two guinea hens, and an Egyptian crane.

Shelley also praised Teresa's looks, but did not comment much on the pair's relationship.

For all that Byron loved Teresa, he wrote very scathingly of her in his letters to his friends. Calling her simply 'the G' and dismissing her, and making fun of her strong Italian accent and lack of subtlety. He made no professions of his love for her to his friends. His variously dismissive and adoring letters are preserved in the library which he mentioned with so little reverence – the Biblioteca Classense, dating from the early eighteenth century. The library of a former monastery, it has good claim to be the loveliest library in the world.

This building is one of Ravenna's less well-known treasures. The halls of books are arranged around a cloistered courtyard, which is home to five gorgeous trees. There is birdsong, and cicadas, and a breeze stirs the young palm fronds from one of the smaller trees. The walls are yellow, and sienna, and terracotta. It is perhaps the calmest place that I have ever been.

Byron came here too. Restless and agitated, waiting to be received by his beloved Teresa, he paced the town, looking at mosaics for which he had little time, rolling his eyes at the mausoleum of Theoderic before eventually acknowledging that this library held a few curiosities of interest to him, as did the tomb of Dante.

The legendary lover-poet's life in Ravenna was a rocky one, beginning with some anguish. The most entertaining thing about reading Byron's letters is to perceive the different personalities he displays to different correspondents. His love affair with Teresa was at first, it seems, nearly all conducted in Italian, and the warmth of the language seemed to allow him to express sentiments he scarcely could in English – for all that he was a master of letters. His relationship with Teresa is one of thorough feeling, and thorough hedonism. Byron's days in Ravenna were spent riding, shooting, loving, dining, and – of course – writing. *Don Juan* was a product of Ravenna.

The Biblioteca Classense allowed me to handle two letters of Lord Byron, the first sent on 22 April 1819, from Venice, where he met Teresa. This letter is perhaps the sweetest artefact from the life of Byron, ringing as it does with the first flush of real passion. The man writing this letter is completely smitten – he's the lover who leaves four voice notes in a row today. He writes that he has covered the letter with his kisses, moved by the thought that she might raise it to her lips.

It is a large sheet of fragile cream paper that has been folded in half like an exercise book, and then folded again and sealed with red wax and addressed to 'Madame la Comtesse Guiccioli, Ravenna'. When Byron wrote '*io tremo scrivendoti*', his hand did indeed falter over '*tremo*' – perhaps for dramatic effect, or not. But the blot is there on the page. His pen, always a lightning rod for raw emotion, here sent his passion for Teresa onto the page. Squeezed into the bottom of the letter, on his second postscript, Byron wrote a few more lines, in haste as the postman was waiting. Cramped in tiny characters at the bottom of the page, using every last scrap of space, he concluded, '*ti bacio 10000 volte*' – 'I kiss you ten thousand times'.

This paper, preserved in carefully controlled temperatures, has known the lips of both Byron and Teresa, who called him '*caro* Giorgio' and '*mio* Byron!' There is joy in knowing the letter has stayed in Ravenna, in the cool interior of this ancient library that doubtless they both visited.

The library is patrolled by two cats. One, a small female with delicate whiskers and pink nose, is called Teresa. She lounges on velvet benches and washes her face in patches of sunlight pooling in the cloisters. She disdainfully accepts my affection, which is better than the other cat, a slightly rangy tom – hard to glimpse for he is always out hunting: his name is Byron.

Perhaps the best relic of their relationship is a pocket-sized copy of *Corinne* by Madame de Staël, printed in Italian and bound in purple velvet. This was a book that belonged to Teresa, and while she was away from the house, Byron sat thumbing it in the garden. In a fit of literary affection, he scrawled a note – in English – on the blank final pages for her (and subsequent generations) to stumble upon at some future point. It was an electric moment when I discovered these pages. I had asked for all of Byron's letters, and was perplexed when the book was delivered; on finding the letter in the back my heart skipped with the surprise, and with the passion of Byron's writing:

My dearest Teresa, –

I have read this book in your garden; – my love, you were absent, or else I could not have read it. It is a favourite book of yours, and the writer was a friend of mine. You will not understand these English words, and others will not understand them, – which is the reason I have not scrawled them in Italian. But you will recognize the handwriting of him who passionately loves you, and you will divine that, over a book which was yours, he could only think of love. In that word, beautiful in all languages, but most so in yours – *Amor mio* – is comprised my existence here and hereafter. I feel I exist here, and I fear that I shall exist hereafter, – as to what purpose you will decide; my destiny rests with you, and you are a woman, seventeen years of age, and two out of a convent. I wish that you had stayed there, with all my heart, – or, at least, that I had never met you in your married state.

But all this is too late. I love you, and you love me, – at least, you say so, and act as if you did so, which last is a great consolation in all events. But I more than love you, and cannot cease to love you.

Think of me, sometimes, when the Alps and the ocean divide us, – but they never will, unless you wish it.

B

But love and life is complicated, and the summer of the romance would not last forever. Teresa loved Byron until the end of her days, and remained dedicated to preserving his legacy, but eventually was pressured into returning to her husband and ending the relationship with Byron, in order to save her father from exile. Byron and various members of Teresa's family had become involved together in radical social plots leaning towards the unification of Italy, bringing further shame.

Partly precipitated by this situation, partly by boredom, and partly by righteous fervour – Lord Byron would sail away from Italy, and from Teresa, forever in 1823. He took a ship for Greece to fight in the Greek war of independence against the Ottoman Empire. Teresa was grief stricken, but Byron thrived in Greece. He committed himself fully to the revolutionary cause, even selling his estates in England to raise money for it. He lived fully in those last years, not least having an affair with a Greek boy, and eventually died of fever in Missolonghi on 19 April 1824.

Teresa continued to live in Ravenna, outliving her husband and marrying again. She preserved all of her correspondence with Byron, and wrote a biography of his life in Italy. When she died, her papers were secreted away by embarrassed relatives, but eventually passed to the care of the Biblioteca Classense, where I was fortunate enough to study them.

In 1861, thirty-seven years after Byron's death in Greece, fighting for a cause of freedom which the Greeks eventually won, Italy itself underwent seismic change. In 1830, Ravenna joined other cities in Romagna in rising up against the authority of the Papal States. Thirst for independence was rife in Italy, and the Greek War of Independence and the beginning of Italian independence and unification were part of a wave of revolutions sweeping across Europe in the wake of the downfall of Napoleon and the terms of the Congress of Vienna. The flag of the Papal States with its crossed keys of St Peter was replaced with the tricolour of modern Italy. This was only a step however on the long and bloody road towards the creation of the unified Kingdom of Italy – finally achieved in 1861. Ravenna was only a small part in this enterprise, but it was the place where the great heroine of this conflict – Anita Garibaldi, Brazilian revolutionary wife of the leader Giuseppe Garibaldi – died. Following fighting in the siege of Rome, and pursued by French and Austrian troops, she fled north, pregnant and ill with malaria, and died in hiding on the outskirts of Ravenna in 1849.

Modern Ravenna has reinvented itself. While the sea has receded, and the meandering waterways that used to form its streets have dried up, a canal still links the city to the sea, and it still functions as a port. It is the industrial port for the region, and passenger ferries carry tourists to and from Croatia, just across the Adriatic.

Since 1972 the Byzantine churches of Ravenna have been recognised by UNESCO as World Heritage Sites.

Following the unification of Italy, more and more august travellers began to descend on Ravenna and be inspired by the beauty of the art they found there. Karl Gustav Jung was so enraptured by the mosaics of Galla Placidia's 'mausoleum' that he had extensive hallucinations, and even delivered a lecture on mosaics that did not exist. He had only dreamed of them, and only realised this when other travellers tried to find the places he described and were unsuccessful. Gustav Klimt, so famous for his golden period, was inspired by Ravenna, and Marc Chagall went there to learn how to make mosaic dreamscapes. The beautifully frescoed palazzo that Count Giuccioli inexplicably lent as a love nest to Byron and Teresa fell into disrepair in the twentieth century, but has undergone extensive restoration in recent years and soon will be opened as a museum dedicated to the pair.

Ravenna is rightly proud of its poetic and artistic heritage. Winding away from Dante's tomb towards one of the historic city gates is the Street of the Poets. Posted at stations down this thoroughfare are quotations from great writers describing their raptures in the city.

But for all the glories of its artistic and poetic past, Ravenna must strive to live more in the present. The identity of the city is too tied to the dead. Modern residents, particularly modern creatives who want to express themselves differently, in new ways, feel their hands are tied.

I interview Marco Miccoli, a skater and street art curator from Ravenna who each year creates an exhibition in honour of Dante. 'People are only interested, we only get permission, if it's about Dante. But with Dante Plus we try to do something different. We do Dante but with augmented reality, with street art, comic book style. We have a huge sculpture of his head made out of scrap metal. We want people to think differently, and we ask subversive artists to do something different with his legacy. We want people to try and see things a new way.'

The scrap metal certainly puts a fresh spin on a centuries-dead poet, and one piece shows Dante sitting and writing the *Divine Comedy* on a MacBook Air. Another shows him dressed in a space suit, with the names of Beatrice and Virgil embroidered on the uniform.

Marco tells me that, of course, Venice and Florence feel some rivalry over Dante. Dante was, undeniably, a Florentine, not Ravennate, but – as Marco says – the Florentines did not want him when he was alive, so why should they have a monopoly on him in death? 'He wrote some of his most beautiful poetry while in Ravenna. He died here. He is buried here, and the people here grow up with Dante as a figure in their minds.' Marco's girlfriend, gallerist Alessandra Carini, asserts that for Ravennate children, Dante is like a relative. And the mosaics are like the sky, they are just there, and part of their lives. They are part of the soul of the city.

Alessandra is passionate about contemporary art, and spent years studying the subject in order to open a contemporary gallery in her family home in Ravenna. She says sharing her passion with her home town has been an uphill struggle, but she will keep trying. It has been challenging to encourage the people of Ravenna to embrace new styles, but little by little she is succeeding.

Alessandra's gallery is a 'home gallery', something common in other places, but not so common in Italy. The building is from the 1860s, and decorated with brightly coloured frescoes that permeate the walls and ceilings. The art displayed contrasts so extremely with the classic, baroque style of decoration, but each style accentuates the other. In what might have been a chic living room in the 1890s, a mosaicked unicorn head presides over the other art objects on display.

At Alessandra's gallery, I meet Nicola Montalbini, an artist in his thirties. His features are quick moving and intelligent, but sceptical. His head is all but shaved, and the hair that is there – artificially or not – is platinum blond. He wears a black shirt, half undone, and jeans. Silver rings adorn his hands, and his eyes glint blue.

He paints vivid watercolours, but it's the sort of work you have to warm up to. But when Nicola talks about them, he comes to life, and his work suddenly coalesces into much more than it might have been.

He explains the skylines he wanted to create, and why he chose hot pink. Despite not being raised Catholic, Nicola has painted San Vitale – he believes the spirituality and significance of the architecture of the basilicas transcend the religions they were built for. 'I love my city very much. I love it and I hate it and I live it and I am part of it. These are the shapes you grow up with as an Italian child, the history and religion cluttering your horizons. You grow up in a small city, but which has this *phantasmic* history, which dwarfs everything the city is in the modern day. That trumps the reality of the city. It's a mistake. Ravenna is so much more than her history, but you grow up with these ghosts. The air is so thick with ghosts that you can't breathe, and you can't see past them.' I agree emphatically. In Syracuse, the ghosts feel like they raise the city up; in Ravenna, Nicola thinks they hold it back. He tells me that he hates Dante: 'If I could kill the memory, I would.' Later, perhaps slightly abashed, he is quick to clarify, 'I don't hate Dante, he was a genius, but I hate the brand. They've made a brand out of his bones – and his nose.'

The obsession with Dante, Nicola says, comes from the Italian obsession with death. 'It's a fetish,' he tells us. 'Dante lived in Ravenna, *for three years*, and the city didn't really care. Florence didn't want him. But as soon as the poet dies, his bones become valuable. Suddenly Florence wants them back, but Ravenna keeps them, and sets them at the very centre of the city. It's a fetish. We fetishise the bones of a dead poet, and build our entire cultural life around them.'

Nicola isn't wrong. One cannot turn a corner in Ravenna without being confronted with the image of the red-robed, laurel-crowned poet. His words hang in the air in the streets, and he lends his name to many of the city's institutions. And yet he only lived here three years.

ANTIOCH

Is this Antioch, the queen of the East, the glory of the monarch, the joy of the evangelist? brought down even to the dust... on every side is the silence of ruin, and the dimness of despair: yet how beautiful and exulting is the face of nature: she sitteth not solitary, with the tears on her cheek, but dwells, as of old, in her loved valley of the Orontes.

– John Carne, Traveller

The ruined walls of Antioch, 1836

In a valley sheltered by two mountain ranges, the Nur Mountains to the west and the Jibal al-Aqra Mountains to the east, lie the remains of ancient Antioch. Before 6 February 2023, these ragged arches were juxtaposed with the high-rise sprawl of the modern city of Antakya, which had steadily grown over the last 150 years to supersede the ancient metropolis. Now the modern city is ruins too. It was razed by two devastating earthquakes that took place on 6 February 2023, and another that struck two weeks later, on the evening of 20 February. The quakes measured 7.8, 7.5 and 6.4 on the Richter scale, and were followed by dozens of aftershocks. More than 50,000 people lost their lives across southern Turkey and northern Syria, and the city of Antakya was rendered unrecognisable. The scale of loss has been unimaginable.

Before this, Antakya was beautiful. At its heart was an old city of winding streets, designed in Ottoman and French styles. Boutiques sold mosaic art, traditional clothing, Turkish ceramics and the *Künefe* for which the city is famous. The population was multicultural, predominantly Alawite Islamic, but also with significant Christian and small Jewish communities, that have continued in the city for over two millennia – since the days of Antioch's founding.

Even now, the loveliness of the location is astounding. Not coastal, like Carthage, Syracuse or Tyre, the beauty of Antioch's situation comes not even from the waters of the Orontes – now called the Asi River – that flow through it, but from the formidable, verdant mountains that cradle the city on all sides. The lands are fertile but treacherous, resting above the meeting point of multiple tectonic plates, that at various points in history have jostled one another and brought down the city above them, tearing up the landscape and producing the vertiginous mountains that surround the city. The natural defences offered by these mountains have been enhanced by the fortifications of numerous civilisations over the centuries. Now that the modern city of Antakya has fallen, visitors must be prepared to camp if they wish to visit the ruins. Nevertheless, hiking in the foothills of these mountains to find the long-forgotten ruins of the ancient city is rewarding. Traces of the once 'impregnable' walls of Antioch can be found, towers, gates and arches that hold firm all these centuries later, grasping the mountainside. Those with clear eyesight can look up from the ruined streets of the old city to the mountain peaks and see the straight line of the Byzantine walls, and wonder at the iron will that dragged the stones so high and built the structures that would survive centuries.

The slopes are steep but climbable.

These walls are all that remain of the ancient city that dominated the

Roman east. Capital of the Seleucid Empire, and then of Roman Syria, for much of its heyday in the Roman period Antioch was second only to Rome. Indeed, scholars have argued that during the decline of Rome in the third and fourth centuries AD, Antioch was the de facto capital of the empire in all but name.* Many emperors used the city as their primary residence. With the eastern expansion of the Roman Empire, Antioch took on a greater status than simply the capital of a province. Governors and emperors continued to reside there from 63 BC to AD 299, notably Vespasian and Diocletian – the persecutor of the Christians. After the fall of Rome, the city's importance would wax and wane.

In the golden days of Antioch the city was a crossing place on the greatest trade route of the age – the Silk Road. This brought it inestimable wealth. It was the gateway to the Levant, and a major city in the eastern Mediterranean. Following the fall of the Seleucids, it became in turn the capital of the Roman Orient, the cradle of Christianity, an Islamic stronghold, a Byzantine trading centre and a crusader capital, before beginning a process of slow decline under the governance of the Mamluks. For a brief period of almost a year from 7 September 1938 to 29 June 1939, it was the capital of Hatay State – an independent state, attached to no country. In 1939, it was controversially annexed by modern Turkey.

For all the sumptuous history, many of the curious European travellers who visited Antioch from the seventeenth to the twenty-first centuries, before the opening of the great Hatay Archaeological Museum, left feeling disappointed by the historical offering they found in Antioch. They were underwhelmed by the crumbling stones, collapsed walls and lack of architectural grandeur that perhaps they had seen recently in Aleppo, Tripoli, Rome and Palermo. Most travellers did not stay long. But, had they had the patience to tarry a while longer, and arm themselves with a trowel and a little curiosity – they might have had their breath taken away. What they would have discovered, had they scratched beneath the soil, was a monumental network of mosaics that lay shrouded in earth beneath the surface of the city.

For thousands of years, from antiquity until the mid-twentieth century, Antioch's golden past has been written in sumptuous tesserae, its wealth and status attested to in extensive mosaic floors, just waiting to be uncovered. And more is discovered all the time. The once flat Roman floors have moved with time. No longer flat, the mosaics now roll like waves, astonishingly well preserved except for these new

* Andrea De Giorgi and A. Asa Eger, *Antioch: A History*.

undulations. They are gorgeous, decadent, and speak to Antioch's past as the capital of Roman Syria, greater even than Damascus. Damascus is the older of the two cities, but the rise of Antioch as the capital of the Seleucid Empire under Seleucus I Nicator spelled a period of decline for Damascus. Despite the recent earthquakes, the majority of the mosaics still survive, preserving the city's heritage under a blanket of new destruction. Miraculously, the structure of the Archaeological Museum escaped practically unscathed, amid a sea of damaged buildings. A blessing for historians, it also stands as a silent reminder that Turkish authorities can build earthquake-proof buildings. The tragedy of Antakya is that such stringent precautions were only taken for the preservation of relics, rather than human life. The vast majority of buildings that collapsed and killed their occupants were residential.

Nevertheless, the history survives. An eerie mosaic preserved in the museum depicts a reclining skeleton, quaffing wine from a jar at a banquet, with loaves of bread and a wine amphora beside him. The mosaic was once in a dining hall, reminding revellers to cheer up, have fun and enjoy the food as death would take them one day. In other panels, hunting scenes are depicted, with big cats and wild boar leaping in all directions. Gods and nymphs are present too, alongside heroes from mythology. So how did this remarkable place come to be? And how did Glorious Antioch – the Queen of the East – contract to become a relatively modest city on the southernmost tip of Turkey?

SELEUCID ANTIOCH: A JEWEL IN THE CROWN

The history of Antakya – ancient Antioch – stretches back 2,300 years, and it was founded quite by chance. The story goes that Antioch, while not technically an Alexandrine city, does indeed owe its existence to a whim of the great general, Alexander the Great, and indeed to Zeus himself. According to a native orator named Libanius, Alexander camped on the site of the city, and mused that it would be a good place to build a city after tasting the deliciously sweet water from the springs. He proclaimed this water was like his mother's milk, and commanded a fountain to be built to channel the spring. He built an altar too, to make a sacrifice to Zeus, thus founding what would become the great temple of Zeus Bottios. Some years later, when Seleucus chose to make a sacrifice to Zeus a little way away, an eagle sent by Zeus himself swooped down and plucked up the thigh meat from the sacrifice and carried it away to the horizon. One of Seleucus's men rode after it on horseback to see where it would take him and saw the eagle deposit the meaty burden on the very altar that Alexander had consecrated several decades before. This was interpreted by all to be a divine omen, suggesting the founding of a city.

In Libanius's account, Seleucus lost no time in rallying to Zeus's command. He felled trees, quarried stones and with great speed raised up his new city, named in honour of his father, a man called Antiochus. He stationed his war elephants around the edges of the city and instructed builders that wherever there was an elephant, there they should construct a tower. It is a loss to urban planning that this method of demarcation is no longer employed as part of the architectural process. He then mapped out his streets with trails of flour brought up by ships on the Orontes. The beginning of Antioch was a prosperous one. Of course, such an account of a city's founding, written by an ardent devotee both of Antioch and Seleucus Nicator, must be viewed almost as sceptically as Syracuse's myth of Arethusa, or the story of Tyre's foundation by Melqart. By the time Libanius was writing in the fourth century AD, Alexander had taken on an almost godlike status in the mythology of the Late Antique world. Associating a place with Alexander was not dissimilar to associating it with a deity, and such associations were deemed essential for bringing prestige to a city.

Seleucus was one of Alexander's most trusted generals. He had been on campaign with Alexander at the time of his supposed construction of the fountain and sacrifice to Zeus. He had risen through the ranks from infantryman to general, and on his king's death his ambition would take him a further leap: he would become *basileus* and founder of his eponymous empire. As has been well documented, Alexander's empire was torn apart when the young general died suddenly of illness at the age of thirty-two, leaving no viable heir or plan of succession. Perhaps he had thought himself invincible, but in all his grand plans Alexander made no provision for his own death. His son was too young to succeed, his regent too weak, his widow too unpopular, his generals too opportunistic and greedy. Chaos ensued, and the greatest empire the world has ever seen cracked into fragments. Seleucus took the lion's share, earning himself his epithet Nicator (the Victorious) with lands stretching from Tenedos, off the Mediterranean coast of Turkey, across Persia. Three power blocks emerged: Ptolemaic Egypt, the Antigonid Kingdom and the sprawling Seleucid Empire.

Who was Seleucus? What can be said of the man who gave his name to this empire, forged from the ruins of Alexander's? In terms of personal accomplishment, Seleucus's meteoric rise from impecunious soldier to lord of an empire that stretched from Anatolia to Persia was just as impressive as the conquests of Alexander himself.

It is not clear who precisely Seleucus's parents were, but we do know that they were not kings. Seleucus was born in obscurity, it seems, around the year 358, and no one is quite sure where. Little is known about his parents beyond their names: his father was Antiochus – it was for him that the great city that is the focus of this chapter was named. His mother, Laodike, also had a city named after her: Laodicea, on the coast of Syria. It can likewise be deduced that they were not paupers, for Seleucus was inducted into the corps of Royal Pages in his teens, and these youths were selected only from the sons of high-born Macedonians. There were myths that his father was in fact the god Apollo, who left a ring for his mother and a birthmark shaped like an anchor on his son. The likelihood of this I will leave to readers to decide.

Seleucus forged a promising career for himself in the army of Philip of Macedon. When the old king was assassinated, he served his son – Alexander the Great. In 334 BC, two years after the death of Philip of Macedon, Seleucus accompanied Alexander to war in Asia. He took several commands and fought in many battles as far east as India, and by 324 BC had garnered himself so much praise and trust from the great general that he was awarded a lofty prize.

Following Alexander's defeat of the Persian King Darius III, he decided to symbolically seal his new-found dominant alliance with the Persians with a great wedding feast. This was an unusual event because not just one couple was married. Alexander, already married to the legendary Roxana, was rumoured to have taken not one but two brides to the altar that same day. He encouraged the great men in his entourage to also marry Persian brides, and the event became known as the Suza weddings. He honoured Seleucus with a bride named Apama, the daughter of the Persian general Spitamenes – Alexander's most tenacious adversary in his Persian campaigns. The daughter of this man was a prize indeed, and Seleucus seemed pleased with Apama, demonstrated in the fact that she gave him children, and he named the fourth city of his Syrian tetrapolis after her – Apamea.

More important in demonstrating Seleucus's regard for his wife was the fact that he did not repudiate her upon Alexander's death. The other Macedonian officials who had taken wives at this ceremony swiftly divested themselves of these spouses at the first opportunity, and Apama was one of the very few who was not sent away by her husband. She remained Seleucus's wife, and when he seized power she became his queen.

It was twenty-three years after the death of Alexander that Seleucus founded Antioch on the site of Alexander's fountain and temple. Despite the method of choosing its site, the environs of Antioch were perfectly suited to hosting a prosperous and well defended city. This perhaps suggests that the site of the city was a result of prudent and strategic assessment, rather than the site of Alexander's camp, or where an eagle dropped some meat – but no textual evidence supports this.

What the sources do make clear is that Seleucus's original city was carefully planned, with or without elephant involvement. It was constructed on a grid system street plan, designed by an architect named Xenarios, which closely mirrored the design of Alexandria, the most enduring of the cities named after Alexander on the northern coast of Egypt.

The first residents of Seleucus's Antioch were a diverse melting pot of peoples, races and cultures. A significant portion were Macedonians, formerly of Seleucus's army, who were encouraged to settle in the new city. Alongside these men were the inhabitants of nearby Antigonia. Seleucus's great rival in the wars for control of Alexander's lands – after Ptolemy himself – was the other great general, Antigonus. This man had founded his own city, just seven miles from the site that would one day evolve into Antioch, and had named it after himself, planning this settlement to be the capital, not of the Seleucid Empire, but the Antigonid Empire. After crushing Antigonus at the Battle of Ipsus, and putting paid to the founder's imperial ambitions, Seleucus forced the population of Antigonia to decamp to his new city of Antioch. Alongside them, according to myth at least, were Cypriots, Cretans, Argives and more. The bulk were probably native Syrians, but there were also significant numbers of Athenians and Jewish settlers, who established their own communities within the new city. Natives and European settlers inhabited different quarters, but integrated nonetheless. A babel of different languages was chattered in the streets.

However Antioch was not the capital of Seleucus's empire during his lifetime. The city he intended as his capital and had named after himself – Seleucia – was some 650 miles east of Antioch, on the bank of the Tigris, south of Baghdad. It is not known when exactly the status of imperial capital transferred from Seleucia to Antioch, but it seemed to rise in importance during the reign of Seleucus's son, Antiochus I.

Seleucus had a good relationship with Antiochus. However, it had a strange, rivalrous undertone, both politically and romantically. For all his regard for his first wife Apama, Seleucus married again – it is likely while Apama still lived. His second marriage was also political, to the daughter of Demetrius, one of the defeated commanders at the Battle of Ipsus, a teenage girl named Stratonice. This marriage proved a bizarre one, not because it was unsuccessful – Stratonice produced a daughter for her ageing husband – but because of the unforeseen complication of Seleucus's eldest son Antiochus falling madly in love with his young and lovely stepmother.

Upon learning of this, the old king was not vengeful, but rather concerned for the well-being of his lovesick son. Eventually he yielded Stratonice to Antiochus. Antiochus was clearly delighted and his new wife gave him five children in quick succession, the first of whom was named Seleucus after her former husband and then father-in-law. Stratonice was not the only prize Seleucus Nicator gave to Antiochus I. In 292 BC, he named his son as co-ruler, giving him rule over the eastern provinces of the Seleucid Empire. In 281 BC, leaving his eastern lands in the hands of his son, Seleucus began to march west, with the aim of conquering Macedon and later Greece. No sooner had he crossed the Hellespont than he was assassinated by Ptolemy Ceraunus, son of Ptolemy I Sotus, his old enemy. Seleucus was seventy-seven at this time, and the last surviving successor of Alexander the Great.

Seleucus had ruled his empire around the time that Agathocles declared himself King of Sicily, and chased the Carthaginians back to Africa, to harry them on their own soil. He had learned from Alexander's example, and left his succession secure. Antiochus I became the next ruler.

A distinct culture emerged in Seleucid Antioch. The city had an identity even from its earliest days, and a cult of worship sprang up around the Tyche of Antioch. A Tyche is a female deity, not exclusive to Antioch, who guards the fortune of a city. Each of the four great Mediterranean capitals of the Roman Empire – Antioch, Rome, Alexandria and Constantinople – had their own distinct Tyche – but the idea preceded the diffusion of this visual currency during the Roman Empire, and the most famous representation of her was cast in bronze by the celebrated sculptor Eutychides of Sicyon in the early third century BC.

This sculpture has been lost, but was imitated many times in later Roman art. It represented a queenly woman in a draped mantle, wearing a turreted crown that resembled the walls of Antioch. In her hand she held a sheaf of wheat, to represent the fertility of the city, and at her feet were waves, indicating the importance of Antioch as a trade centre. Curiously, in those waters swam a male figure – the personification of the River Orontes, the life blood of Antioch and the surrounding region.

The rock on which she rested represents the mountains surrounding and protecting the city.

Alexandria was Antioch's nearest neighbour and closest rival among the Mediterranean capitals. In the aftermath of Alexander's demise, Alexandria became the capital of Ptolemaic Egypt, and vied with Antioch for control of the eastern Mediterranean.

At its height, the Seleucid Empire held lands stretching from Thrace to India. However, like so many empires before and since, it was destined to contract and collapse. Seleucus's descendants ruled the empire, and heirs were always close at hand, but serious enemies would emerge to both east and west, and the empire began to lose lands to the Romans, Armenians, Parthians and more. In the early second century BC, Antiochus III failed in efforts to expand still further westwards into Greece, rebuffed by Roman and Greek alliances. This marked the beginning of slow but determined decline and fall.

In 83 BC the empire was dealt a heavy blow by Tigranes the Great of Armenia, and in 63 BC, what was left of the Seleucid Empire (not much more than Antioch itself) clashed with the Roman general Pompey under the nominal reign of Antiochus XIII. Pompey had previously defeated Tigranes, and now killed Antiochus, and annexed Antioch and the surrounding lands into the ever-expanding Roman holdings, creating the Roman province of Syria, with Antioch as its capital. It was during this period of its existence that Antioch became its most magnificent.

QUEEN OF THE EAST: ROMAN ANTIOCH

> Yet I can say this of my native city – that it is the fairest
> thing in the fairest land under heaven
>
> – Libanius, *Oration XI*

The emperors of Rome saw the importance of Antioch, and soon it rose to become one of the foremost cities of the empire, and the gateway to their Asian possessions. Early in its Roman absorption, it was granted the status of 'free city' – giving it a greater status over other cities in the region, a certain amount of autonomy, and tax breaks as well. Under Roman rule the city expanded and enjoyed a commercial boom. Emperors favoured the city, and its location was of strategic importance.

This said, the transition to Roman rule was not without hiccups.

Julius Caesar confirmed Antioch's status as 'free' following his civil war with Pompey, and began a lavish construction programme in the city. This served as a clear visual representation of imperial favour and Antioch's elevated status. Caesar's assassination precipitated a crisis in Antioch as elsewhere in the empire, with the Jews of the city being persecuted and deprived of their lands and possessions, only to have them returned to them by Mark Antony on his eventual defeat of Cassius and Brutus, Caesar's assassins. Mark Antony's stay in Antioch was brief, and his departure with his army left the city vulnerable, resulting in the Parthians* besieging it in 51 BC, and the Persians managing to occupy it for nearly a year from 40–39 BC, when Mark Antony returned and freed it once again.

During the tenure of Mark Antony, Antioch's primary function became that of an imperial base in a campaign against the Parthians, and for the defence of the eastern Roman territories. The defeat of Mark Antony and the rise of Octavian marked the beginning of Augustan Antioch, and this meant a drastic administrative reorganisation of the region of Syria.

With Roman absorption, and the years of peace – the Pax Romana – that Augustus brought in came a Roman makeover. The strategic importance, renown and wealth of the city was not lost on the emperors, and if the city was to become a thriving Roman centre, a bastion of Roman prosperity and civilisation in the east, it had to look the part. Caesar had already begun this with his construction programme, bestowing on it an aqueduct, a theatre and a pantheon. Augustus and his successors sought to outdo Caesar in the scale of their benefaction. Before long a Roman colonnaded street ran the length of the city and temples sprang up everywhere, including the famously lavish revamp of the temple of Jupiter Capitolinus, complete with gilded interiors. Tiberius put the most Roman stamp of all on the city, erecting a bronze statue of the she-wolf of Rome suckling Romulus and Remus at one of the city's gates. Not only was Antioch's prestige enhanced with baths, temples, theatres, statues and the like, but the city was also geographically expanded. New neighbourhoods were built, and Tiberius's most important addition to Antioch was an encircling fortifying wall which enlarged the boundary of the city significantly from the Seleucid times. In thanks for Tiberius's many building projects to expand the glory of the city, the citizens of Antioch repaid him with a statue.

Despite being given the external appearance of an imperial capital under this succession of Roman emperors – many of whom visited the

* The Parthian Empire was a major power in ancient Iran from 247 BC to 224 AD.

city multiple times – Antioch retained its own distinct identity. Even after the wide distribution of citizenship by Caracalla, Roman Emperor from 198 to 217, the people remained Antiochenes first, and Romans second. Latin was not spoken in the winding streets of the urban centre, nor in the hinterland. Greek was the most common language in the city itself, and away from the centre, Syriac was more common. Antioch began life as a Greek city, and became – for 700 years – a Roman one, but it always existed in a Semitic landscape,* and retained vestiges of Hellenic culture at its heart. Despite the proliferation of Roman temples, the worship of the 'old gods' continued in many parts of the territory of Antioch and wider Syria. At this time, Rome's priority was not to 'Romanise' a people, to interrogate their souls and beliefs, but to establish order and force citizens to submit to Roman systems of government and extract taxes. With this in mind, they left language and religion alone – for the time being at least. Antioch's large Jewish population is not recorded as being particularly harried by the Roman rulers.

Indeed, it is in the Roman period that we know the most about Antioch. The archaeological record is most complete, as is the written history. Little architectural evidence remains from the Seleucid period, and little besides is known about life in the city except for the diversity of its inhabitants and the fact that it rose steadily to become the capital of the Seleucid Empire, displacing Seleucia – most likely in the reign of Antiochus I. It was certainly a thriving centre of Hellenic culture, and during the reigns of Seleucus's son and grandson, Antiochus I and II, and Seleucus II and Antiochus the Great, it saw a particular flourishing of arts and culture.

Roman Antioch was exquisitely described by Libanius, and the archaeological record testifies to far more. It was a wondrous place. Enjoying the same gorgeous situation as the modern city of Antakya, it was a wealthy and colonnaded Hellenic city, and far greater than Tyre. Slow-limbed Libanius describes the size of the city in laborious terms: 'If you try to walk from beginning to end, it is a hard job, and you would need the help of a carriage.' In reality, this colonnaded street that stretched from the Aleppo gate at the north of the city to the Daphne gate at the south was just two miles long, but still apparently too much for Libanius, a man who preferred to journey with his mind rather than his feet.

Little of ancient Antioch remains standing; this is due in no small part to the sequence of devastating earthquakes that befell the city, and

* Andrea De Giorgi and A. Asa Eger, *Antioch: A History*.

because the city has remained continuously inhabited rather than being abandoned, as has been the case with other great Hellenic cities such as Ephesus. This means that centuries of construction have taken place, making use of the stones of ancient sites, and building over them. The closest comparison, to which we might be able to look for a glimpse of Antioch, albeit on a more modest scale, are the ruins of Apamea, the sister city of Antioch, founded by Seleucus and named in honour of his wife Apama. Apamea's central colonnaded street survives. Crumbled yes, and also reconstructed by modern hands, but beautifully done with minimal modern additions.

We can glimpse in these ruins the grandeur of the streets of ancient Antioch, and get a sense of the great porticos which would have stood at the four gates of the city. Between the columns would have been stalls for the various vendors who made up the commercial life of the city – another element of Antioch's urban identity attested to by Libanius. The streets of Antioch bustled with trade and there were goods for every budget. Libanius paints a picture of a city of plenty, a veritable cornucopia: 'Every part teems with human beings, so it teems with goods on sale [...] exquisite delicacies vie with necessities, for in our city they cater for both purses.'

Libanius's words sound too good to be true. The archaeological record attests that the poor suffered a meagre existence in antiquity, and it is hard to imagine that Antioch was so prosperous as to be immune from that. Libanius does however claim that the city's 'proudest boast' was that it could 'care for the poor in various ways; it ensures them not merely a bare existence, but a pleasant existence'. He claims that the rich are fed from the sea, the poor are fed from the lake, but all are fed. He praises the Orontes once again for watering the fields that yield up the corn, and for the fact that the grain is easily transported to the city by the river. The city's ancient harbour was in Seleucia Pieria, 'and so ships put in from every port with the produce of the whole world, Libya, Europe, Asia, the islands and the highlands. The choicest products of everywhere are brought here.'

For all this, ancient Antioch was not a cramped and crowded thoroughfare, for at regular intervals and intersections sweeping, open plazas had been built, where citizens could happily mingle. Schoolboys with wax tablets would jostle with tradesmen and philosophers, and a hubbub, dominated by Greek but infused with snatches of Aramaic, Hebrew, Persian, Coptic and Syriac, would rise over the throng.

In ancient Antioch five bridges were built across the Orontes, all of which have collapsed and have now been replaced by modern ones – most of which are still functional following the earthquakes of February 2023. Another major feature of the urban landscape that has disappeared from modern Antakya was an urbanised island on the River Orontes. This was at first the site of the Seleucid palace, but in later Roman times was replaced by the Great Church of Constantine, known as the *Domus Aurea* – or Golden House. This church would become a fierce point of contention between the Christians of Antioch and the Emperor Julian in the fourth century.

Today, as then, paths wind their way up the mountains from the city, leading to homes built on the mountainside, commanding views of the river and city. Libanius asserts that 'everything is in harmony, like the perfectly matched colours of a painting' and he compares Mount Silpius to 'a protecting shield held high' sheltering the city both from the elements and invasion.

Ancient Antioch was certainly an opulent city. There were sumptuous temples with 'gleaming marble, coloured pillars, glistening paintings'. The hippodrome was 'big enough to satisfy the fastest of horses', and the theatre '[resounded] with contests of flute, lyre and voice and the manifold delights of the stage'; and of course there were the baths, the gloriously mosaicked remains of which are still preserved in the Hatay Archaeological Museum.

So much for the external beauty of Roman Antioch. At the same time that these gorgeous imperial buildings were evolving, something far more interesting was happening in the minds of the citizens, and starting a process that would reshape the Roman Empire: Christianity.

CRADLE OF CHRISTIANITY

In the third and fourth centuries AD Antioch underwent yet another transformation, which would become one of the defining periods in the history of the city. It became Christian. While Augustus had been busy propagating peace and beautifying the city, a baby was born in Bethlehem and the cult that would develop around him would change the face of history across both east and west. While the cult surrounding Jesus Christ, believing him to be the son of God, struggled to gain traction with the Roman populace during his lifetime, the early evangelists including St Paul were met with more success. Paul based his early church and missionary work in Antioch. Antioch is hailed as the first Christian church, and the place where – according to the Book of Acts – the followers of Christ first took the name 'Christians'. Christian tradition holds that St Peter led this early Church, and was the first bishop of Antioch – however this makes the early Church potentially sound grander than it was. The early Christians, unwelcome as they were, met in caves surrounding the city. In the aftermath of the 2023 earthquakes, families took shelter in these caves. The natural shelters in the mountains were safer than the man-made ones in the destroyed city centre. These caves have survived the centuries, weathering countless earthquakes and storms.

One of the early cave churches is still marked today. It is – apparently incorrectly – named the Cave Church of St Peter, after that famous first bishop. It is found amid the slopes of the hills that rise up from the valley of Antioch, and is well signposted today. In Late Antiquity however it would have been hard to find, outside the limits of the city and carved into the sheer cliff face. It is not a particularly deep cave, but it is well sheltered, and well hidden, which is perhaps what the early Christians were looking for. The walls are rough and mottled inside. Today, it has the remains of three naves constructed within it and an impressive white stone facade in the medieval style. Inside is a stone altar, over which a statue of St Peter was placed in 1939. In 1963, Pope Paul VI designated this cave church a place of pilgrimage. Nevertheless, its origins seem somewhat spurious.

While the cave church on the slopes of Mount Staurin is attested to in several historic documents from the nineteenth century, it is referred to as the Church of St John rather than the Church of St Peter. Beyond this, it is not mentioned at all in the accounts of travellers to and citizens of the city of Antioch before that time. Neither Byzantine nor crusader sources testify to the existence of a church in which St Peter preached, and thus this is likely to be a later fabrication, based on the tradition that early Christians did indeed meet in caves beyond the city limits out of necessity. Furthermore, crusader accounts of the city from the high Middle Ages do not rhapsodise about this shrine, which they certainly would have done had they known that St Peter's first church was close at hand. The crusaders arrived in Antioch riding a wave of religious fervour, and when the cult of relics was at its highest. While it does seem the place of worship was known and enhanced by the crusaders, if they had believed it to be the original church of St Peter, they would have mentioned it in their chronicles and glorified it. While it has certainly been a place of Christian worship for centuries, the authenticity of its Biblical origins is called into question.

That said, it is clear that it is not simply a cave that later Christians stumbled upon and made into a church. Any visitor can see that the architecture inside has a distinctly twelfth-century appearance, and the remnants of mosaics on the floor are much older – clearly Byzantine. The only medieval chronicler I have found who references this cave is William of Oldenbourg, who associates it with Paul rather than Peter.

However, the cave church is mentioned in travel writing of the eighteenth century, and in a way that implies it has been there for some time. In 1738 a travelling anthropologist name Richard Pococke observed:

> Towards the iron gate, is the church of St. John, which is hewn out of the rock, being a sort of grotto open to the west; there is no altar in it; but the Greeks, who have their service there every Sunday and holiday, bring an altar to the church, and near it they bury their dead.

There is evidence from another traveller named John Buckingham that under the Ottoman Empire it did indeed become a site of Christian worship. Out of necessity and the fact that the attempts to build a church were all foiled, the Christian community resorted to worship in this very cave. Buckingham wrote:

> The Christians have made several unsuccessful efforts to build a church for themselves here; but, though they are not wanting in wealth, and successive firmans have been obtained from Stamboul for that purpose, yet, the fanaticism of the Turks and some unfortunate fatality which they think attached to the town itself, has hitherto always obstructed its execution. They resort, therefore, to a cave on the east of the town for the performance of their religious duties.

Thus, unfortunately for the faithful, it seems unlikely that the cave marked in modern Antakya as the Church of St Peter was in fact an early and secret place of Christian worship. However it is known that during the long history of the persecution of Christians in Asia Minor and Syria, devout Christians did in fact congregate in caves and other hidden places, and this cave was clearly embellished with decorations in both the Byzantine and crusader periods, and did seem to have some connection to the early Church Fathers – though it is unclear which. Perhaps this was a sacred place – secret or not – whose exact origin has fallen out of the written record and has been blurred by the many sackings and razings of the city. What is clear at least is that it is an ancient and venerated place, associated in some way with early Christianity – if not Peter himself. The miracle of this church is that, of all the buildings I visited in February 2023, the Cave Church of St Peter was the only building that had escaped completely the ravages of the earthquakes. The stone facade was just as I had left it, gleaming in the sunlight with its star-shaped windows and arched doors. The Byzantine mosaic floor was intact, as were the vaulted brickwork arches built in the twelfth century overhead. The altar was uncracked, and the statue of St Peter still stood affixed to the wall, raising a hand to the faithful. The cave church was the first building I 'checked on' when I arrived in Antakya in February 2023, and when I entered to see everything exactly as it had been, I burst into tears. They were the first tears of many to be shed that day – and the only happy ones.

Prior to the 2023 earthquakes, the Christian community was alive and well in Antioch. The Greek Orthodox Church had approximately 4,000 worshippers, who were well integrated into the community of modern Antakya. However, the Orthodox church was completely destroyed by the earthquakes – the serene courtyard and soaring domes reduced to rubble, through which the gilded tabernacle could just be glimpsed. The ruins were hard to find amid a sea of destroyed buildings, and piles of wreckage many storeys high over which new makeshift roads had been constructed to allow for aid workers to reach residential homes.

In recent years, Antakya prided itself on being a city of tolerance, where religions live side by side. New Christian communities were founded as well. A pastor named Jerry from Michigan created a new church in Antakya, and prior to the disaster ran it out of the back room of a coffee shop. Not quite a cave, but it had a similar feeling to the surreptitious and dissident meetings of Christians. His congregation was mixed, and was reduced by Covid-19 – but still the faithful came. At the time of writing, the group was forty strong. They believed in charismatic worship and practised glossolalia (speaking in tongues) when the spirit moved them. Jerry told me that the Turkish government is strongly opposed to Christian missions and conversion. He said that within Christianity there are three types of churches: the museum keepers, the settlers and the pioneers. The pioneers are the men who are feared. Jerry's theory rings true, as Protestants in Turkey have faced a new wave of persecution in recent years.

Jerry first came to Antakya thirty-five years ago, and his four children were born and have been raised in the city. When he arrived, he tells me, there were perhaps a hundred Protestant believers in all of Turkey, but now there are perhaps 10,000, and most are converts from a Turkish Muslim background. They had only a handful of worshippers in Antakya, but he was determined to build a church, and he began in the basement of a house: 'The church is not the building; the people are the church,' he asserts. Steadily their numbers grew, going back to the nuts and bolts of Christianity. He worries each day that his church and congregation and those similar will be abolished, and leaders like him will be forced to leave Turkey. More and more, those involved with Protestant churches in Turkey have been targeted by the government and persecuted, the most famous case being that of the American pastor Andrew Burnson, who after living for decades in the country was arrested on suspicion of espionage, causing a major diplomatic incident with the USA. The Orthodox community is part of the fabric and the furniture of Antakya, and their leaders are unafraid of government interference. When questioned about this, Jerry smiles. The Orthodox Christians, he argues, are guarding and preserving tradition – like museum keepers – and their numbers are shrinking not expanding; as a result, they pose no threat.

Jerry was one of the first people I texted after being woken by the first major earthquake in my bed in Beirut. 'I have never felt such a violent shaking,' he told me. 'Our building still stands but is badly damaged. Many buildings have fallen into the streets.' They took shelter with friends outside the city, and he asked me to pray for them. He told me the church buildings were all collapsed, but the members had all survived. In the weeks following the earthquake, he and his family evacuated to Istanbul, but planned to return to Antakya in June to rebuild what they had lost.

Antioch's place in the history of early Christianity is well documented. A sizeable community of Christian converts grew here in the first century, made up of Jews and Gentiles alike. It was in Antioch that Christianity first began to gain traction as a new, Gentile religion – separate from Judaism. Most scholars agree that Matthew's Gospel was written from Antioch. It was a key early Christian centre, in which the saints Peter and Paul both spent much time, and was the site of the famous incident at Antioch – a disagreement between these two Church Fathers over whether or not Gentiles who became Christians should have to adhere to the strict laws of Moses from the Old Testament, particularly with regard to dietary rules. Antioch would serve as a base for the missionary journeys of St Paul. Christianity would make slow and steady progress, spreading from Antioch around the Mediterranean.

As Christianity spread and took hold, it melded with Roman culture to create a distinct culture of Roman Christianity, which married central tenets of Christianity and Christian worship with Roman values and administrative policies.

In the early third century, the Roman Empire was in a state of crisis, unravelling at its edges, its seams and its heartland. Both military fail-ures and economic pressures fed into this, humbling the empire that had annihilated Carthage and dominated the Mediterranean.

The Emperor Diocletian restored some balance, and attacked the Christians in the empire. The Diocletian persecutions are well docu-mented, and made a great many martyrs for the early Christians to ven-erate – most importantly in this book, Lucia of Syracuse and Perpetua of Carthage. The persecutions did not come from any great hatred of Christians from Diocletian himself, but rather from a fervent desire of his advisors to preserve the status quo, from which they benefitted. An oracle was purported to have announced that the presence of Christians in society blocked Diocletian's contact with the gods, and thus a decision was made to root them out. Punishments were meted out to those who would not make sacrifices to the gods of the polytheistic Roman faith – usually burning alive. Many men in Antioch fell victim to these purges. However, Diocletian eventually called a halt to this unproductive and bloody exercise, and just ten years after Diocletian threw the Christians to the lions, the Emperor Constantine issued the Edict of Milan,* accept-ing Christianity and legalising its practice. He formally converted, and while the empire did not suddenly shift to Christianity, by the end of the fourth century it had become the main religion. This marked the great-est ideological shift in the history of Rome. The tenets of Christianity were fundamentally at odds with the tenets of Roman paganism, and the cultural tensions that had been raised between Christians and pagans in the Roman Empire only intensified with Constantine's conversion. The Christians were legitimised, and became bolder. A religion that had once been scorned as the religion of women and slaves, because it promised salvation for the wretched, and that 'the last shall be first and the first last', suddenly became embraced by the elite of Roman society.

Julian the Apostate – a nephew of Constantine – tried to back-pedal from this wide acceptance of Christianity, but found himself ridiculed and disrespected by the people of Antioch as a result. Tolerance between Christians and pagans existed in the fourth century after the end of the persecutions, to the extent that Libanius, who wrote so proudly and lovingly of his native city, became a tutor to John Chrysostom, a Christian orator from Antioch. However, what was to become thornier

* This is not an edict, and not issued in Milan, and not issued by Constantine. It was in fact a letter written by Constantine's imperial rival Lacinius, who controlled the eastern empire, and he wrote it following a meeting with Constantine in Milan. However it has been attributed to Constantine for simplicity's sake, as it is a pivotal moment in the legislat-ive freedom in Milan.

was the relationship between the newly dominant Christian community and the ancient Jewish community, which had inhabited Antioch since the earliest days. Not only had Jews been present in Antioch since its founding (Jewish mercenary soldiers were among the early settlers) but the community expanded to all strata of society and Jews numbered among the peasant farmers of the hinterland all the way to the wealthy and educated elite of the city, during both Hellenic and Roman times.

Until February 2023, a small community of nineteen Jews remained in Antakya. For the most part they had stayed in order to preserve their synagogue, and their traditions in the historic city. They had not been driven out by any persecution, but rather there had been a great exodus to Israel in the 1950s, given the geographical proximity to the newly formed Jewish state. Since then, many of the younger generations had moved to the bigger cities of Turkey, primarily Istanbul, in order to find better opportunities for work. In the centre of Antakya, among the ruins are the now abandoned remains of what was a modest but beautiful synagogue on the main street, its entrance marked with Stars of David and tucked between two shops. The building was equipped to meet the needs of the small community of worshippers. During one of my visits to Antakya, I am introduced to a member of the community, Azra, who speaks to me in Arabic – like so many of Antioch's citizens he is fluent in both Arabic and Turkish – and tells me that his city is a tolerant place. He is friends with Christians and Alawites alike – they are one community. He is happy to show me the synagogue, and prays while I explore. It is built around a small courtyard with an orange tree, and inside the main room is wood panelled, with a lofty, white-painted ceiling from which hang crystal chandeliers. The walls are decorated with Hebrew text, and the Aron Hakodesh – the holy space facing Jerusalem in which the Torah scrolls are kept – is curtained with blue velvet, richly embroidered in gold, depicting a crown, two menorahs and a sea of six-pointed stars.

The leaders of the Jewish community of Antakya were Saul and Fortuna Cenudioglu, an elderly couple, who were killed when their home collapsed in the 6 February earthquake. The other community members recovered the Torah scrolls from the damaged synagogue and took them to safety in Istanbul. The entire community has now evacuated, marking the end of approximately 2,300 years of Jewish Antioch.

The tolerance known in recent decades has not always been the norm for the Jews of Antioch, who have suffered persecution since the rise of Christianity in the city. Their status dwindled under Christian governors: John Chrysostom, Libanius's pupil, would spread vitriol against them in an effort to prevent members of his Christian community fraternising with them, and even attending the synagogue – as many still did given the ancient links in their traditions. As the star of the Christians waxed in Antioch, the star of the Jews waned. Antioch was to become a major centre of Christian theology, which would intensify the pressure on citizens to conform and enhance the zealotry of the Christian leaders in the city.

The Christians eventually prevailed, and the Roman temples were destroyed. This changed the urban landscape of imperial cities, and Antioch was no exception. In particular, the altars of blood sacrifice were destroyed. Julian tried to reverse this but his efforts were met with little enthusiasm by the Antiochenes who accused him of 'turning the world upside down'.

Many saints and martyrs are associated with early Antioch, and while the most famous martyr was certainly Ignatius – the bishop of Antioch killed on his way to Rome – two other famous saints far exceed him in fame and popularity in Late Antiquity and in the Middle Ages. The first is St Pelagia of Antioch, known initially as Pelagia the Harlot and then as Pelagia the Hermit. Pelagia was a prostitute who had a religious awakening and did a complete 180 to become a hermit disguised as a man, living simply beyond the city limits. Her immodest decadence of bare-headedness and see-through gold clothes was well documented before her repentance and conversion. Still more famous than Pelagia, however, was St Simeon Stylites the Younger, after whom Antioch's port would come to be named. St Simeon perched himself atop a sixty-foot pillar and stayed elevated between heaven and earth for decades. Dedicated followers would bring him food and tend him in sickness, but still he lived without shelter under the blistering summers and the freezing winters of northern Syria, never wavering in his resolve. His father had been killed in an earthquake, and following this – still a young child – Simeon climbed the pillar on the outskirts of Antioch to live out his days thinking about God. His youth is attested to as he writes that he lost his baby teeth atop that pillar. Eventually, as an ordained priest, he would dispense communion from his perch to ladder-bearing disciples. After his death, he was buried on the outskirts of Antioch, and a monastery constructed around the site of his pillar. The remains of this monastery can still be visited between Antakya and Samandağ, today commanding views not only of the hills but of wind turbines. Local women sell jars of honey nearby.

As Antioch rose as a Christian centre it also became a centre for dissent. In the fourth and fifth centuries the theological school of

Antioch reached its zenith. It began to preach that the two natures of Jesus, human and divine, were distinct and separate. This was known as Dyophysite doctrine, and stood in direct contrast to the Monophysite theology taught in Alexandria. The result of this conflict was the expulsion of the theological school of Antioch; its dedicated followers relocated to Edessa – modern Urfa in Turkey – and eventually to Nisibius.

As has been seen, at the same time as these ecclesiastical battles were raging, Antioch had transitioned firmly into the Late Antique period. Rome had fallen, and the Empire had moved eastwards, now headquartered in Constantinople and known to later generations as the Byzantine Empire.

BYZANTINE ANTIOCH:
A TIME OF CATASTROPHE AND THE CITY OF GOD

Antioch thrived under Byzantine rule, despite occasional periods of difficulty, until the sixth century, when the city would go through a series of catastrophes during which it was repeatedly destroyed.

One of the greatest emperors of the Byzantine period was Justinian, who we have already encountered in our discussions of Ravenna. He had the misfortune to preside over Antioch at a time when it would be hit by a series of expensive and devastating calamities that would do much to undo the centuries of splendour and progress it had been enjoying – even with its religious disputes and persecutions.

Antioch's history has been undone as much by nature as by war. Just as in February 2023, severe earthquakes struck the antique and medieval city, the greatest being that of 526, which occurred a year before Justinian came to power, and which levelled most of the central city and equally destroyed the neighbouring settlements. Just as Samandağ was hard hit in 2023, the port of Seleucia and the religious 'garden suburb' of Daphne were brought down by the earthquakes of 526. The main tremor struck in mid-May, and killed at some estimates around 250,000 people. Antioch sits on a junction where three tectonic plates meet; nevertheless, earthquakes of this destructive scale are not common. The number of casualties was particularly high as the populace had gathered in the city to celebrate Ascension Day, and the damage so extensive not only due to the earthquake itself but also due to the fires that raged for days afterwards. One of the most notable casualties was Bishop Euphrasius of Antioch, whose house collapsed into a wine factory below. His body was found in a cauldron of burning pitch beneath his house.

John Malalas, a native of Antioch, recorded the devastation. His account is eerily similar to contemporary news reporting about the human tragedy and scale of devastation caused by the earthquakes in February 2023:

> those caught in the earth beneath the buildings were incinerated and sparks of fire appeared out of the air and burned anyone they struck like lightning. The surface of the earth boiled and foundations of buildings were struck by thunderbolts thrown up by the earthquakes and were burned to ashes by fire... flames consumed even those in the earth who were crying out. As a result Antioch became desolate... no holy chapel nor monastery nor any other holy place remained which had not been torn apart. Everything had been utterly destroyed.

Just as modern newspapers continued to report miraculous rescues over a week after the February 2023 earthquakes, Malalas writes in wonder of women who had delivered newborns under the rubble being saved long after such rescues were thought impossible. The earthquake of 526 was followed by significant aftershocks, and by another devastating quake in November 528. Approximately 5,000 further citizens died, and much of the reconstruction work that had been begun with the aid of 3,000 pounds of gold from the imperial coffers was undone. The new Emperor Justinian once again sent relief funds and exempted the city from taxes for three years. It was also at this time that Antioch officially changed its name to Theopolis – the city of God – presumably to try to curry favour with the Lord who was so furious with them as to send these manifold disasters.

That said, Antioch's – or Theopolis's – luck was not about to change just yet.

Rebuilding was not the only item on the city's agenda, which now also had the Persians to contend with. Antioch served as a military HQ for the eastern branch of the Byzantine Empire, and was central to communication and strategy. In 528, the year of the second great earthquake, fighting broke out once again – ending the truce between Byzantium and Persia. It was following a raid in 529, which was not successfully repelled by the then general Hypatius, that Justinian's legendary general Belisarius was instated as *Magister Militum* and dispatched to Antioch to defend the city and see off the Persians.

War continued, heavily impacting the city. In one moving episode, a group of captured Antiochenes, held hostage by the Persians, sent a message to their people, begging them to raise their ransoms. The city turned out its pockets, and coins and items of value were collected in the churches of the city. The target was reached, the gold sent and the captives freed.

Nevertheless, despite the best efforts of the citizens of Antioch, its soldiers and General Belisarius, the Persian threat could not be repelled, and the Persians succeeded in capturing and sacking the city in AD 540. It is one of the most vivid and best documented events in the life cycle of the ancient city – even if it proved its undoing. Justinian's prolific but snide court historian Procopius, who wrote so damningly of the early life of Theodora, immortalised the events in his chronicle.

The year 540 was highly significant for Justinian. Not only was this the year that Belisarius, Justinian's most successful general, succeeded in driving the Goths from Ravenna, but it was the year the Persians sacked Antioch, the third largest city of the empire. It had not yet recovered from the devastating earthquake of 526.

The Byzantine army had extensive borders to guard. When Belisarius left Antioch, he was not replaced as *Magister Militum* of the east. The 'eternal peace' was in place, and perhaps Justinian optimistically thought that it would hold, despite the fact that he had left some of the wealthiest cities of his empire relatively unguarded and open to plundering. When Khusraw, the great Persian leader, descended upon Antioch, leaving a trail of sacked cities in his wake, Belisarius was nowhere to be seen, and was in fact encamped outside the gates of Ravenna, gunning for the victory that would see him immortalised in gleaming tesserae amid the gold eternity of San Vitale's apse. What that mosaic depicting the triumphant and resplendent imperial entourage does not reflect is that in the same year that Byzantine forces recaptured Ravenna, they lost Antioch, in an ignominious and shocking defeat that would see the city almost totally razed and its population forcibly deported.

The defence of the city was in the hands of a commander named Bouzes, who had little choice but to hang back and watch as the monumental Persian host marched across the lands he had been tasked to defend. Doubtless he sent word to the emperor asking for assistance, and Justinian dispatched his cousin Germanus with several hundred men to take control of the defence of Antioch.

Germanus, however, was pessimistic about the odds of success if the Persian army did besiege the city. He inspected the walls, and concluded that in areas they were too easily assailable. He tried instead to bribe Khusraw to turn away from Antioch, but he was unsuccessful. Germanus also abandoned the city, and withdrew to Cilicia.

In June, the Persians arrived outside the city walls. Citizens began to flee, converting what valuable possessions they could into gold. When Khusraw's army surrounded the city, they intentionally left one gate unblockaded from which the cowardly could flee. Some of the first to leave were the imperial troops. They smelled defeat, and did not fancy making martyrs of themselves for a hopeless cause. With the professional soldiers gone, the only men left to mount the defence were the two teams of blues and greens – the overzealous rival factions who had originated as something similar to modern football hooligans, except they were fans of chariot racing. These men, passionate as they might have been, were no match for the Persian war host.

The sacking of a city is never a pleasant thing, and has already been described in this book. The bloodshed does not need reiterating, but it is worth saying that the Persian assault on Antioch was brutal and relentless. The population was largely spared once the city had capitulated, but the city itself was symbolically destroyed. Khusraw attempted to do to Byzantine Antioch something akin to what the Romans had done to Punic Carthage. Anything lootable was looted, anything valuable was stripped, and what was left of the city was demolished and burned. Khusraw, demonstrating the flair for dramatics which was evident throughout his reign, re-enacted the progress of conquerors of old, who washed their weapons in the sea. He passed on to Seleucia Pieria and swam in the Mediterranean, ostensibly basking in his triumph in the summer sun of Syria, and washing off the filth of war.

Justinian's reputation in the east was in tatters. He paid off Khusraw, agreeing to pay him 5,000 pounds of gold, and 500 a year thereafter, in exchange for leaving Byzantine territory. Antioch was lost – reduced to rubble – because Justinian and Belisarius had been focused on western reconquest. An estimated thirty thousand citizens of Antioch were taken prisoner, and marched into Persia. Khusraw settled them at a new city, crudely named 'Better-than-Antioch'. Nevertheless, Justinian did rebuild Antioch, and even if his efforts could not quite restore the city to its former glory, he did construct new baths, theatres and churches.

The Persian sack of Antioch did not spell the end of the city's misfortunes, conclusive as it seemed to have been. In fact, it would prove to be the least of Justinian's problems. Plague was about to ravage the Byzantine Empire, and Antioch and its displaced citizens would be no exception. The first outbreak was recorded at Pelusiem, near Suez in Egypt.

Procopius described the plague as a threat to all mankind. This is, of course, an exaggeration. The Justinianic plague largely affected the

Byzantine Empire and wider Mediterranean region rather than the entire world, and it troubled different regions at different times. While there is evidence of Justinianic plague further afield, and it is clear the disease did circulate widely and possibly touch nearly every corner of the globe, this was over several centuries, and while it was the scourge of the Byzantine Empire in the sixth century, it did not rage everywhere.

The main symptoms described by contemporary authors – Procopius and the Antiochene chronicler who observed the plague in Antioch itself, Evagrius Scholasticus – were a severe and sudden fever, and also buboes, swellings in the groin and armpit. After that it depended on the person: some became demented and delirious, some comatose, some stayed sound of mind, some died slowly, some died quickly, some recovered. Needless to say, panic surrounded this disease. John of Ephesus recorded going to bed each night, frightened he might not wake up in the morning. Procopius said the initial outbreak lasted around four months, and that five to ten thousand people a day were dying; John of Ephesus says even higher, and if the claims are true than half the population died. But of course, record keeping for an event of this scale was hard, and so this may have been an exaggeration. However, the archaeological evidence testifies to massive loss of life. Plague pits – emergency mass graves – have been discovered containing *Yersinia pestis* – the plague bacterium – from the sixth century, and the disease caused by this bacterium does indeed have a 50 per cent mortality rate or higher, which makes Procopius's claims about the scale of the loss of life credible.

It's unclear where the outbreak started. It comes onto Procopius's radar in Egypt, near the modern Suez Canal, but other sources suggest it came up various other routes, from Abyssinia or Yemen, among others. But the plague may have been circulating in other regions for hundreds of years before it devastated the Mediterranean and reached Antioch.

The plague did not die out quickly. It struck Antioch three times. Evagrius was a boy when he first started writing about it and it became a fact of life. He wrote that it had prevailed over 'the whole world' for 'fifty-two years'.

There was no pattern to how or when the disease would strike, or what age group it would attack. There was some evidence of immunity: the households which were unaffected one year were invariably the ones to suffer the next. Two years before he wrote his account, Evagrius lost his daughter and grandson in Antioch: 'At the commencement of this calamity, I was seized with what were termed "buboes", while still a schoolboy, and lost by its recurrence at different times, several of my children, my wife, and many of my kin.'

Even following these disasters Justinian was determined to rebuild the city of Antioch, indicating that at least some of the population survived the various misfortunes or were able to return. Procopius asserts that Justinian rebuilt the city to even greater heights than it had stood before, but the archaeological record and other written sources fail to corroborate this. Procopius, with one notable exception – the scandalous *Secret History* – was effusive to the point of being inaccurate in his praise of his sponsor – and in this respect he misrepresented Justinian's achievements. That said, some of his explanations of Justinian's improvements to the fortifications do seem to be accurate. In addition to rebuilding homes and internal infrastructure, Justinian thoroughly rebuilt the enclosing walls. He rerouted the Orontes to better serve the city – a move which contributed to the disappearance of the island – and built over it a great gate in the hinterland behind the city, on the slopes of Mount Silpius, with sluice gates to allow the passage of the Parmenius stream (a seasonal affluent of the Orontes) beneath.

Today, this is the most magnificent of the ruins still standing from Justinian's time. Keen travellers must climb over the hills behind the Cave Church of St Peter and follow a dry riverbed, before scrambling up steep and unmarked mountain paths. When I decided to follow this route, nothing prepared me for the experience of rounding the corner and beholding the mighty section of the Byzantine wall, known as the Iron Gate of Antioch. Monumental, touchable, climbable, the Iron Gate is the most impressive monument of the ancient city, standing as tangible, stone testament to Antioch's venerable past. In a rare blessing, this building has survived the 2023 earthquakes, and still stands guarding the ancient road to Aleppo.

It alone of all that is left calls to mind the splendid history, the epic battles and the intrigue that undid the city of Antioch. Earthquakes have not levelled it, and modern urbanisation has not superseded it. It stands twenty metres high, and the river does not rush beneath it, but rather trickles. Its edges are jagged where the walls around the gate itself have collapsed, and new piles of powdered rubble where looser stones were shaken free in February 2023 pool at its base. It straddles the river between two mountains, with craggy, shrub-strewn slopes rising on either side, crested by the remains of the walls and ancient arches high above. A few metres from the gate, just a little further up the slopes, are traces of the walls that once connected to it, and encircled the Byzantine and medieval city. It is possible to climb onto the wall and sit in the arched opening where Byzantine soldiers might once have kept watch. After visiting the cave church in February 2023, I hiked to the gate with a lump in my throat. I had seen the devastation in the modern city and was prepared for the Iron Gate to have disintegrated too. Relief washed over me when I saw it still standing, protecting the pass between the mountains. I sat down with Adnan, a local resident and owner of Barron, the vicious Kangal hound that guards the mountain paths, to drink a beer to celebrate the survival of the gate. Adnan too was relieved; he has known the Iron Gate his whole life, and visits it often to sit in silence and reflect.

Justinian's reconstruction of the city – along with this mighty gate – gave Antioch a new lease of life, but did not render it impenetrable to assault. The city would see a succession of emperors, and for another eighty years would stand strong as a Byzantine possession, but it would eventually fall once again.

It was under the Emperor Heraclius that Antioch was lost, first to the Sassanid Persians, and then to the Rashidun Caliphate as the Arab conquests of the seventh century swept across the Middle East. It was in response to these conquests that Heraclius would foster the idea of Christian Holy War, and galvanise his empire with a mighty propaganda campaign not just to retake cities like Antioch, but to reclaim Jerusalem which had also fallen.

In 611 Sassanid Persians under Khusraw II captured and occupied Antioch, and while several battles were fought to reclaim it, Heraclius was ultimately unsuccessful until Khusraw's son sought to make peace with him, and as such evacuated many of the cities his father had taken over the course of the Byzantine–Sassanid wars.

What Heraclius did not expect was that in less than a decade he would lose this famous city again, and this time would not live to see it reclaimed. In 634 the Arab conquests swept across Palestine and Syria and cities fell like dominoes under the might of the armies of the Rashidun Caliphate. Heraclius made Antioch the nerve centre of his defence initiative, but abandoned it when he realised resisting the invaders was futile following their decisive victory at the Battle of Yarmuk. As the cities of Syria fell, citizens were given the option either to leave and go to Byzantine territory, or remain and pay high taxes for their freedoms. In 638 the Rashiduns took Antioch with little resistance, and some but not all of the inhabitants left.

The Caliphate held Antioch for three centuries, and contrary to common perception this period was not one of unmitigated decline for the city. While Antioch was not given capital status in the Rashidun

Caliphate, it was a still a valuable city, usefully situated with much of the Byzantine defences remaining. The city did not decline, but it did transform.* Churches were converted to mosques, but given the relative brevity of the Rashidun interval the fundamental character of the city did not change. The Byzantine Empire would eventually win back the city through the efforts of the army of Nicophorus II Phocas in AD 969. In AD 1084 however it would change hands again, this time taken by the Seljuk Turks of the Sultanate of Rum in a second round of Islamic expansion. The Seljuks did little to change the face of Antioch, short of converting the churches to mosques and so forth. That said, they did not hold the city for long.

CRUSADER ANTIOCH: A FRONTIER PRINCIPALITY

William of Tyre – the archbishop of Tyre who served as court historian to King Amalric of Jerusalem and wrote the crusader chronicle *A History of Deeds Done Beyond the Sea* – is clear on the importance attributed to the city of Antioch in the Middle Ages. He names the city as certainly third and potentially even second after Rome in its importance. One of the foremost historians of the Middle Ages, William did however make some mistakes in his account of the early history of Antioch, ascribing its foundation to Antiochus, rather than Seleucus, and mixing it up with the ancient city of Reblata, but beyond these errors his writing is sound, based on first-hand observations. His lengthy descriptions of the city, its walls and the Iron Gate demonstrate that the fortifications built by Justinian still held strong in the medieval period, encircling the city and climbing the mountain heights, with defensive towers at regular intervals, leading to the citadel itself.

Medieval Antioch was still an awe-inspiring place. It had tumbled from its Seleucid and Roman splendour, but it was still a city of opulence and renown that made the travelling Europeans of the First Crusade catch their breath. Its architecture would have blended Syrian, Greek and Islamic styles, and the food and culture would have blended these traditions too. The natural beauty of the valley in which it is situated, and the majesty of the Orontes, was unchanged then as now, and Justinian's walls – still so impressive today – were complete and fortified when the crusaders arrived. William of Tyre rhapsodised that the city

* Andrea De Giorgi and A. Asa Eger, *Antioch: A History.*

had never been conquered; this is not quite true, but that was the impact its fortifications had on the mind: it was the unconquerable city.

In the minds of medieval writers, Antioch stood akin to Troy. And the chronicles describing Antioch and the medieval sieges are littered with references to Homeric and Virgilian epic. This is in no small part due to the epic and extended nature of the crusader siege of Antioch, which lasted from 20 October 1097 to 28 June 1098.

In 1097, when the armies of the First Crusade arrived before them, the walls of Antioch encircled an area of at least three and a half square miles. These were the walls built under Justinian, although of course they had undergone restoration in the five centuries since the emperor erected them. There were 400 towers at rough intervals throughout the defences; the remains of a handful of these still stand today, as indeed do fragments of the medieval citadel, although these were depleted somewhat by the 2023 earthquakes.*

The Seljuk ruler of the city at this time was Yaghi-Siyan, who had been given control following the capture of the city from the Byzantines in 1086. When the armies of the Franks became visible from the parapets, the city was gripped by fear. The horde of Christians was immense, and the Antiochenes were glad of their high walls. Yaghi-Siyan knew that the key to Antioch's capture was always sedition rather than military failure, so in addition to stockpiling food and resources, his first act in defence of the city was to expel the native Christian population. To do this, he set them the task of cleaning the trenches that surrounded the city walls, which kept them busy until nightfall. When they arrived back at the city gates expecting to be let in to return to the safety of their homes for rest and a hot meal, they were denied entry. Homeless and without provisions or possessions, they were left to fend for themselves in the darkness. It seems the women and children were permitted to remain within the city, and the Muslim chronicler Ibn Al-Athir testifies that Yaghi-Siyan placed them under his personal protection. This is, of course, a biased account. The Christian sources tell a different story, with the patriarch of Antioch being imprisoned, and – in a gesture designed to incense the crusaders – the Cathedral of St Paul turned into a stable for Yaghi-Siyan's horses. To add insult to injury, at various points during the ensuing siege, Yaghi-Siyan had the captured patriarch – John

---

* The existence of this mountaintop citadel is attested to, and played a major role in the defence of the city since the sixth century. However the remains that stand today are largely Latin in character, suggesting that extensive renovation took place during the crusader period.

the Oxite – hung upside down from the walls of the city, and burned his feet with hot irons to taunt the Latin Christians below and show them what the people of Antioch thought of their crusade.

Somewhat more practically, in addition to persecuting the Christian residents of his city, Yaghi-Siyan sent emissaries to the lords of the surrounding Islamic territories, requesting aid against the Franks. So serious was this mission, and also the threat of the Franks, that he sent his own sons as messengers. Ridwan of Aleppo – his nearest neighbour – ignored his pleas, but Duqaq of Damascus pledged aid, and began to muster a relief force. Ridwan's reluctance should not be surprising. Politics in the region were tense. Duqaq and Ridwan were brothers but vicious rivals nonetheless, competing for control of Antioch, and Yaghi-Siyan was well known for playing the brothers against each other and vacillating in allegiance between the two.

The crusaders meanwhile fixated on the city of Antioch, and the army would not move towards Jerusalem without first capturing the impregnable city. This was not for religious reasons, despite Antioch's important Christian heritage, but rather due to its strategic importance – they would never be able to settle in Jerusalem if Antioch remained a threat. No doubt aware of the scale of what they were undertaking, all the leaders of the crusade swore a solemn oath not to abandon their siege. Winter was coming, and if progress was slow the temptation to desert would be high. Stephen of Blois – a French lord who would indeed desert – was sceptical from the start. In a letter to his wife he described the city as 'fortified with incredible strength and almost impregnable' – not the words of a man optimistic about Antioch's capture.

The attacking force was led by the European lords Godfrey of Bouillon, Raymond of Toulouse, Bohemond of Taranto, his nephew Tancred, the papal legate Adhemar of Le Puy and a Byzantine general there to provide local advice and keep an eye on the crusaders – Tatikios.

How was it that this tenacious horde of Christians from western and southern Europe came to find themselves encamped at the foot of Antioch's splendid walls, settling in for what would be one of the most gruelling and testing sieges of the Middle Ages?

As has been seen, the Seljuk Turks wrested the city from Byzantine control in 1084. The loss of Antioch to the Muslims to some extent precipitated the inception of the crusading movement. The Byzantine Emperor Alexios Komnenos, a wiry man with flashing eyes and streaks of red in his long dark hair, incensed by the territorial gains the encroaching Muslims were making at the expense of his empire, sent one of the most fateful letters in history. He wrote to Robert the Count of Flanders, but the letter was also read by Pope Urban II. Alexios urged his readers to call Europe to arms, to regain the Christian territory lost to Muslim expansion. He wrote emotively of the slaughter and abuses eastern Christians were suffering at the hands of Muslim oppressors, and begged his fellow Christians to rise to the challenge and ride to his aid, for the sake of their shared faith. He described the desecration of the holy places, and the slaughter of pilgrims. Urban II called for a crusade at the Council of Clermont, and after rallying their forces many of the great magnates of medieval Europe set off for the east. The siege of Antioch would be their most testing challenge of all.

The siege began, after lengthy preparations, on 20 October 1097. It was clear to the crusaders that they could not form a complete blockade of the city. Logistically, this would have been impossible even for an army of their size, as there were five kilometres of defensive wall to patrol, and six gates. Instead of blockading, the crusaders focused their attack on the north-west section of the city walls, stationing troops outside the St Paul Gate, the Dog Gate and the Duke's Gate. They ignored the inaccessible Iron Gate, and the two southern gates: the Bridge Gate and the Gate of St George.

The unmanned gates meant the Seljuks of Antioch could come and go from the city as they pleased, both to bring in supplies and to attack the crusaders. They shot arrows into their camps from the heights of Mount Silpius, and launched daring raids, harrying them with arrows shot from horseback. The crusaders were also attacked by support troops sent from the fortress of Harim east of Antioch. They rebuffed these attacks, and ultimately they did not represent a serious threat, but nevertheless they were a continual irritant.

Via the Orontes and the port of St Simeon, the crusaders had access to the Mediterranean, which would prove vital. It was the source of letters from home, but also more crucially of supplies and new recruits. In November, ships arrived from Genoa laden with soldiers and, importantly, engineers and craftsmen skilled in building the apparatus of siege warfare. The result of this was a makeshift fortress erected near St Paul's Gate, which offered some protection to the armies encamped there. The crusaders' next step was to neutralise the threat offered by Harim. Bohemond of Taranto, an Italian Norman and one of the leaders of the crusade, was chosen to deal with the problem. He laid an ambush for the soldiers and deftly annihilated the army of Harim.

As the siege developed, the tactics on both sides took a turn for the nasty, with the crusaders beheading prisoners in front of the walls of Antioch, and the Seljuks responding in kind by catapulting the heads of executed Christians over the walls into the crusader camps. These acts, while seeming wantonly brutal to modern readers, were standard fare in medieval siege warfare. What would truly catch the crusaders out would be hunger, and cold.

The harsh Syrian winter was the most testing obstacle the crusaders would encounter, and was the best hope for the Seljuks repelling their foe. William of Tyre paints a grim picture of conditions in the Christian camps before the walls of Antioch that winter:

> the famine grew [...] in addition, the pavilions and tents in the camp rotted. Thus many who still had food perished because they could not endure the rigorous cold without protection. Floods of water fell in torrents, so that both food and garments moulded and there was not a dry place where pilgrims might lay their heads.

He goes on to relate that, as a result of these gruelling conditions, 'pestilence' broke out in the camp, and many more perished of the disease. So high were the fatalities that there was no room to bury the dead or conduct funerals. Godfrey of Bouillon himself, one of the great leaders, fell sick around Christmas.

Christmas in the camp was lean, and on 28 December Bohemond of Taranto took 20,000 men away from the camp to forage for food. They could not sit and wait. Yaghi-Siyan exploited this opportunity, knowing that the crusader army was depleted and struggling with low morale. He attacked, but Count Raymond of Toulouse rebuffed his ambush, and pushed him back, but not without deaths on both sides. Meanwhile, the foraging party was about to stumble across more than wild berries. Duqaq of Damascus's relief force was approaching the city, and Bohemond's foraging party was unwittingly marching right towards it.

The two forces clashed in the village of Albara, south of Antioch, which today lies in ruins in the north of modern Syria. The battle was inconclusive, with Duqaq driven back, but the crusaders lost most of the food they had gathered and were forced to return to the siege at Antioch with much less than they had promised. One in seven men was now dying of starvation. With the famine worsening, and the siege no closer to completion, many men – including leaders such as Peter the Hermit – began to desert. In February, the crusaders' Byzantine advisor Tatikios did the same.

It seems that over the winter months, Yaghi-Siyan had managed to mend his bridges with his neighbour Ridwan of Aleppo, who agreed at last to send aid to Antioch. Perhaps Ridwan had accepted that the crusaders were not planning on going anywhere, and that if Antioch were captured by Christians it would be a major threat to his rule in Aleppo and the surrounding territories. He succeeded in taking Harim, and prepared to advance on the crusaders. Bohemond of Taranto however mustered what was left of the crusader cavalry – now only around seven hundred mounted knights (many of the horses had either starved or been eaten) – and pre-empted his attack. They clashed several times and Ridwan was eventually driven out of Harim and back to Aleppo – for the time being at least.

The siege continued through the spring, with much intrigue and many skirmishes. At least the advent of spring had brought more food for the crusaders, and those that had remained must have at least had the comfort that the worst was behind them. In May 1098 word arrived in the Christian camps of another army making its way towards them. This army was led by an emir as yet unknown to the crusaders – but whom they knew by formidable reputation – Kerbogha, Lord of Mosul. He had joined forces with Ridwan of Aleppo and Duqaq of Damascus, forcing the brothers into an unlikely co-operation, and had also swelled the ranks with troops from Persia. It was an impressive force. The crusaders, for their part, were heavily depleted. Of the 100,000 men that had set out from Europe, only 30,000 remained before the walls of Antioch. When Kerbogha's armies arrived, the crusaders would be caught between the walls of Antioch and the far larger Muslim force coming to the city's aid. They would be trapped. The situation was desperate.

The fate of the First Crusade and medieval Antioch was changed forever by the unlikely friendship struck up between an Italian nobleman and an obscure Armenian soldier, known only to history as Firuz.

Throughout May, learning of Kerbogha's approach, the crusaders were on the brink of panic, casting around for a strategy to extricate themselves from their impending doom. One of the leaders, more daring than most, made an offer to his comrades. He told them he had a plan to break through the defences, and to take the city. He asked his fellow commanders whether if his plan were successful, and he saved all their skins, they would agree to give him control of the city of Antioch. The other leaders were less than enthused at this suggestion. Firstly, they doubted that even this prince – Bohemond of Taranto – could make good on such a claim, and secondly, if he did, to give him control of the city would be to break their oaths to the Byzantine Emperor Alexius: in exchange for his help they had promised to restore to him any conquered Byzantine territory once they recaptured it, including the city of Antioch. However, circumstances forced their hands, and they begrudgingly struck the deal with Bohemond.

Bohemond was the second son of the self-made Italian warlord Robert Guiscard, who had already fostered a reputation for carving principalities out for himself from among lands traditionally controlled by the Byzantine Empire. It was Bohemond's uncle, William Iron Arm of Hauteville, half-brother of Robert Guiscard – who single-handedly struck off the head of the Emir of Syracuse during the Norman siege of the city.

Thanks to the somewhat rapturous descriptions left by the Byzantine chronicler Princess Anna Komnene, we have a good record of Bohemond's heroic appearance. He was well above average height, with light blond hair and flashing blue eyes that betrayed the indomitable spirit he shared with his father. His skin was paler than you would expect of a southern Italian today, a salute to his Scandinavian heritage, but suffused with colour. He was well made, conforming to the ideal standards of beauty of his day. We know this because his appearance so impressed Anna Komnene that despite her hatred for him she described his physique and colouring in minute detail. She borrowed language from Homer to describe her father's marauding adversary, characterising him as a classical Greek anti-hero.

Anna's description did not stop at his beauty and took pains to emphasise his objectionable spirit, and the horrid sound of his laughter. Not a prince charming, then, but a real, flawed human being filled with ambition, an expedient approach to morality and a gratingly raucous laugh.

Perhaps it is due to Anna's simultaneously lavish and scathing description that Bohemond stands as the most famous of all the leaders of the First Crusade, who reaped all the glory and yet never set foot in Jerusalem. He was hailed as a hero in Europe during his lifetime, and given a French princess to wed. He was a daredevil, handsome and silver-tongued, motivated for the crusade less by religious zeal and Christian ardour than by personal greed. He sought fame, wealth, land and adventure. His father's marriage to the formidable Sichelgaita and the birth of their son saw Bohemond's standing in the world disintegrate, as his father made the son from his new marriage his heir. All of a sudden the restless Bohemond had to fight tooth and nail for his inheritance, waging war against his brother, resulting in the creation of the Principality of Taranto. However Taranto was, even in medieval times, an obscure and lacklustre region to rule. Bohemond's sights were set higher, and when the call from the east came, he saw an unparalleled opportunity to rewrite his destiny and lift himself from obscurity. For all his moral shortcomings he played a decisive part in the success of the First Crusade, and his impact was most felt at this crucial moment during the siege of Antioch.

In the early hours of 3 June 1098, a single ladder appeared against the tower of the Two Sisters on the western side of the city. One by one, a small band of Italian Christians furtively scaled the walls. They were met at the summit by the Armenian Firuz, who had struck a bargain with Bohemond. He would give the crusaders access to the city through the tower he commanded, probably in exchange for gold and power. As the crusaders ascended the battlements, adrenalin was high.

Firuz wavered in his resolve when he saw the number of soldiers who had joined him. Nervously he exclaimed at how few they were, beginning to doubt the wisdom of their enterprise. He asked where the invincible Bohemond was, and was relieved when the prince appeared moments later. His courage renewed, he sprang into action alongside them, stealing along the city's battlements, quietly killing the sentries, including his own brother.

Crusader control of Antioch began with fratricide and betrayal.

Bohemond's assault force overpowered the guards on the battlements then swiftly opened the gates of the city to allow the other crusaders to pour in. The sleeping city was taken completely by surprise, unprepared for such an attack. What ensued was mayhem and slaughter. No citizen was spared on account of age, gender or religion: women and children were hacked to death in the streets, and Christians, Jews and Muslims fell alongside one another. When the crusader bloodlust was sated, the streets of Antioch were piled high with corpses, and even the crusaders could scarcely stand the stench of their crimes.

Still, the capture of the city was far from complete. In the heat of the carnage that followed the crusader entry, the Seljuk leaders of Antioch attempted to flee to safety. Yaghi-Siyan fled the city – most probably out of the Iron Gate and into the hills in the direction of Aleppo. His son, Shams ad-Daulah, instead made for the citadel of the city, and barricaded himself within with his garrison. When the crusaders attempted to storm the citadel, their efforts failed. Yaghi-Siyan's attempt to escape was less successful than his son's. He was thrown from his horse on the uneven terrain outside the city wall and left for dead by his panicked comrades. An opportunistic butcher found his body and promptly beheaded it, offering the grisly trophy to the victorious Franks.

Bohemond's plan to take Antioch was successful, and earned him a reputation as an exceptionally cunning and resourceful leader. Yet while the crusaders seized control of the city of Antioch, they failed in their assault of the citadel, which still stands 500 metres above the city on the summit of Mount Silpius. For the moment, this did not stop them enjoying their captive city, and Adhemar of Le Puy immediately released John the Oxite, the imprisoned patriarch, and reinstated him. Some reports say he was so injured by his ordeal that he was unable to stand, but in any case this did not prevent him resuming religious duties. While the crusaders made themselves at home in captive Antioch, Yaghi-Siyan's forces – now commanded by his son – looked down from above. Just as the city walls were virtually impregnable, so too was the citadel, which relied on its high positioning and inaccessibility as its greatest defence. It was almost a separate entity from the city itself, and there they would have to endure a second siege should it come. They watched, and they waited.

The show was only just beginning and Yaghi-Siyan's supporters did not have to wait long for the second act. The crusader besiegers were about to become the besieged, and Shams and what was left of the army had a prime view of all that would unfold, perched as they were high on the mountainside.

Kerbogha's much-anticipated army arrived after just two days. The streets of Antioch were still wet with the blood of its slaughtered inhabitants and the crusaders still recovering from their assault. Kerbogha arrived and set about besieging the crusaders, who – although they had captured Antioch – still had next to no food, and stores within the city had also run low during the many months of war. They were not in a good position, caught between the hostile resisters in the citadel, and Kerbogha's army of fresh troops eager for vengeance beyond the city walls.

However, hope might not have been lost, if not for the faintheartedness of Stephen of Blois. Following his desertion on the eve of Bohemond's victory, he began to make his way back to Constantinople. On the road, he met the Emperor Alexios, who was bringing an army to assist the crusaders. Not yet knowing his comrades had succeeded in capturing the city, Stephen persuaded Alexios that the cause was lost, and convinced him to turn back.

Kerbogha immediately targeted one of the siege fortifications erected by the crusaders near the Bridge Gate. This protected the Bridge Gate and indeed the crusaders' only open supply line with the port of St Simeon. The Franks, realising they could not hold this fort, burned it so that Kerbogha's men could not benefit from it, and withdrew into the walls of the city. In besieging Antioch, Kerbogha had a significant advantage that the crusaders had not had during their assault, and that was the co-operation of the commander of the citadel. Shams was eager for Kerbogha's aid and was willing to defer to his command.

The citadel had been built to withstand attacks from both outside the city and from within it, and was fortified on all sides. Today the remains of the once formidable defences still look out over the city of Antioch. The ruins of vaulted medieval halls and stout defensive towers crown Mount Silpius, and can be reached by the committed hiker, who can follow the line cut by the remains of the Byzantine walls over the surrounding hilltops. The citadel not only provided a defensive position where Shams could wait for assistance, but also gave him access to the vast stretch of the walls which connected directly to the citadel, and a path to the city. Thus, with Shams in the citadel and controlling large sections of the walls, the crusaders' grip on Antioch was significantly compromised, and they would never be able to withstand a long siege by Kerbogha.

Kerbogha and Shams coordinated their efforts, and launched a simultaneous attack on the Franks within Antioch. Shams sent his men out of the citadel and down the slope to the city below, while Kerbogha's men assaulted the walls. The fighting was relentless and lasted for days, as Kerbogha had no shortage of men to send into the battle. The crusaders had time neither to eat nor drink, and there were many near misses, with even Bohemond himself being struck down and needing to be rescued from death by his comrades. Despite this however, the crusaders managed to weather the storm, and Kerbogha's attack was unsuccessful against the manic determination of the Frankish crusaders – cornered men fight hard.

Kerbogha turned to another strategy: starvation. He managed to blockade the crusaders' routes out of the city, and thus shut them up in a city that had already endured an eight-month siege and had few supplies left. Before long, the crusaders were in the grip of a second period of starvation more severe than even that of the winter, with many soldiers resorting to eating stewed weeds and their own leather shoes.

The morale of the crusaders reached rock bottom. It was at this time of sheer desperation, when hope seemed a distant memory, and soldiers were secretly deserting over the walls left, right and centre, that a miracle struck. Or at least it seemed that way to the more credulous crusaders. A peasant from Provence in southern France, named Peter Bartholomew, approached the leaders of the crusade to tell them that he had had a vision. St Andrew, accompanied by Christ himself, in glorious raiment, had appeared to him, and revealed the place where the relic of the Holy Lance was buried, within Antioch itself. This was the lance that had pierced Christ's side as he hung on the cross, and thus was tipped with the Saviour's blood. It was a relic of almost unparalleled significance to Christianity, particularly during the Middle Ages when the cult of relics was at its zenith.

Peter Bartholomew told the generals that he had been instructed by his saintly guide to lead them to the place where the lance was buried, so that it might be recovered, and used to bring victory to the Franks against their infidel enemies. Sceptical as the lords might have been, four days later they did indeed command excavations in the spot where Peter asserted they would find the relic, and lo and behold, a fragment of metal was unearthed in that very spot – beneath the floor of the Church of St Peter.

This discovery was met with jubilation by the exhausted crusaders, who took it as a sign of God's favour returned to them. They did not however, as some sources claim, immediately ride this tidal wave of confidence to charge out of the gates and annihilate their enemy. No, rather they waited two weeks, as the leaders debated their best chance of survival. By then it must have been woefully apparent that no Byzantine troops would be coming to their aid, and that they would either have to talk or fight their way out of there. Peter the Hermit, a silver-tongued preacher from southern France, was sent to negotiate with Kerbogha, presumably to ask for terms of surrender. Kerbogha, it seems, rebuffed his entreaties, and it was then that the crusaders decided to make a final stand – exhausted and completely outnumbered as they were.

As dawn broke on 28 June 1098, the crusaders assembled what was left of their armies by the Bridge Gate. This battle would either signify their salvation, or their destruction. Rationing ceased, and horses and men ate through all the remaining food stores in the city. Every ounce of strength was needed, and the men knew that they would either succeed in driving away Kerbogha's armies, and therefore gain access to the surrounding pasture lands, or they would not be returning to the city – and why leave it fully stocked for their conquerors? This battle would mean all or nothing for the crusaders; it would be a fight to the death.

Bohemond was elected temporary military commander, and the night before, the men prepared for battle through spiritual cleansing: prayer, repentance, processions and fasting. That said, most of the men had been in a near perpetual state of fasting for some months. As the crusaders assembled to march out of the Bridge Gate, the priests and non-combatants lined the battlements to bless them and wish them well. Only 200 rideable horses remained in the crusader army, so their cavalry unit – usually their secret weapon – was greatly depleted. Nevertheless, every remaining soldier was battle hardened. The weak had died, the cowardly had fled, and those who no longer believed in the cause had deserted. Every man there was fully committed to the cause and was fighting for his very survival. Despite being significantly smaller in number than Kerbogha's force, it was arguably more terrible. It was certainly more motivated. Desperation makes hard men.

The crusaders' best chance of success was to fight sections of Kerbogha's army sequentially. Kerbogha made this easy for them. The crusaders, when they had besieged Antioch, had opted against blockading every gate as they did not want to spread their army over such a large area, thus rendering it vulnerable. Kerbogha had done the opposite. He had completed the blockade but spread his army thinly, and while he had indeed forced the crusaders out, he had essentially created a burning battering ram, a tight unit of fierce soldiers who would hammer his army, one piece at a time.

When the crusaders marched out, and rebuffed the small part of Kerbogha's force stationed by the Bridge Gate, the counter-strike by the rest of the army was disorganised and panicked. This proved Kerbogha's undoing. The crusader army numbered no more than 20,000, and only 200 mounted knights, whereas Kerbogha's force was nearly double that number, and far fresher. Against the odds, the crusaders held their ground, even when surrounded on all sides, and scattered their opponents. They chased them through their own camp and drove them into a disordered retreat.

Victorious and ecstatic, the crusaders plundered Kerbogha's camp, falling ravenous upon the food supplies and seizing anything of value. One chronicler in Bohemond's army recorded: 'the enemy left his pavilions, with gold and silver and many furnishings, as well as sheep, oxen, horses, mules, camels and asses, corn, wine, flour and many other things of which we were badly in need'.

Of course, Shams had been looking on first with interest and then with horror from the citadel as the battle unfolded below him. He had not attempted to retake the city while the crusaders were attacking Kerbogha, presumably as he did not wish to jeopardise his position which had kept him alive until that point. Now however, he saw that to resist further was hopeless. No aid would come, and the crusaders had proven their might – he prepared to surrender. For nine months the crusaders had endured unimaginable hardships besieging Antioch; finally, it was theirs. This was the beginning of a new chapter in Antioch's story, and the beginning of a new period of Christian rule. The city would fall to Egyptian Mamluks in 1268, and never again would it come under Christian control.

For now, for the first time since its Seljuk conquest, the city would have a Christian ruler, and it was not Alexios Komnenos. Instead, it was Bohemond of Taranto, soon to be named Prince of Antioch – the man who had masterminded the entire scheme and brought Antioch under Frankish control, as it would remain in for 170 years.

Bohemond announced his intention to stay in Antioch, to rule the principality he had won with his resourcefulness and military skill. His ambition was not well received by his fellow crusaders who were there to get to Jerusalem. The idea of a man peeling off from the crusade to enjoy the fruits of his labour was somewhat jarring to them – especially when it was clearly done out of self-interest rather than as a tactical sacrifice to help the cause. Furthermore, Bohemond had revealed himself to be the most capable general of the army and the crusade was far from over. It would not be good for the morale of the other men for Bohemond stay behind in Antioch while the rest of the army marched into the unknown.

But the crusaders weren't marching anywhere just yet. Summer was heating up, and they had no intention of marching through Syria and Palestine under the scorching sun of July and August, especially without local guides or knowledge of where they would find water. They bedded down in Antioch and its environs – beautifully appointed and well supplied with water as they were – and they set about cleaning the city of the filth of war, restoring the damaged defences and reconsecrating the Christian churches and holy places, starting with St Peter's Basilica, where the Holy Lance had been discovered. Despite Latin capture, the Church in Antioch remained Greek, for the time being at least. Antioch's future was uncertain. While Bohemond would succeed in achieving the status of prince and control of the city, back in Constantinople Alexios was fuming. The crusaders had promised to restore Antioch to him upon its capture, but that said, Alexios had failed to aid them in their darkest hour and it was Bohemond's cunning that saved the day. Bohemond for one believed that that rendered Alexios's claim null and void.

While these disputes simmered, another trial struck Antioch. Disease broke out, and swept through those within the city like wildfire. Adhemar, the spiritual leader of the crusaders, died. After much bitterness and discord, Bohemond was left in control of Antioch.

The Antioch captured by Bohemond was a wealthy city. Ralph of Caen reports a line of columns of Parian marble, crystalline paving, buildings and furnishings made of fragrant Lebanese cedar wood, marble from the Atlas Mountains, glassware from Tyre, Cypriot gold, and English iron. Once the threat of violence was over, the returning population was diverse. Sixteen years after the crusader conquest a Latin chronicler recorded hearing the babel of many languages competing in the streets: French and Italian dialects, Greek, Syriac, Armenian, Arabic and more rang through the narrow alleys of crusader Antioch. The Norman Italians Bohemond and Tancred were practised in ruling over heterogeneous cities – since the Norman conquest of Sicily, Norman noblemen had had hands-on experience governing a diverse and majority-Islamic populations.

Despite this, tensions simmered in the new-won principality. Twenty years after crusader conquest, the non-Latin population would rebel against the Latin rulers and it would take the intervention of the King of Jerusalem to quell the unrest. Similarly, there was conflict between the pre-existing Greek Church hierarchy in the city, and the new Latin Catholic Church. When Bohemond was captured in 1100, and Tancred stepped in as regent, he threw all the high-ranking Greek clergy out of the city.

Under Bohemond's rule, Antioch would grow to become an extensive and important crusader state in the Latin East, one of the four distinct territories which made up the region known in the Middle Ages as Outremer, or the land beyond the sea. It was a region defined by its otherness and distance from Europe, and during the crusader period, from 1098 to 1268, Antioch revived still more of her former glory and became a bustling and wealthy metropolis. Its politics and fate were defined largely by the personalities of Bohemond's family and descendants, as it was ruled first by him, and then by his nephew Tancred while Bohemond was in disgrace.

The enmity sown between Bohemond and Emperor Alexios when the former took control of Antioch would never abate, and would in fact prove to be Bohemond's undoing. What he had in military skill and personal gumption he lacked in diplomacy, and even the former skills would let him down later in life. In the meantime however, the Prince of Antioch was a hero. The siege of Antioch was celebrated by Europeans as a second Trojan War, a seemingly unending siege filled with bravery, suffering, intrigue and eventual victory for the Europeans, and – if the more zealous of the sources were to be believed – sprinkled with a healthy dose of divine intervention (some chroniclers swore they saw an angelic host riding with them in the final battle against Kerbogha). Bohemond was celebrated far and wide.

As the other crusaders marched on to Jerusalem, Bohemond would solidify his holdings and look to his own prospects. When the First Crusade succeeded and captured Jerusalem after a far shorter and less interesting siege, Bohemond's reputation as a military icon and medieval heartthrob was cemented. He had gone out to Outremer as a disinherited second son of a man who divided opinion, and came back with the title Prince of Antioch. He was offered a French princess, Constance, as a wife by the King of France – the ultimate status symbol. His nephew Tancred also received a royal French bride – the Lady Cecile.

Despite Bohemond's popularity in Europe, his career was on the decline. Likely with an inflated sense of self-importance and confidence in his own invincibility, he decided to challenge his old rival, Emperor Alexios Komnenos, directly. He should have known that the Prince of Antioch was no match for the Emperor of Constantinople. Overplaying his hand badly, Bohemond attacked Alexios at Dyrrhachium in modern-day Albania. He was swiftly and decisively defeated, and forced to make a negotiated surrender. Under the terms of the Treaty of Devol, Bohemond surrendered Antioch to become a vassal state of Alexios, and agreed to take pay from the emperor, making him less than an ally or even a vassal – an employee in fact. It was abject humiliation, and while Bohemond managed to return to Italy, to see his wife and the baby son she had given birth to (dutifully christened Bohemond II), he never returned to the shores of St Simeon and his beloved principality. A broken man, he died six months after the Treaty of Devol, and is buried in a simple mausoleum in Canossa – a small town in northern Italy.

Tancred would rule the principality after his uncle's death, and when his own time came a year later, Antioch passed first through a period of regency and then went to Bohemond's son once he came of age.

Crucially, the Treaty of Devol, aside from disgracing Bohemond and potentially hurrying his death, had little or no effect on the status of Antioch. Had Bohemond lived, the treaty might have been binding, but his successor Tancred argued that it applied to Bohemond only, and he had never agreed to the terms. He refused to honour the treaty, and the Byzantine Empire was too preoccupied with other things to come and besiege the city. However, Alexios and his successors were disgruntled in the extreme, and would not let the matter rest until 1158, when they finally managed to bring a Prince of Antioch to heel.

The Principality of Antioch was a frontier state. On a recent research

ANTIOCH   237

trip, I idly put 'kalesi' (Turkish for castle) into Google Maps and was
overwhelmed by the results. Dozens of pins fanned out across the
hinterland of Hatay, showing the vast array of documented crusader
and Byzantine fortresses abandoned in the hills surrounding Antioch.
They stand as testament to the region's status and strategic importance, guarding the Belen Pass and the gateway to Syria and the Holy
Land. It was an area constantly contested, fought over by countless
armies. In the twelfth and thirteenth centuries it was harried by the
lords of Aleppo, Damascus, Mosul and more, as well as by Armenian
neighbours, Byzantines and eventually by the Mamluks and Mongols.
It would be Egyptian Mamluks who eventually sacked the city.

The man who succeeded Tancred as regent for Bohemond II was
Roger of Salerno, a fellow Italian-Norman cousin of Tancred. He ruled
well, until he along with most of Antioch's fighting elite were uncere-
moniously wiped out at a battle with Ilghazi of Mardin, the Artuqid
ruler of Aleppo, on 28 June 1119. This conflict was so bloody that it
became known as the Battle of the Field of Blood. The battle turned
Antioch into a city of widows and orphans overnight and forced the
King of Jerusalem to ride to the city and defend it, installing a garrison
and bringing it under his control. The king formally ended his regency
in 1126 when Bohemond II finally arrived in Outremer to claim his
inheritance, and Princess Alice of Jerusalem as his bride. Against the
odds, it was Alice who would have a far greater influence on events in
Antioch than her long-anticipated husband.

Bohemond II fathered one daughter with Alice, a princess named
Constance, before he too was killed in battle. The princes of Antioch
had the highest fatality rate of any rulers in the Latin East, standing as
further evidence of the instability of the principality and potentially also
the risk-taking of its Norman rulers. Bohemond II was beheaded in a
skirmish in Cilicia, and his head – as beautiful and golden in life as his
father's – was struck off and sent to the Caliph of Baghdad as a grisly
trophy. It was then that Alice became a major player in the politics of the
principality. She and her daughter Constance are two of the most often
overlooked and important figures in the medieval history of Antioch.
Alice made three attempts to take control of the city, and was foiled each
time, in increasingly spectacular fashion.

Her daughter would have more long-term impact. The constant peril
and short lifespan of male rulers in the Principality of Antioch created
an environment in which noblewomen could wield real power, playing
the leading roles usually reserved for men.

Constance was married at the age of eight to a French lord, Raymond of Poitiers. Raymond had tricked Alice into believing he wished to marry her and for them to rule Antioch together, but instead he kidnapped her daughter and married the child-bride. The marriage was functional at least: when Constance was older she gave her husband children – including the future Bohemond III of Antioch – and Raymond proved a stable and zealous ruler for the frontier principality.

In 1144 the neighbouring crusader territory of Edessa fell to the Atabeg Zengi and sparked the Second Crusade. This brought King Louis of France, and his wife the redoubtable Eleanor of Aquitaine, to Antioch. Hailing from southern France, Eleanor was a niece of Raymond of Poitiers.

Louis and Eleanor had faced a gruelling march to Antioch, and fell with relief through the gates of the storied city. Antioch was at the height of its crusader prosperity, despite friction with the ruler of Aleppo. The city was luxurious and exotic to the eyes of the road-weary Europeans, and they stayed for a month. It seems Eleanor was charmed not only by the beauty of the city, but by the charisma of her uncle, and the two spent a great deal of time closeted together, to the extent that Louis soon became viciously jealous – either because he believed Raymond was helping her plot to divorce him, or because he believed they were conducting a full-blown affair. The truth will never be known, but the rumours spread like wildfire and have echoed down the ages.

Whatever happened in the alleged love triangle, Louis refused to support Raymond in attacking Aleppo, and rode on to Jerusalem to launch an ill-fated attack on Damascus. Shortly after this, Raymond was killed along with much of the army of Antioch at the Battle of Inab. This left Constance in charge of the city, and – crucially – single. Meanwhile, Zengi's son Nur ad-Din pressed his advantage and retook several key fortresses in the region, and – in the style of Seleucus Nicator and Khusraw – rode to the sea and bathed in the Mediterranean to celebrate his victory.

Constance fended off husbands for four years, until eventually she shocked the entire court of Antioch and Jerusalem by having a love affair and hasty marriage with a French mercenary knight, Reynald de Chatillon. In marrying Constance, Reynald became the new Prince of Antioch – and would lead a tumultuous period for the crusader city. He began with the brutal persecution of the city's Patriarch Aimery, when he refused to give Reynald access to Church gold.

Constantinople still wrangled for control of Antioch, but with obedience not forthcoming from the new ruler, the Emperor Manuel offered to pay Reynald for his assistance against the Armenians of Cilicia.

Reynald defeated the Armenians at Alexandretta in 1155 and ceded the lands conquered, however the reward Manuel had promised never materialised. Enraged, Reynald decided to teach the emperor a lesson and allied with the Armenian king to raid the Byzantine-held island of Cyprus. His attack was thorough and ferocious.

It was now Manuel's turn to exact vengeance. In an unprecedented demonstration of the power of the Byzantine Empire, Manuel marched his armies across Anatolia and into Antiochene territory. This was the first time since the foundation of the states of Outremer that the Byzantine Empire had mobilised their troops on this scale and invaded Frankish territory. Manuel chased out the Armenian lords of Cilicia, and held court at the town of Mamistra. He summoned Reynald to attend him there, and the chastened prince obeyed. There, he was ritually humiliated and paid spectacular homage to Manuel. He surrendered the city too; at last, Byzantium had won Antioch. Reynald would remain Prince of Antioch, but now as a vassal of the Emperor Manuel. On 12 April 1159, Manuel made a triumphal entry to Antioch on horseback in Roman imperial style; behind him on foot walked a presumably dejected King of Jerusalem and the Prince of Antioch.

Antioch's independence was over for the moment. From that point onwards, the principality was beset by a host of challenges. Reynald would be captured in 1161 and spend thirteen years in captivity. Constance and the patriarch would rule on behalf of her son Bohemond III until he came of age in 1163. He would rule Antioch until 1201.

During the reign of Bohemond III, the Kingdom of Jerusalem would fall to Saladin, sending shock waves across Outremer, Byzantium and Europe. Rising rapidly from his relatively humble origins, Saladin exploited the power vacuum left by the death of Nur ad-Din, coupled with disunity and religious fervour and a tactical marriage, to unify the territories of Aleppo, Damascus and Egypt under his control. With this combined force, the coastal cities of the Holy Land fell like dominoes to him – culminating in the infamous Battle of Hattin and his successful conquest of Jerusalem on 2 October 1187. Antioch was one of the last crusader strongholds to hold out against Saladin. Saladin did in fact besiege Antioch the following year, following the capture of the essential fortresses surrounding the city, including Bagras. However, the siege wore his army out and he agreed surrender terms: he left Bohemond III in charge of the city itself, and the port of St Simeon on the Mediterranean, in exchange for the release of all Muslim prisoners. And he kept the surrounding land. The crusader principality was on its knees.

This started a chain of misfortune and disaster that would eventually wipe the Christian principality off the map. Vicious internal wars of succession would destabilise and destroy what was left of crusader Antioch. Following Bohemond III's death in 1201, not only did Antioch face an Islamic threat, but also a Christian threat from the Armenians of Cilicia.

King Levon of Cilicia had a vested interest in who would succeed Bohemond III – Bohemond's eldest son had died, leaving a grandson who was a nephew of Levon. Levon recognised this child as heir to Cilicia, and wanted him to succeed to the throne of Antioch. However, Bohemond III had another surviving son, Bohemond IV, who was adult and already Lord of Tripoli, and wished to take over what was left of his father's principality. This plunged Antioch, under the newly recognised Bohemond IV, into a twenty-year war with Levon.

Bohemond IV finally managed to retake and solidify his control of Antioch in 1219, and ruled until his death in 1233. The succession of Bohemond IV was smooth, with his son Baldwin V taking control and ruling until 1254, and he in turn was succeeded by his son Baldwin VI. The tension with the Armenian Kingdom of Cilicia had continued, but was eventually neutralised when Baldwin VI married the Princess Sibylla of Armenia, the daughter of the then Armenian king, Hethoum.

Somewhat unsurprisingly, Antioch was not left to enjoy a period of peace in the aftermath of the succession wars. Two powerful forces were rallying against it, threatening attack from the east and the south. The Mongols and the Mamluks were mustering their armies, and setting their sights on Antioch.

The Mongol Empire was, during this period, still in a phase of relentless expansion. Since the death in 1227 of the great Genghis Khan – the most famous of all Mongol leaders, and the man who assembled the greatest empire the world had ever seen – the throne had passed to his sons and grandsons, and had seen a gradual splitting up of the empire, beginning in 1259. One of the semi-autonomous khanates to emerge from this fragmentation was the Ilkhanate, ruled by Genghis's grandson Hulagu. No longer directly under the official rule of the Great Khan – who at this time was Kublai Khan – Hulagu made his own decisions, and employed his own strategies. Like his grandfather before him, Hulagu employed a policy of submission rather than destruction where he could – wishing to absorb cities and peoples into his empire rather than annihilating them. However, when a people refused to submit, they were massacred and their cities burnt. His lands in 1256 included Iraq, Iran, the Transcaucasus region and large swathes of eastern Asia Minor and western Turkestan. Lying just west of these lands, Antioch and indeed Syria was a natural area in which the Ilkhanate would wish to expand. In 1258 the Ilkhanate Mongol forces under Hulagu captured and sacked Baghdad in modern-day Iraq. The scale of the slaughter and destruction appalled all who witnessed it, and struck terror into the hearts of the Levantine cities that were presumably next on Hulagu's list. Centuries of learning was lost as books were burned, and tens of thousands of citizens were slaughtered. The Mongols, superstitious about the spilling of royal blood on the earth, rolled the Abbasid Caliph of Baghdad in a carpet and trampled him to death by riding their horses over him. The Christians of the Latin East celebrated this great Mongol victory, with some even comparing Hulagu and his wife Dokuz Khatun to Constantine and Helena, as instruments of God's will on earth.

When Bohemond VI of Antioch heard that they were coming for his city, he favoured a course of diplomacy and submission. His father-in-law, King Hethoum of Armenia, had been observing the movements of the Mongols in the region for some time – in 1243 they had won a major victory over a Seljuk army, and he had predicted that before long they would be back for more. With this in mind Hethoum had dispatched friendly diplomatic embassies to the Mongol court as early as 1248. During this time he had indicated willingness to become a Mongol vassal. While certainly not Christian themselves, the Mongols were not badly disposed towards Christianity, and Hethoum for one certainly regarded the menacing khanate as a potential ally for eastern Christians against the various Muslim factions.

Furthermore, the alternative reaction of the Christians in the east was pure panic in the face of the advancing enemy: there was no way the depleted and diminished Christian states of Asia Minor and Outremer could stand up to the Mongol armies. Thus, Armenian Cilicia submitted, and so too did Antioch; and thus Antioch became a vassal state of the Mongol Empire in 1260, and came under their protection, while Bohemond VI stayed in nominal control. The army of Antioch assisted the Mongol capture of Aleppo and Damascus. As a reward, Bohemond VI found territories previously lost to the Muslims unexpectedly returned to him, and he co-operated with the remaining knights of the military orders in the east to re-expand his territory south and east.

However, while the protection of the Mongols may have appeared highly desirable to Bohemond VI at a time when his other option seemed to be the total annihilation of his city and being trampled to death, it was to have far-reaching consequences for the principality. Unlike Antioch and the Armenians, the Mamluks of Egypt did not choose to submit to the Mongols and instead pitched themselves against them in open war. They would check Mongol progress in the Levant, and drive them from Syria.

MAMLUKS: THE DESTRUCTION OF THE ANCIENT CITY

The Mamluks who now ruled in Egypt were descendants of the nomads from tribal cultures in the steppes. Kidnapped and enslaved, they were trained to become soldiers and formed an elite branch of the Egyptian military. In 1250 this enslaved soldier class rose up and successfully overthrew its leaders to establish the Mamluk Sultanate. The triumphant Mamluks consolidated their holdings in North Africa, then swept up through Palestine to meet the Mongols in pitched battle.

Just eight months after their successful conquest of Aleppo, the Mongol invading army clashed with the armies of the Mamluks of Egypt in September 1260, in Ain Jalut in southern Galilee, about seventy miles north of Jerusalem. The Mamluks were commanded by the rival sultans Qutuz and Baibars. This would be the first major blow to Mongol expansion in sixty years, and the first time their westward expansion was definitively checked. The Mamluks won the day and were rewarded with a conquered Syria laid at their feet. With the Mongols retreating, the Mamluks only had to advance to gather up their newly subjugated territories. They snapped up Aleppo and Damascus with minimal resistance, destroyed Cilicia and the Armenian capital at Sis, and in 1268, Baibars besieged Antioch as well.

Bohemond VI was absent at this time – ruling from the County of Tripoli, so Antioch was under the command of his constable Simon Mansel. The garrison was insufficient to man the extensive walls, and the city was taken after a short and ineffectual struggle. Baibars was not kind to the inhabitants of Antioch. His secretary wrote a letter to Bohemond VI, chiding him for his absence at such a crucial moment and detailing the destruction that had been visited upon his ancestral city:

> Death came among the besieged from all sides and by all roads: we killed all that thou hadst appointed to guard the city or defend its approaches. If thou hadst seen thy knights trampled under the feet of the horses, thy provinces given up to pillage, thy riches distributed by measures full, the wives of thy subjects put to public sale; if thou hadst seen the pulpits and crosses overturned, the leaves of the Gospel

torn and cast to the winds, the sepulchres of thy patriarchs profaned; if thou hadst seen thy enemies, the Mussulmans trampling upon the tabernacle, and immolating in the sanctuary, monk, priest and deacon; in short, if thou hadst seen thy palaces given up to the flames, the dead devoured by the fire of this world, the Church of St Paul and that of St Peter completely and entirely destroyed, certes, thou wouldst have cried out 'Would to Heaven that I were become dust!'

Antioch had always been one of the richest cities of the crusader states, and its wealth was now frenziedly divided among the Mamluk armies. Most of the population was slaughtered – indeed the gates of the city were shut to prevent the escape of civilians – and those who did escape the carnage were immediately enslaved. The Mamluks did not stop with Antioch, and in 1291 expelled the crusaders from Acre, and finally from Ruad (Arwad) in 1303, thus driving the Franks completely from the Holy Land.

In the crusader period, Antioch had been key to the control of the region, as it had been in the Roman and Seleucid period. It was a meeting point between Asia Minor, Mesopotamia and Syria. However, following the Mongol conquests, and the Mamluk sack of St Simeon, Antioch had ceased to be a major trading centre. Therefore, following their destruction and plundering of the city, the Mamluks were not motivated to rebuild the capital to its former glory. In the popular imagination, it was this sack that marked the end of Antioch's significance as a Mediterranean capital. The popular imagination is not wrong: this was the beginning of Antioch's descent into obscurity; however it was not the end of the city. It was not forgotten nor left to languish and decay after this sacking, thorough as it might have been. The city would recover, as it had recovered countless times before, and became an important commercial and religious hub.

The Mamluks would hold Antioch until the Ottoman conquest of Syria in 1516, in which the Sultan Selim the Grim and the Mamluk Sultan Qansuh-al-Ghawri clashed in the Dabik Plain. It would form a sub province, a dependency of the greater Province of Aleppo. They did not leave the city to fall into decline during this time. This is evidenced by the beautiful hammams, remarkably still functioning in Antakya until February 2023, two of which dated from the Mamluk period. The city was important enough, and home to important enough inhabitants, to prompt the construction of these monumental bathhouses as well as mosques in Antakya. The madrasa of the Habib al-Najjar mosque bears an inscription referencing Baibars, thus suggesting it was built in the years following the Mamluk conquest of the city. The Ulu mosque also dates from Baibars' rule. Cindi hammam was built by Baibars, and has remained in continuous use until the earthquakes of 2023. It was a family-run business, and was popular with locals. Until 2023, it was still open, as were the three other hammams of Antakya. The Sakka hammam and Bayseri hammam were both also built under Mamluk rule.

On my second trip to Antakya, I visited Yeni hammam. I was told about it by a Turkish girl I met, but it is hard to find. Unlisted on Google Maps, I had to muster my best Turkish and Arabic to find directions to the pretty street of pastel-painted houses in the old city, just next to the Habib'i Neccar mosque. The locals knew where to point me, after all, it had been there for over 500 years.

'Yeni hammam' translates as 'new bath'. Built in the Ottoman period, it was considerably newer than some of Antakya's other bathhouses. The architecture was lofty and monumental. Built before electricity, in an environment where candles would be ineffective and windows too invasive (privacy was essential), daylight was necessary but complicated. Windows allowed for prying eyes, so the walls were made high and the domes steep and sweeping. These domed ceilings were perforated with light wells, circular and star shaped, that allowed trickles of Anatolian sunlight into the hall, filtered by the steam.

In the entrance hall, which also served as an accounting area, tea salon and changing room, a circular skylight hovered over the centre of the arched and vaulted room.

Even then, while fully functional, Yeni hammam was not in good shape. Plaster crumbled, paint peeled, pieces of stone and unidentified debris clustered at the foot of the walls. The place was clean, but crumbling. Hammam culture itself seems to be heading in a similar direction. Since hot water came into people's homes, the functionality of the hammams' remit has been in decline. When telephones, technology and social media emerged, the social function declined as well. During my visit to Yeni hammam, there was a greenish tint spreading over many of the walls, giving the whole place a slightly subterranean atmosphere, like entering a cathedral long lost to the sea, and the passage of time.

Privacy is in short supply in Turkish baths, and women entering Yeni hammam for a bath were obliged to strip off in front of the fully clothed receptionist. I did the same. Then I was ushered into the warm room, the first in a series of chambers kept at different temperatures and humidities, to begin the ritual purification.

Inside the stone hammam chamber other women had spread their foutas on the central slab of marble, and lay languidly outstretched on them, breathing in the steam-filled air in an echoing silence. One woman, with more foresight than the rest of us, had brought a flask of tea. The women were of all ages, shapes and sizes. I copied them, laying out my foutas, and gingerly arranging myself on it. Lying on my back, I stared up at the domed ceiling, the only light source the concentric rings of small round and star-shaped channels that perforated it and allowed daylight to trickle through.

Domes are shapes that appeal to people of all faiths and of none; they encourage contemplation, with no edges for thoughts to snag on. Hammams across the Middle East have their domed roofs in common. Most were traditionally built alongside mosques, and follow the pattern of this religious architecture designed to inspire reverence and elevate the mind. Baths were also places where differences were stripped away, and people of different religions and social classes mixed. The outer trappings of religion and status could be removed, and people were equalised. Lying on the hot square of marble in Yeni hammam that day, I felt connected not only to the women around me, but to the centuries of bathers who came before me to this place – when Antakya was still called Antioch, and it was traditional clothes rather than American denim hanging in the entrance hall.

Previously, visits to the hammam were essential for hygiene purposes and socialising. For women in particular, they represented safe, female-only spaces which women could visit freely and unsupervised to wash and gossip. It was also the place where marriages were brokered. Mothers would come to inspect the bodies and 'natural beauty' of prospective daughters-in-law, who at all other times might be veiled. The hammam is still part of the wedding ritual in modern days, but thankfully now it is more of a celebration/bachelorette party setting rather than a cattle market.

I was woken from the trance into which I had slipped by the arrival of a bridal party. Women, some with babies, flooded into the steam chamber, shattering the calm, and bringing with them food, music and effervescent joy. Thirty strong, they danced in sodden slips and towels, beating drums and singing in the tepid chamber of the hammam, before piling into the steam room to be thoroughly scrubbed down and anointed by the attendant, an older woman with a no-nonsense demeanour named Inje. Gentle but firm in her approach, she soon had dark ribbons of dead skin spooling from the skin of her customers.

As Inje worked, aunts washed their nieces' hair and sisters scrubbed each other's backs, all amid a cacophony of happy chatter. Soon it was my turn, and Inje pushed other women out of the way to make a bigger space for us for my scrubbing. A girl called Nurgul pulled me over to a corner, and told me to sit tight while her aunt did my hair. As she kneaded in the shampoo, I thought my head would come off, but Nurgul laughed and said it was part of the experience.

In the cooling room, picnic rugs were laid out on the central marble slab and regional food alongside Pepsi, Fanta and cake was happily shared. One of the women, who visited the hammam frequently, told me it was designed by Mimar Sinan, the favourite architect of Suleiman the Magnificent. I look up at the sweeping domes above us, and I believe her. Conducting research later, this is hard to verify, as even the dating of the original structure of Yeni hammam is hard to pin down. Nevertheless, it is pleasing to think that the crumbling hammam that catered to women in the back streets of Antakya may have been sketched by the same hand as the great Suleiman Mosque of Istanbul.

Whatever the origins of Yeni hammam, it is certainly true that in the early modern period Antioch was enriched with Islamic architecture that combines both pre-Ottoman and Ottoman styles, often making dating difficult. Among these hybrid structures is the mosque of Habib'i Neccar. Just around the corner from Yeni hammam, stood one of the most prominent monuments in modern Antakya, which housed the remains of this Islamic martyr. A particularly curious case, Habib the carpenter was persuaded by the Christian apostles John, Jude and Peter to join them in preaching the Gospel to the citizens of Antioch, but was stoned to death.

A key fact of Islam often misunderstood or simply unknown to Western Christians is that Muslims do in fact recognise Jesus as the Messiah, and as an important prophet – but they do not believe in his divinity or that he was a son of God. They also believe he was the forerunner of the Prophet Muhammad, and foretold his coming. In this way, Habib'i, the carpenter who preached Jesus's teaching and was stoned to death for it, is also a martyr to Islam. Until 2023, this mosque was one of the central monuments of modern-day Antakya; the original structure that Baibars reconsecrated as a mosque and expanded on his conquest of Antioch no longer stood. Earthquakes laid this building low, and it was rebuilt in the Ottoman period. Similarly, the Ottoman structure was largely destroyed by the earthquakes of February 2023. Both Yeni hammam and the mosque collapsed. The pretty pink building opposite Yeni hammam fell onto it and crushed it. When I went looking for the remains of the hammam in the ruined streets of Antakya, I thought I was lost and must have my location wrong – until I realised the rubble on which I stood was, in fact, all that was left of the hammam. Likewise, the dome of Habib'i Neccar Mosque fell, leaving a shell of the building and the decorative yellow plaster work exposed. The walls of the historic courtyard still stood, filled with heaps of fallen stones. The minaret snapped, and lay across one of the walls, the crescent hanging by a thread of metal, dangling in the street below: a poignant symbol of the broken city.

INTO THE EMPIRE: OTTOMAN ANTIOCH

Antioch fell into Ottoman hands, along with much of Syria and Egypt, in 1517 following Selim I's campaign against a possible Mamluk–Safavid alliance.

The Ottomans divided Syria into three separate provinces, centred on Aleppo, Damascus and Tripoli. Antioch was not a provincial capital, but was demoted to the rank of *kaza* – or district – in the sphere of influence of the Aleppo Vilayet.

During this time the population remained small compared to previous centuries, only approximately six thousand people in 1536, but this figure rose to nearer seven thousand by 1584, which demonstrates the efforts the Ottomans made to improve the city. At this time, the vast majority of the city's inhabitants were Muslim, although it is likely that small minorities of Jews and Christians lived on who are not recorded in official documents.

The Ottomans improved the economy of Antioch in the wake of the devastation brought by the Mamluks. Antioch began to be famed for its textiles, known for its exports of fine cottons and silks. As peace was gradually restored to the region under Ottoman rule, the economy once again began to benefit from Antioch's position on the pilgrimage route to Jerusalem.

But this would not last. While the Ottomans took a laissez-faire approach to government in the region, relying mostly on local governors, in the seventeenth and eighteenth centuries the empire and the government in Antioch came under significant pressures. Wars with rival empires including the Hapsburgs and the Safavids, as well as drought, disrupted supply chains and provisioning in the empire, causing unrest and crime to rise dramatically in the region.

Following several failed attempts to deal with these issues, resulting in the decentralisation of government, several noble or Ayan families came to take control of the cities – with only nominal deference to larger authority figures. This autocratic rule was resented by the people, not least because it went hand in hand with a period of conscription and increased taxation.

In the nineteenth century the provinces of the Ottoman Empire were falling into disarray. Security was dwindling fast, which prompted attempts to recentralise the government of Antakya and oust the Ayan ruling class. However external pressures were too great to effectively reform and stabilise the government. Multiple rebellions shook the empire in this period, not least the revolt of Muhammad Ali Pasha of Egypt, and there was also the Russo-Ottoman war playing out.

Antioch was occupied by Egypt from 1832–40 under the rule of Muhammad Ali Pasha. This man, a nobleman of Albanian origin, invaded Syria in 1832. Portraits of him show a man in military dress, girded with a golden sword, and sporting an impressive – indeed nearly spherical – white turban, and a still more impressive white handlebar moustache. Over the course of his life he had at least thirteen wives, the first of whom was a noblewoman of Circassian origin named Amina. In his early career he had clashed with and driven Napoleon's troops out of Egypt. When he masterminded the invasion of Syria, he was already in his sixties.

His commander in Syria was his son by Amina, Ibrahim Pasha. Ibrahim Pasha's plan was to take Damascus, Hama and Homs before defeating the Ottomans decisively in a major battle outside Antioch. He achieved exactly this, despite the superior numbers of the Ottomans. Ibrahim Pasha made the newly conquered city of Antioch the seat of his temporary government, and the reforms he enacted within the city and wider region to reduce corruption and increase security served to make him very popular.

A British traveller, who roved across the Middle East at the same as Ibrahim Pasha waged his wars, described a scene of hospitality in Antioch. He was invited into the bustling and luxurious house of an Antiochene Christian named Girgius. Here he was fed and watered handsomely, and offered *naguileh*. On one evening, the table was set for guests, and among them were Christians, Turks, merchants, men from Aleppo dressed in furs, men of all faiths – for Girgius was a generous host. One of the guests was 'a young Pole' of medical background, personally in the employ of Ibrahim Pasha. The man, whose master's manifold faults were related to him during the dinner, answered every criticism with the nonchalant phrase: '*Monsieur, il paie bien ses employés.*'

For all his munificence with his entourage, and his success outside the gates of Antioch, Ibrahim Pasha would not be successful: the

Egyptian forces would be forced to evacuate Syria in 1841, leaving Antioch once again under Ottoman control, presumably to the delight of Girgius and his guests from many nations.

MODERN ANTAKYA

As a result of its unique history and its fluid administrative boundaries, Antakya today has a distinct cultural and political identity. It is a different city to the rest of Turkey, in no small part because for fifteen years in recent history – from 1923 to 1938 – Antakya was a separate entity to Turkey. Before that, it was part of Ottoman Syria. Old travel books still caption engravings of Antioch as '*Antioche en Syrie*'. Syria still asserts claims over the territory, but the international community and Turkish authorities are deaf to these calls to return the land, and for the entirety of my lifetime, Syria has also had bigger fish to fry. That said, in official maps of Syria, Hatay Province is still claimed as Syrian.

Visitors to Antakya today will find a quiet city. Looking at the map, this might come as a surprise, given that it is positioned perilously close to the Syrian border, with Idlib province – one of the regions hardest hit by the Syrian civil war – just a handful of miles away. Many Syrian refugees did flee across the border into Antakya, including an educated businessman, Mahmoud, and his family. His wife is a nurse and they have three children in their teens. They all came as young children and have assimilated well – learning Turkish and attending Turkish schools – but it was harder for their parents. They have not learned the language, and feel discrimination strongly in nearly every aspect of their lives. Following the earthquake, the family relocated immediately to Bursa. They were lucky to escape with their lives.

For a long time, Mahmoud made his living aiding war correspondents to cross the border from Antakya into Idlib, to report on the conflict and interview refugees. Mahmoud had a good relationship with his neighbours, and had Turkish friends in the town. Partly why this is possible is because many of the residents of Antakya speak Arabic.

For centuries Antakya has been a bilingual city. Indeed, for millennia, this has been the case, but the languages have not always been Turkish and Arabic. Prior to the thirteenth century the main languages would have been Greek, Syriac and a spattering of Norman French.

Turkey's modern borders were more or less laid out in the 1920 Treaty of Sevres, and while they were extended still further southwards by the Treaty of Lausanne, they never reached Antakya. In French

Mandate Syria, Antakya was the centre of the semi-autonomous region of Hatay State in Greater Syria.

The population in the French mandate was ethnically, religiously and linguistically mixed. It still is today. The 1936 French census showed that while 39 per cent of the population were Turks – the greatest homogenous ethnic group – the number of Arabic speakers was higher. Twenty-eight per cent were Alawites, 10 per cent Sunni Arabs, and 8 per cent non-Armenian Christians – the result was that 46 per cent were Arabic-speaking. The Armenian population was still significant and had good reason to fear Turkish governance. Thus, when an election was called to decide the status of Antakya, the Arab portion of the population was unable to mobilise voters in the same way as the Turkish population. The French closed the border to Syria, while the Turkish border remained open as a result, and Hatay and Antakya were annexed by Turkey in 1938. Many of the Arab and Armenian inhabitants initially saw the French departure as no less than betrayal. Large numbers left as refugees for Syria. Within two months of Hatay's annexation 47,000 residents left, including 22,000 Armenians. This was an Arabic-speaking exodus.*

Those who remained did not see their customs and language protected. The residents of Antakya became Turkish citizens, and in many cases were given Turkish surnames. Arabic education was prohibited, and there were reports of assaults by officials on those speaking only Arabic. Mahmoud, despite living in Antakya for many years, still encounters discrimination for speaking Arabic. The headmaster of his son's school, despite speaking fluent Arabic, speaks to him only in Turkish, and he is forced to bring his trilingual son to translate.

Arabic is shrinking in Antakya today. Bilingualism is declining in the new generations. Even the Greek Orthodox Church, which had always functioned in Arabic, in early 2023 was conducting parts of its services in Turkish.

For all these tensions in recent years, Antakya still valued its reputation as a diverse city, and its unique identity. In 2007 a choir – the Antakya Civilisations Choir – was formed from the different ethno-religious groups in Antakya, and in 2012 it was nominated for a Nobel Peace Prize. The choristers comprised Turks, Armenians, Orthodox Christians, Jews, Sunni Muslims, Alawites and Catholics, and represented the many cultures blended in Antakya. They sang

* Smith/Kocamahhul, Joan, *In the Shadow of Kurdish: The Silence of Other Ethnolinguistic Minorities in Turkey.*

songs in Arabic, Turkish and English, and sang hymns from different faiths. They dedicated many of their songs to the victims of the Syrian conflict happening on their doorstep. In 2012, they performed for the US Congress in Washington. The choir said it represented the unique mosaic of people who lived in the city, and the city's particular history.

CONCLUSION

The beach at Samandağ, formerly the port of St Simeon, is made of dark sand. Here and there are pieces of litter and sharp stones. Gingerly, I tiptoe among the rocks and seaweed and step into the water. The snow-capped mountain of Saman Dag dominates the view. It is February, and the water is cold, but nevertheless I brace myself and dive beneath the surface. I want to wash off the rubble of Antakya, which is thick in my hair, under my nails and between my toes. Dust has filled my boots. I have just been walking in the ruins of the city, a ghost town save for soldiers and rescue workers. Streets are blocked with the remains of shattered buildings, and shattered lives. To date, more than 50,000 people have been confirmed dead. In among the rubble I have seen children's colouring books, menus from restaurants where I once ate, family photo albums, spectacles. Passing one destroyed house, I see a lone woman sitting silently on a pile of bricks and staring at the wreckage. I ask her if she is all right; she tells me the heap I see before me was her mother's house. She has come here to be with her mother, whose body has still not been recovered. Her mother's name was Gül, Turkish for rose. The devastation in the city is profound.

The sea is a little drive from Antakya, but I have made the journey because it seems to be a historic tradition to swim here after some kind of struggle. Unlike Seleucus Nicator and Nur ad-Din, I have not emerged victorious from a conquered Antioch, but have stumbled shell-shocked from a fallen one. I have not triumphed at all, instead I have witnessed the devastation of a city I have loved – brought down by the inexorable force of nature. I have climbed the walls, and done my best to digest, distill and relate two and a half millennia of history, and come to terms with Antakya's destruction. I had written about the earthquakes that destroyed Antioch, and Tyre, and Syracuse, but now I have witnessed their effects myself. More than that, I have shuddered through one. A third major earthquake hit on 20 February, while I was visiting the city.

Driving between Antakya and Samandağ, the world suddenly lurched, and threw me backwards and forwards. The gas station we had just left collapsed, and the earth roared beneath us. It was like thunder, but coming from below, and far more furious than any other sound I have ever heard. I felt the road would split beneath us.

Immersed in the cold water, I feel reborn, and I think of swimming in Tyre. The two cities are close – maybe six hours' drive down the coast from each other. The same rare loggerhead turtles that nest on the beach in Tyre nest here as well. But with two closed borders separating the territories of Turkey and Lebanon it might as well be another continent.

With their block physicality, and the momentous ruins left behind, it's sometimes hard to think of cities as fragile; but they are. The fate of Antakya has proven this to me in a way I could never have imagined.

Down the centuries cities have been born, have thrived, contracted and died under the harsh rays of the Mediterranean sun. Tyre, Carthage, Syracuse, Ravenna and Antioch have been rocked by war, famine, pestilence and a plethora of natural disasters. They have also struggled with changing trade routes, and changing cultures. There were many reasons why ancient cities failed. Ancient cities were nothing like their modern counterparts, nothing like even our conception of them. Ancient cities loom large in our minds. But the reality is that the majority of great urban centres of antiquity were tiny by modern standards and highly vulnerable to destruction and to failure. Most would, at best, be called a town by modern metrics. Syracuse in its heyday had fewer than 150,000 inhabitants – that's less than New York's Upper East Side. Tyre had as few as 30,000 people, and yet the imprint it has left on history is huge. For all their precarity and relative daintiness, the concept of the classical city is one of the prevailing images of antiquity, because ancient writers picked it up and ran with it. The literature of Ancient Greece and Rome has filtered down to us, and for ancient writers their urban centres represented the confluence of all that was good in their societies. Cities were celebrated and eulogised, and made larger than life. Classical writers exaggerated, and spoke in superlatives, and we have believed them. Beyond this, we revere the memories of ancient cities because in many cases we have their physical remains. We wonder how, at Baalbek, ancient men moved the megaliths, and stare in awe at the Colosseum of Rome, and we lament the splendours that are beyond our reach: the Hanging Gardens of Babylon, the Colossus of Rhodes. The legacy of these cities is not the stones that are left behind, but the collective memory society has of them, and the literature that has sprung up around them.

Nowhere is this more true, or the sense of what has been lost greater, than among the ruined walls of Antioch. On my last day there, I looked up to the hills rising high above the city, and set myself a target. And up I went. I climbed for hours. I wanted to reach the highest arch that I could see. I walked past the Cave Church of St Peter, miraculously preserved, into the ravine of the Iron Gate. I dragged myself over hills, past half-collapsed homes with dilapidated armchairs set outside facing the view, and Barron the chained Kangal shepherd dog that has always put one in mind of the Molossian hounds of old. His furious barks echoed all around me as I climbed. I went up the steep slopes, grasping shrubs and bushes to pull myself higher, slipping in gravel and tearing my clothes. I went up to the highest arch – brick, solemn and stately – and looked down over what had been Antakya, and the crumbling remains of all that was left of Antioch the Golden. From so high up, the city did not look ruined at all.

Clambering along what was left of the ancient walls, shards of ancient and medieval pottery mingled with the stones under my feet. I stooped and picked up a fragment that had caught the light, glazed green with a yellow pattern in the Islamic style. I put it in my bag, alongside a roof tile I had taken from the ruins of Konak Restaurant – which had served the best lamb chops in Turkey.

The names of Tyre, Carthage, Syracuse, Ravenna and Antioch have endured, but the true reality of the ancient cities has been lost. These cities are not the same as they were, and their glory has dimmed. But a city only dies when the ideas it was built with fade, as much as when fires tear down its walls or earthquakes shatter them. The ideas of these cities have persisted. Their memories remain. Not always necessarily in the minds of residents, but preserved in texts, and the stone monuments that still grasp the earth around the Mediterranean. The air in these cities hangs heavy with legend. The history, the memories are engulfing. Walking in the streets of Ortygia or Tyre, of Antioch or Ravenna, even in desolated Carthage, one can feel the past. People will remember Antakya and, God willing, it will be reborn.

> The poetry of history lies in the quasi-miraculous fact that once, on this earth, once, on this familiar spot of ground, walked other men and women, as actual as we are today, thinking their own thoughts, swayed by their own passions, but now all gone, one generation vanishing into another, gone as utterly as we ourselves shall shortly be gone, like ghosts at cockcrow.
> – G.M. Trevelyan

BIBLIOGRAPHY

Due to the intertwined nature of the history of these cities, to avoid repetition I have put all my primary sources together, but grouped modern, secondary sources by city. This is not an exhaustive list, though does include all those texts without which I could not have written the book.

PRIMARY SOURCES

Agnellus of Ravenna, *The Books of the Pontiffs of the Church of Ravenna,* ed/ trans. D. M. Deliyannis (Washington DC, 2004)

Al-Idrīsī Muḥammad Ibn-Muḥammad, and **Michele Amari,** *L' Italia Descritta Nel 'Libro Del Re Ruggero',* (Salviucci, 1883)

Ambrose, *Epistles in Some of the Principal Works of St Ambrose,* tr. H. De Romestin, E. De Romestin and H. T. F. Duckworth (Oxford, 1869)

Ammianus Marcellinus, *History,* ed/trans. J. Rolfe, 3 vols (Cambridge, MA, 1935–9)

——, *The Later Roman Empire (A.D. 354–378),* tr. W. Hamilton, intro. A. Wallace-Hadrill (London, 1986)

Anon., *The Acts of the Christian Martyrs,* tr. H. Musurillo (Oxford, 1972)

Apollodorus, *The Library* I, trans. James George Frazer (London, 1921)

Appian, *Roman History [inc. Civil Wars],* ed/trans. H. White, 4 vols (Cambridge, MA, 1912–13)

Aristophanes, *Acharnians, Knights,* ed/trans. B. Bickley Rogers (Cambridge, MA, 1930)

Aristotle, *On Colors,* 'Minor Works', trans. W. S. Hett (Cambridge, MA, 1995)

Arrian, *Anabasis Alezandri* I and II, trans. E. Iliff Robson (London, 1929–1933, reprinted 1954)

Athenaeus, *The Deipnosophists* IV, trans. Charles Burton Gulick (Cambridge, MA, 1957)

Augustine, *Augustine: Anti-Pelagian Writings,* vol. 5 of *Nicene and Post-Nicene*

Fathers 'On the Soul and Its Origin', trans. P. Holmes (Peabody, MA, 1994)

——, *City of God*, trans. H. Bettenson (Hardmondsworth, 1972)

——, *Confessions*, trans. R. S. Pine-Coffin (New York, 1980)

——, *Letters*, vols 4 and 5, trans. W. Parsons (New York, 1955–6)

Aurelius Victor, *De Caesaribus*, trans. H. Bird (Liverpool, 1994)

Baha' al-Din, *The Rare and Excellent History of Saladin*, trans. Donald S. Richards (Aldershot, 2002)

Brydone, P. and **Mr Swinburne**, *The Present State of Sicily and Malta* (London, 1788)

Buckingham, J. S., *Travels Among the Arab Tribes, Inhabiting the Countries East of Syria and Palestine, Including a Journey to Bozra, Damascus, Tripoly, Lebanon, Baalbeck, and by the Valley of the Orontes to Seleucia, Antioch, and Aleppo with an Appendix* (London, 1825)

Byron's letters

Carne, J., *Syria, The Holy Land, Asia Minor &c C.*, illustrated. *In a series of views drawn from nature by W. H. Bartlett, William Purser (Thomas Allom), &c. With descriptions of the plates by L. Carne* (London, 1853)

Chronicon Salernitanum, ed. Ulla Westerbergh (Stockholm, 1956)

Cicero, *De Natura Deorum*, trans. H. Rackman (Cambridge, MA, 1956)

——, *Letters to Friends*, ed/trans. D. Shackleton Bailey (Cambridge, MA, 1937)

——, *The Verrine Orations*, ed/trans. L. Greenwood (Cambridge, MA., 1928–35)

——, *Tusculan Dispitations*, trans. J. E. King (London, 1927)

Codex Theodosianus, *The Theodoisan Code and Novels*, ed. T. Mommsen, trans. C. Pharr (New York, 1952)

Columella, *On Agriculture*, ed/trans. E. Forster and E. Heffner, 3 vols (Cambridge, MA, 1941–55)

Cornelius Nepos, 'Hamiclar, Hannibal, Timoleon', in *Lives of Eminent Commanders*, ed/trans. J. Rolfe (London, 1929)

Cyprian, *Saint Cyprian: Letters*, trans. Rose Bernard Donna (Washington DC, 1964)

Dio Cassius, *Roman History*, ed/trans. E. Cary, 9 vols (Cambridge, MA, 1917–27)

Diodorus Siculus, *The Library of History*, ed/trans. C. Oldfather et al. 12 vols (Cambridge, MA, 1960–67)

——, *Diodorus of Sicily*, trans. R. M. Geer (Cambridge, MA, 1962)

Diogenes Laertius, 'Clitomachus', 'Herillus', in *Lives of the Eminent Philosophers*, ed/trans. H. Hicks, 2 vols (Cambridge, MA, 1925)

Dionysius of Halicarnassus, *The Roman Antiquities*, ed/trans. E. Cary, 7 vols (Cambridge, MA, 1948–50)

Estoires d'Outremer et de la Naissance Salehadin, ed. Margaret A. Jubb (London, 1990)

Euripides, *The Bacchanals* III, trans. Arthur S. Way (Cambridge, MA, 1950)

Eusebius of Caesarea, *The Ecclesiastical History* I and II, trans. Kirsopp Lake and J. E. L. Oulton (Cambridge, MA, 1957–1959)

——, *Evangelica Praeparatio [Preparation for the Gospell]*, ed. H. Gifford (Oxford, 1903)

Eusebius, *The History of the Church*, trans. G. A. Williamson (Harmondsworth, 1984)

Fulcher of Chartres, *A History of the Expedition to Jerusalem, 1095–1127*, trans. F. Ryan, ed. H. Fink (Knoxville, TN, 1969)

Gabrieli, Francesco, *Arab Historians of the Crusades* (Routledge, 2010)

Gesta Francorum et Aliorum Hierolsolimitanorum, ed/trans. Rosalind Hill, Nelson's Medieval Texts (London, 1962)

Gesta Francorum: Histoire Anonyme de la Premiere Croisade, ed. L. Brehier (Paris, 1924)

Guibert of Nogent, *Dei Gesta Per Francos et cinq autres textes*, ed. Robert B. C. Huygens (Turnhout, 1996)

Guiccioli, T., *Lord Byron's Life in Italy* (2004)

Hanno the Carthaginian, *Periplus of Circumnavigation [of Africa]*, ed/trans. A. Oikonomides and M. Miller (Chicago, 1995)

Herodian of Antioch, *History of the Roman Empire*, trans. Edward C. Echols (Berkeley and Los Angeles, 1961)

Herodotus, *The Histories*, ed. John M. Marincola, trans. Aubrey de Selincourt (London, 2003)

——, *The Persian Wars*, ed/trans. A. Godley, 4 vols (Cambridge, MA, 1920–25)

History of the Martyrs in Palestine, trans. William Cureton from an ancient Syriac manuscript (London, 1861)

Homer, *The Iliad* I and II, trans. A. T. Murray (Cambridge, MA, 1962)

Hostein, S., *La Corinna* (Florence, 1808)

Houel, J. P. L., *Voyage Pittoresque des Isles de Sicile, de Malte et de Lipari* (Paris, 1782–87)

Ibn al-Athir, *The Chronicle of Ibn al-Athir for the crusading period from al-Kamil fi'-ta'rikh*, parts 1 and 2, trans. D. S. Richards, Crusade Texts in Translation (Aldershot, 2006, 2007)

Ibn Al-Qalanisi, *The Damascus Chronicle of the Crusades,* trans. H.A.R. Gibb (London, 1972)

Ibn Jubayr, *The Travels of Ibn Jubayr*, ed/trans. R.J.C. Broadhurst (London, 1952)

Imad al-Din al Isfahani, *Conquete de la Syrie de la Palestine par Saladin*, trans. Henri Masse (Paris, 1972)

Isocrates, *The Orations of Isocrates* III, IX, 'Evagoras' trans. La Rue Van Hook (Cambridge, MA, 1954)

Itinerarum Peregrinorum et Gesta Regis Ricardi, ed. Helen Nicolson (Aldershot, 1997)

Jansen, Katherine L., et al. *Medieval Italy: Texts in Translation* (Pennsylvania, PA, 2009)

Jerome (Eusebius Hieronymus), *Commentary on Ezekiel* 27.3; Jacques Paul Migne, *Patrologia Latina* 25.303–304

John of Salisbury, *Memoirs of the Papal Court*, ed/trans. Marjorie Chibnall (London, 1956)

Jordanes, and Charles C. Mierow, *Jordanes: The Origin and Deeds of the Goths* (Princeton, NJ, 1908)

Josephus Flavius, *'Against Apion'*, *Josephus* I, trans. H. St. J. Thackeray (Cambridge, MA, 1961)

——, *Jewish Antiquities*, ed/trans. H. Thackeray et al. 13 vols (Cambridge, MA, 1930–65)

——, 'The Jewish War', *Josephus* II. trans. H. St. J. Thackeray (Cambridge, MA, 1961)

Justin, *Epitome of the Philippic Histories*, trans. Rev. John Selby Watson, ed. Giles Laurén. (Atlanta, GA, 1994)

King James Bible (Oxford, 2010)

Komnene, Anna, *The Alexiad*, ed. Peter Frankopan, trans. E. R. A. Sewter (London, 2009)

L'Estoire d'Eracles Empereur, in RHC Occ. vols 1 and 2 (1859)

La Chronique d'Ernoul et de Bernard le Trésorier, ed. Louis de Mas Latrie (Paris, 1871)

La Continuation de Guillaume de Tyr 1184–1197, ed. Margaret R. Morgan (Paris, 1982)

Libanius, trans. A. F. Norman (Cambridge, MA, 1969)

Liber Pontificalis. Texte, Introduction et Commentaire, ed. L. Duchesne (Rome 1886–92)

Livy, *Hannibal's War* (Oxford, 2006)

——, *History of Rome [inc. Epitome]*, ed/trans. B. Foster et al. 14 vols (Cambridge, MA, 1961–7)

Lucan, *The Civil War*, ed/trans. Susan H. Braund (Oxford, 2008)

Machiavelli, Niccolò, *The Prince*, ed. Anthony Grafton, trans. George Bull (London, 2003)

John Malalas, *The Chronicle of John Malalas*, trans. E. Jeffreys, M. Jeffreys, R. Scott (Melbourne, 1986)

Martin Hoffman, Lars, 'Theodosius of Syracuse', in: *Christian–Muslim Relations 600–1500*, ed. David Thomas, accessed online 16 January 2023: //dx.doi.org/10.1163/1877-8054_cmri_COM_23823

Matthew of Edessa, *Armenia and the Crusades, Tenth to Twelfth Centuries: The Chronicle of Matthew of Edessa*, trans. A. Dostourian (Lanham, MD, 1993)

Matthew Paris, *Chronica Majora*, ed. Henry Richard Luard (London, 1872–83)

Nonnus, *Dionysiaca* I–III, trans. W. H. D. Rouse (Cambridge, MA, 1955)

Odo of Deuil, *De Profectione Ludovici VII in Orientum*, ed/trans. Virginia Gingerick Berry (New York, 1948)

Paul the Deacon, *Historia Langobardorum*, ed. G. Waitz, trans. W. D. Foulke (Philadelphia, 1974)

Plato, *Complete Works*, ed. J. M. Cooper (Indianapolis, 1997)

Pliny the Elder, *Natural History*, ed/trans. H. Racklam, W. Jones and D. Eichholz, 10 vols (Cambridge, MA, 1962–7)

Plutarch, *De Herodoti malignitate [On the Malice of Herodotus]*, ed. W. Goodwin (Boston, 1878)

——, *Fall of the Roman Republic: Six Lives*, ed. Robin Seager, trans. Rex Warner (London, 2005)

——, *Lives of the Noble Grecians and Romans*, trans. J. Dryden (London, 1934)

——, *Makers of Rome*, ed/trans. Ian Scott-Kilvert (London, 1965)

——, *Parallel Lives*, ed. and trans. B. Perrin. 11 vols (*Camillus, Cato Major, Lucullus, Thermistocles* – vol. 2, *Fabius Maximus, Pericles* – vol. 3, *Marcellus, Pompey* – vol. 5, *Timoleon* – vol. 6, *Alexander* – vol. 7, *Marius, Pyrrhus* – vol. 9, *Gaius Gracchus, Flaminius* – vol. 10) (Cambridge, MA, 1914–26)

——, *The Age of Alexander, Lives of Dion, Timoleon, and Pyrrhus* (London, 1973)

Pococke, Richard, *A Description of the East and Some Other Countries* (London, 1743–1755)

Polybius, *The Histories*, ed/trans. W. Paton, 6 vols (Cambridge, MA, 1922–27)

——, *The Rise of the Roman Empire*, trans. Ian Scott-Kilvert (London, 1979)

Procopius, *History of the Wars*, ed/trans. H. B. Dewing (Cambridge, MA, 2006)

——, *The Secret History*, ed. Peter Sarris, trans. G. A. Williamson (London, 2007)

——, *Works*, ed/trans. H. B. Dewing (London, 1916)

Quintilian, *The Orator's Education,* ed/trans. D. Russell, 5 vols (Cambridge, MA, 2001)

Quintus Curtius Rufus, *History of Alexander the Great,* ed/trans. J. Role, 2 vols (Cambridge, MA, 1946)

Ralph of Caen, *The Gesta Tancredi,* ed/trans. Bernard S. Bachrach and David S. Bachrach (Aldershot, 2005)

Raymond d'Aguilers, *Le Liber de Raymond D'Aguilers,* ed. John Hugh and Laurita L. Hill (Paris, 1969)

Richard of Devizes, *Chronicon,* ed/trans. John T. Appleby (London, 1963)

Roger of Howden, *Chronica,* vols 1–3, ed. William Stubbs (London, 1868–71)

Seneca, *Ad Lucilium Epistulae Morales,* trans. R. M. Gummere (Cambridge, MA, 1967)

Silius Italicus, *Punica* I, trans. J. D. Duff (Cambridge, MA, 1961)

St Perpetua in Muncey, R. Waterville, *The Passion of Perpetua: An English Translation with Introduction and Notes* (London, 1927)

Strabo, *The Geography,* trans. Horace Leonard Jones (Cambridge, MA, 1989)

Sturluson, Snorri, *The Heimskringla; or, Chronicle of the Kings of Norway,* trans. Samuel Laing, ed. J. C. Nimmo (London, 1889)

Suger, Abbot of St-Denis, *Vita Ludovici Grossi Regis,* ed/trans. Henri Waquet (Paris, 1964)

Swinburne, Henry, *Travels in the Two Sicilies, in the Years 1777–1780* (London, 1790)

Tacitus, *A History of the Monks of Syria,* trans. R. M. Price (Kalamazoo, MI, 1985)

——, *Annals,* trans. C. Damon (London, 2012)

——, *Complete Works of Tacitus,* trans. A. J. Church (New York, 1942)

——, *The Annals of Imperial Rome,* trans. M. Grant (London, 2003)

Tertullian, *Apologetical Works and Minucius Felix,* trans. R. Arbesmann et al. (New York, 1950)

——, *Disciplinary Moral and Ascetical Works,* trans. R. Arbesmann et al. (New York, 1959)

——, *Fathers of the Third Century: Tertullian, Part Fourth.* vol. 4 of *Ante-Nicene Fathers.* (Peabody, MA, 1995)

——, *Latin Christianity: Its Founder, Tertullian,* vol. 3 of *Ante-Nicene Fathers* (Peabody, MA, 1995)

——, *The Address of Q. Sept. Tertullian to Scapula Tertullus, Proconsul of Africa,* tr. D. Dalrymple (Edinburgh, 1790)

——, *The Apology, The Crown* and *Spectacles* in *Christian and Pagan in the Roman Empire: The Witness of Tertullian,* ed. R. Sider (Washington DC, 2001)

——, *The Writings of Q. S. F. Tertullianus*, trans. S. Thelwall, P. Holmes (Edinburgh, 1869–1870)

The Book of the Pontiffs (Liber Pontificalis), The Ancient Biographies of the First Ninety Roman Bishops to AD 715 (Liverpool, 1989)

The Conquest of Jerusalem and the Third Crusade, trans. Peter. W. Edbury (Aldershot, 1996)

Theocritus, *The Idylls*, ed. Richard Hunter, trans. Anthony Verity (Oxford, 2002)

Theodosian Code, trans. Clyde Pharr (Princeton, NJ, 1952)

Theophanes, *Chronicles*, ed/trans. Harry Turtledove (Pennsylvania, 1982)

Thomson, W. M., *The Land and the Book: Or, Biblical Illustrations Drawn from the Manners and Customs, the Scenes and Scenery of the Holy Land* (London, 1891)

Thucydides, *History of the Peloponnesian War*, ed/trans. C. Smith, 4 vols (Cambridge, MA, 1919–23)

Tudebode, Peter, *Historia De Hierosolymitano Itinere*, ed. John Hugh and Laurita L. Hill (Paris, 1977)

Tudela, Benjamin Ben Jonah, and B. Gerrans, *Travels of Rabbi Benjamin, Son of Jonah, of Tudela; through Europe, Asia, and Africa . . . Faithfully Translated from the Original Hebrew, and Enriched with a Dissertation, and Notes . . . by the Rev. B. Gerrans* (London, 1783)

Usamah ibn-Munqidh, *An Arab-Syrian Gentleman and Warrior in the Period of the Crusades: Memoirs of Usamah Ibn-Munqidh*, trans. P.K. Hitti (Princeton, NJ, 1929)

Vergil, *Aeneid*, ed/trans. H. Rushton Fairclough, 2 vols (Cambridge, MA, 1916–18)

Vivant, D., *Voyage en Sicile* (Paris, 1788)

Wilde, Oscar, *The Complete Works of Oscar Wilde* (Oxford, 2007)

William of Tyre, *Deeds Done Beyond the Sea*, ed/trans. Emily A. Babcock and August C. Krey (Columbia University Press, 1943)

Wright, Thomas, *Early Travels in Palestine: Comprising the Narratives of Arculf, Willibald, Bernhard, Saewulf, Sigurd, Benjamin of Tudela, Sir John Maundeville, De La Brocquière and Maundrell* (London, 1848)

SECONDARY SOURCES

TYRE

Abulafia, D., *The Great Sea: A Human History of the Mediterranean* (London, 2011)

Cameron, A. and Amelie K., eds., *Images of Women in Antiquity* (Detroit, 1985)

de Lima, R. A., 'Herakles/Melqart, the Greek façade of a Phoenician deity' in *Revista Hélade: Dossiê Fenícios, 5(2)* (2019), pp. 186–200 https://doi.org/10.22409/rh.v5i2

Flemming, W. B., *The History of Tyre* (New York, 1915)

Gardiner, A. H., *Egyptian Hieratic Texts, Transcribed and Translated by Alan H. Gardiner, Part 1, The Papyrus Anastasi I and the Papyrus Koller, Together with the Parallel Texts* (Hildesheim, 2007)

Gastrad, B., 'Nebuchadnezzar's Siege of Tyre in Jerome's Commentary on Ezekiel' in *Vigiliae Christianae*, vol. 70: no 2; pp 175–192 (2016)

Gore, R., 'Who were the Phoenicians?' in *National Geographic*, October 2004, vol. 206, Issue 4, pp. 26–30

Harris, W., ed. *Rethinking the Mediterranean* (Oxford, 2005)

Horden, P., and Nicholas Purcell, *The Corrupting Sea: A Study of Mediterranean History* (Oxford, 2015)

Jidejian, N., *Tyre Through the Ages* (Beirut, 1996)

Joyce, P. M., *Ezekiel: A Commentary* (London, 2009)

Lantschner, P., 'City States in the Later Medieval Mediterranean World' in *Past & Present*, vol. 254, issue 1, February 2022, pp.3–49

Maguire, S., Bergby, S., Majzoub, M., *Tyre City Profile* (UN Habitat, 2017) https://unhabitat.org/sites/default/files/download-manager-files/TyreCP2017.pdf

Malkin, I., 'Herakles and Melqart: Greeks and Phoenicians in the Middle Ground', (2005), in *Cultural Borrowings and Ethnic Appropriations in Antiquity*, ed. E. Gruen pp. 238–58 (Stuttgart, 2005)

Moscati S., *The World of the Phoenicians*, tr. Alastair Hamilton (London, 1968)

Norton, A. R., *Hezbollah* (Princeton, NJ, 2014)

Noureddine, I., Miorm, A., *Archaeological Survey of the Phoenician Harbour at Tyre, Lebanon* https://honorfrostfoundation.org/wp-content/uploads/2019/07/2013-Tyre-Summary_HFF.pdf, accessed June 2021

Quinn, J. C., *In Search of the Phoenicians* (Princeton, NJ, 2019)

Ṣalībī, K., *A House of Many Mansions: The History of Lebanon Reconsidered* (London, New York, 2021)

Spencer, D., *The Roman Alexander: Reading a Cultural Myth* (Exeter, 2002)

Sultan, C., *Tragedy in South Lebanon: The Israeli–Hezbollah War of 2006* (Minneapolis, MN, 2008)

Ward, W. A., *The Role of the Phoenicians in the Interaction of Mediterranean Civilizations: Papers Presented to the Archaeological Symposium at the American University of Beirut, March, 1967* (Beirut, 1968)

Zalloua P. A., et al. 'Identifying genetic traces of historical expansions: Phoenician footprints in the Mediterranean', *American Journal of Human Genetics*, 2008 Nov; 83 (5) :633-42. doi: 10.1016/j.ajhg.2008.10.012. Epub 2008 Oct 30. PMID: 18976729; PMCID: PMC2668035

CARTHAGE

Anderson, G. D., Fenwick, C., & Rosser-Owen, M. (eds), *The Aghlabids and their Neighbors* (Leiden, 2017)

Bagnall, N., *The Punic Wars: Rome, Carthage and the Struggle for the Mediterranean* (London, 1999)

Bonnet, C., *Melqart: cultes et mythes de l'Héraclès tyrien en Méditerranée* (Leuven, 1988)

——, 'On Gods and Earth: The Tophet and the Construction of a New Identity in Punic Carthage' in *Cultural Identity in the Ancient Mediterranean*, ed. Gruen, Erich S. (Getty Research Institute, 2018)

Briquel, D., 'Hannibal sur les pas d'Herakles: la voyage mythologique et son utilisation dans l'histoire', in *Voyageurs et antiquité Classique*, ed. H. Duchene, pp. 51–60 (Dijon, 2003)

Brown, P., *Religion and Society in the Age of St Augustine*, (New York, 1972)

Camps, G., 'Les Numides et la Civilisation punique' in *Antiquités Africaines* 14, pp. 43–53 (1979)

Dronke, P., *Women Writers of the Middle Ages: A Critical Study of Texts from Perpetua to Marguerite Porete* (Cambridge, 1984)

Frost, H., 'The Prefabricated Punic Warship', in *Studia Phoenicia*, ed. E. Lipinski and H. Devijver, pp. 127–35 (Louvain, 1989)

Hardem, D., 'The Topography of Punic Carthage', in *Greece & Rome*, vol. 9, no. 25, pp. 1–12 (1939)

Hitti, P. K., *History of the Arabs* (London, 1958)

Hoyos, B. D., *Carthage: A Biography* (Abingdon, 2021)

——, *The Carthaginians* (Abingdon, 2010)

——, *Hannibal's Dynasty: Power and Politics in the Western Mediterranean 247–183 BC* (London, 2003)

——, *Truceless War: Carthage's Fight for Survival, 241–237 BC* (Leiden, 2007)

Little, C., 'The Authenticity and Form of Cato's Saying "Carthago Delenda Est"', in *Classical Journal*, vol. 29, pp. 429–35 (1934)

Melliti, K., *Carthage: Histoire d'une métropole méditerranéenne* (Paris, 2016)

Miles, Richard, *Carthage Must Be Destroyed* (London, 2010)

Nelson, J. Raleigh, 'Dido: A Character Study' in *School Review*, vol. 12, no. 5, 1904, pp. 408–19. *JSTOR*, http://www.jstor.org/stable/1075844. Accessed 17 Jan. 2023

Nixey, Catherine, *The Darkening Age: The Christian Destruction of the Classical World* (London, 2017)

Quinn, J. C., 'The Cultures of the Tophet: Identification and Identity in the Phoenician Diaspora' in *Cultural Identity in the Ancient Mediterranean*, ed. Gruen, Erich S. (Getty Research Institute, 2018)

——, and Nicholas C. Vella, *The Punic Mediterranean: Identities and Identification from Phoenician Settlement to Roman Rule* (Cambridge, 2018)

Rawlings, Louis, *Hannibal the Cannibal?: Polybius on Barcid Atrocities* (Cardiff, 2007)

Salisbury, J. E., *Perpetua's Passion: the Death and Memory of a Young Roman Woman* (New York, London, 1997)

Shelby Brown, S., *Late Carthaginian Child Sacrifice and Sacrificial Monuments in their Mediterranean Context* (Sheffield, 1991)

Tahar, M., *Les Grecs et Carthage* (Tunis, 2010)

Walbank, F. W., *A Historical Commentary on Polybius*, 3 vols (Oxford, 1957–79)

SYRACUSE

Abulafia, D., *Frederick II: A Medieval Emperor* (London, 2002)

Amato, et al. *The History of the Normans* (Woodbridge, 2004)

Amore, A., *San Marciano di Siracusa* (Vatican City, 1958)

Bonna Westcoat (ed.), *Syracuse, the Fairest Greek City* (Rome, 1990)

Braudel, F., *The Mediterranean* (London, 1974)

Casson, L., *Ships and Seamanship in the Ancient World* (New York, 1995)

Champion, J., *Tyrants of Syracuse: War in Ancient Sicily* (Barnsley, 2021)

Crawford, Francis Marion, *The Rulers of the South: Sicily, Calabria, Malta: In Two Volumes* (New York, 1900)

Dummett, J., *Syracuse, City of Legends: A Glory of Sicily* (London, 2010)

Finley, M. I., *A History of Sicily; Ancient Sicily to the Arab Conquest* (London, 1968/first published online 2010)

Granara, William, *Ibn Hamdis the Sicilian: Eulogist for a Falling Homeland* (London, 2021)

Guido, M., *Syracuse: A Handbook to Its History and Principal Monuments* (London, 1958)

Kleinhenz, Christopher, et al. *Medieval Italy: An Encyclopedia* (London, 2004)

Lomas, K., 'Tyrants and the Polis: Migration, Identity and Urban Development in Greek Sicily', in *Ancient Tyranny*, ed. Sian Lewis (Edinburgh, 2006)

Lomas, K. (ed.), *Greek Identity in the Western Mediterranean: Papers in Honour of Brian Shefton* (Leiden, 2004)

Mack Smith, D., *A History of Sicily: Medieval and Modern Sicily* (London, 1968)

Malaterra, Geoffroi, and Kenneth Baxter Wolf, *The Deeds of Count Roger of Calabria and Sicily and of His Brother Duke Robert Guiscard* (Michigan, 2005)

Marcuse, L., *Plato and Dionysius; a Double Biography*, trans. Wilson Follett (New York, 1947)

Metcalfe, A., *Muslims and Christians in Norman Sicily: Arabic Speakers and the End of Islam* (Abingdon, 2013)

Morrison, J., and Coates, J., *The Athenian Trireme: The History and Reconstruction of an Ancient Greek Warship* (Cambridge, 1986)

Prigent, V., 'Pour en finir avec Euphèmios, basileus des Romains' in *Mélanges de l'École Française de Rome, Moyen Age*, vol. 118, no. 2, pp. 375–380 (2006)

Rowland, Ingrid D., *The Divine Spark of Syracuse* (Waltham, MA, 2019)

Sarris, Peter, *Empires of Faith: The Fall of Rome to the Rise of Islam, 500–700* (Oxford, 2011)

Van Ooijen, J.A., 'Resilient Matters: The Cathedral of Syracuse as an Architectural Palimpsest' in *Architectural Histories*, vol. 7, no. 1, 2019, 26, pp. 1–12

Walbank, F. W., *Polybius, Rome, and the Hellenistic World: Essays and Reflections* (Cambridge, 2002)

——, *Polybius* (Berkeley, 1972)

Zambon, E., 'From Agathocles to Hieron II: The Birth and Development of Basileia in Hellenistic Sicily', in *Ancient Tyranny*, ed. Sian Lewis, pp. 77–94 (Edinburgh, 2006)

——, ' "Κατὰ δὲ Σικελίαν ἦσαν τύραννοι" Notes on Tyrannies in Sicily Between the Death of Agathocles and the coming of Phyrrus (289–279 BC)' in *Greek Identity in the Western Mediterranean: Papers in Honour of Brian Shefton*, ed. K. Lomas (Leiden, 2004)

RAVENNA

Arnold, T. F., *The Renaissance at War* (London, 2001)

Burns, T., *A History of the Ostrogoths* (Bloomington and Indianapolis, 1984)

Christensen, A. S., *Cassiodorus, Jordanes and the History of the Goths: Studies in a Migration Myth* (Copenhagen, 2002)

Cormack, R., *Byzantine Art* (Oxford, 2018)

Deliyannis, D. M., *Ravenna in Late Antiquity* (Cambridge, 2010)

Doig, A., *Liturgy and Architecture: From the Early Church to the Middle Ages* (Aldershot, 2008)

Goldsworthy, A., *The Fall of the West: The Death of Roman Superpower* (London, 2009)

Heather, P., *The Goths* (Oxford, 1996)

——, *The Fall of the Roman Empire: A New History* (London, 2005)

Herrin, Judith, *Ravenna: Capital of Empire, Crucible of Europe* (London, 2021)

——, *The Formation of Christendom* (Princeton, NJ, 1987)

——, and **Jinty Nelson** (eds), *Ravenna: Its Role in Earlier Medieval Change and Exchange* (London, 2016)

MacCarthy, F., *Byron: Life and Legend* (London, 2002)

Nelson, R. S., 'Modernism's Byzantium, Byzantium's Modernism,' in *Byzantium/Modernism: The Byzantine as Method in Modernity*, eds Betancourt, R. and Taroutina, M. (Leiden, 2015)

Origo, Iris, *The Last Attachment* (London, 2017)

Raffa, G. P., *Dante's Bones: How a Poet Invented Italy* (Cambridge, MA, 2020)

Salisbury, J. E., *Rome's Christian Empress, Galla Placidia Rules at the Twilight of the Empire* (Baltimore, MD, 2016)

Santagata, M., *Dante: The Story of His Life*, trans. R. Dixon (Cambridge, MA, 2018)

Sivan, H., *Galla Placidia: The Last Roman Empress* (Oxford, 2011)

Starks, M., *Understanding Ravenna* (Stroud, 2018)

Redonet, F. L., *How Julius Caesar Started a Big War by Crossing a Small Stream*, Accessed 14/6/22: https://www.nationalgeographic.com/history/history-magazine/article/julius-caesar-crossing-rubicon-rome

ANTIOCH

Asbridge, T., 'Alice of Antioch: A case study of female power in the twelfth century', in *The Experience of Crusading*, vol. 2, *Defining the Crusader Kingdom*, ed. P. Edbury and J. Phillips, pp. 29–47 (Cambridge, 2003)

——, *The First Crusade – A New History: The Roots of Conflict Between Christianity and Islam* (Oxford, 2005)

Barber, M., *The Crusader States* (New Haven, CT, 2012)

Brown, P., *Power and Persuasion in Late Antiquity: Towards a Christian Empire* (Madison, WI, 1992)

De Giorgi, Andrea U., *Ancient Antioch, from the Seleucid Era to the Arab Conquest* (Cambridge, 2016)

——, and **A. Asa Eger,** *Antioch: A History* (Routledge, 2021)

Downey, G., *A History of Antioch in Syria from Seleucus to the Arab Conquest* (Princeton, NJ, 1961)

——, *Antioch in the Age of Theodosius the Great* (Norman, OK, 1962)

Gowers, E., 'Augustus and "Syracuse"' in *Journal of Roman Studies*, vol. 100, 2010, pp. 69–87, https://doi.org/10.1017/s007543581000002x

Hintlian, K., *History of the Armenians in the Holy Land* (Jerusalem, 1989)

Kondoleon, C., *Antioch: The Lost City* (Princeton, NJ, 2000)

Mayer, H.E., *The Crusades* (Oxford, 1998)

Meeks, W., *The First Urban Christians: The Social World of the Apostle Paul* (New Haven, CT, 1983)

——, et al. *Jews and Christians in Antioch in the First Four Centuries of the Common Era* (Missoula, MT, 1979)

——, *The Moral World of the First Christians* (Philadelphia, PA, 1987)

Phillips, J., *Defenders of the Holy Land: Relations Between the Latin East and the West, 1119–1187* (Oxford, 1996)

——, *The Second Crusade: Extending the Frontiers of Christendom* (London, 2007)

——, *Holy Warriors* (London, 2010)

Runciman, S., *A History of the Crusades* (London, 1991)

Smith/Kocamahhul, Joan, 'In the Shadow of Kurdish: The Silence of Other Ethnolinguistic Minorities in Turkey', in *Middle East Report,* no. 219, 2001, p. 45, https://doi.org/10.2307/1559256

Tyerman, C.J., *God's War: A New History of the Crusades* (London, 2006)

——, *The World of the Crusades* (New Haven, CT, 2019)

Wallace-Hadrill, D. S., *Christian Antioch: A Study of Early Christian Thought in the East* (Cambridge, 1982)

INDEX

Page numbers in *italic* indicate illustrations

ACKNOWLEDGEMENTS

This book is the product of many hands and many minds. Despite all the challenges I encountered – not least a pandemic – I will forever be grateful for having had the opportunity to spend three years of my twenties immersed in Mediterranean history and culture, and on the shores of the sea itself. Thank you to my publishers for backing me during this time, and to my friends and family for supporting me during the process.

Particular thanks must go to Alan Samson for the help and inspiration I received while writing – he not only commissioned the book and fed ideas into its inception, but went above and beyond and continued to give vital feedback throughout the process, even when he was no longer my editor. I also need to thank my godfather Alan Beechey – who, likewise, stepped in to edit at short notice, and whose combative stance on commas, general enthusiasm and speed with a red pen were invaluable. My agent Rachel Conway helped me navigate the challenges I met with patience and sangfroid, and Jo Roberts-Miller lent a fantastically steady hand to the final stages of production.

My mum read the manuscript through various iterations, and my dad was a great support throughout. My friends Nancy Hervey-Bathurst, Fred Shan and Professor Jonathan Phillips also read and critiqued the MS in rough forms, and Professor David Abulafia was extremely generous with his time and insights on the Bronze Age Mediterranean, and approaches to the history of the region in general. Professor Paul Joyce at KCL explained key elements of Ezekiel's prophecy and the historical context of the Old Testament and Professor Andrea de Giorgi lent his expertise to my Antioch chapter. My other editors at W&N, Maddy Price and Ed Lake, also gave helpful insight and comments.

Beyond those who helped with the construction and editing of the book, I need to thank the people I met around the Mediterranean who were so generous to me. In Syracuse, thank you to Anna and Francesco Pusateri for hosting me and making many introductions. Thank you to Alice, Lucia, Claudia, Idris, Carmelo, Gabriele, Dino, Helene, Stephano, Xavier and

Claudia for sharing knowledge and stories about Syracuse and their love for the city, and to Costanza for her help with translation. Thank you to Pucci Piccione for hosting my launch event and also to Francesco Italia and Antonio Calbi, for talking to me about the living legacy of Syracuse's ancient past.

In Tyre, I am grateful to Hanna and Bachir, Marina, ZouZou, Anushka, Celine, Thouraya and the Sisters of St Joseph of the Apparition, and Xavier who helped with translation. Professor Pierre Zalloua was very helpful in sharing his research and elucidating the conclusions to be drawn, and Dr Francisco Nuñez and his team were generous with their time and knowledge of Tyre's archaeology, as was Dr Ali Bedawi. Paco went a step further and attempted to correct several of my mistakes; any that remain are entirely my own. In Ravenna, Sara and Nemo were hospitable and helpful, as were Silvia and the members of the city's artistic community, Alessandra Carini, Marco Micoli, Nicola Montalbini and Luca Barberini. In Antakya, Mahmoud, Gamze and Cenk were fantastic friends to meet, and I am so sorry for everything that they have lost. In Tunis, I owe thanks to Philippa Day and Moez Kamoun for their helpful hospitality, and to the Ben Nacefs for sharing their culture. Particular thanks must go to Yusra Ben Meriem who was so generous in showing me around her city and the ruins of Carthage, and taking me to her university to meet her professors, who shared insights and gave me many books.

I could not have completed this project without generous hosts passionate about sharing their history and culture, and I have been so moved by the kindness and brilliance of the people I have met and who have helped me so much. I am also grateful to the libraries who opened their doors to me, IFPO in Beirut and the Biblioteca Classense in Ravenna, who offered beautiful, air-conditioned spaces to work in, and access to some of the treasures in their collections.

I also must thank the friends who travelled with me and who kept me writing at difficult times, including Matt and Lizzy who came out to Italy, and Stephanie Glinski who travelled with me to Antakya after the earthquakes and photographed what was left of the city's built heritage. Maria, John, Atalanta and Anna helped me through rough patches and inspired me with their friendship and creativity. In Beirut, thank you to the brilliant community of artists, writers, diplomats and humanitarians who became my family in Lebanon. Tom Young's artistic insight into all things Tyrian has been a brilliant foil.

Last but not least, the animals who slept at my feet or purred on my lap while I wrote – Manoucheh, Shadow and Hanoun – also deserve a mention for keeping me warm during Lebanese winters. Finally, Eerik and Leon, thank you for taking me sailing in Sicily. I would never have had this idea without you.